DANCING TO AN INDIAN TUNE

Mary Searle-Chatterjee

DANCING TO AN INDIAN TUNE

AN EDUCATION IN INDIA

Matador
9 Priory Business Park,
Wistow Road, Kibworth Beauchamp,
Leicestershire. LE8 0RX
Tel: 0116 279 2299
Email: books@troubador.co.uk
Web: www.troubador.co.uk/matador
Twitter: @matadorbooks

ISBN 978 1800461 376

British Library Cataloguing in Publication Data.
A catalogue record for this book is available from the British Library.

Printed and bound by CPI Group (UK) Ltd, Croydon, CR0 4YY
Typeset in 12pt Minion Pro by Troubador Publishing Ltd, Leicester, UK

Matador is an imprint of Troubador Publishing Ltd

'I want the world to recognise with me the open door of every consciousness... My final prayer, O my body, make of me always a man who questions'

(F. FANON, *BLACK SKIN, WHITE MASKS*, LONDON: MACGIBBON & KEE (1952), 1968, PP.229 & 232.

TABLE OF CONTENTS

In 1963 the city was known both as Banaras, and as Varanasi.
The station has only ever been known as Varanasi.
Some personal names have been changed.

PART I

BEGINNINGS

CHAPTER 1

1953–55 IMBIBING ENGLISH VISIONS OF THE EAST

I WAS BORN ON EMPIRE DAY, 24ᵀᴴ MAY 1942. BUT MY INTEREST in Asia only began in 1953, five days after my eleventh birthday. A newsreader on BBC radio choked with emotion as he announced that Edmund Hillary and Sherpa Tensing had at last achieved the impossible summit of Mount Everest – 8848 metres. Honorary Brits had now vanquished the highest pinnacles of our planet. Newspapers carried the heroes into our homes – conquerors sanctified by an ivory backcloth of dazzling snow and ice, imbued with the unearthly purity of the peak on whose flanks so many men had willingly sacrificed themselves.

From the windows of our home in North Yorkshire, we could see the distinctive summit of Ingleborough – 723 metres – up which my parents had hauled me at the age of six. A large heap of pruned branches and grass cuttings occupied the bottom corner of our garden.

'Let's name it Everest,' I said to Richard, my younger brother.

'To do it properly you need to break a bottle.' He charged off to the kitchen with his short trousers flapping around his knees.

The bottle was smashed against the wall and I declaimed in ringing tones, 'I do hereby name this mound, Everest.' Richard stood to attention and saluted.

On dry days, we escaped to the open horizons of fields and moors. When it rained, I devoured books on the Himalayas, that world of alluring beauty. *Seven Years in Tibet*, by Heinrich Harrer, appeared in paperback later that year. The grandeur of the mountains, untainted by the blemishes of family life, blended with the mystery of Tibetan society and religion. Richard gave me a book on Tibetan Buddhism for my birthday. School friends followed this at Christmas with Maurice Herzog's *Annapurna*, first on sale the year before. James Hilton's *Lost Horizon* arrived next. His romance of a hidden Himalayan valley, *Shangri La*, where nobody grew old, had formed the basis of a box office hit in 1937.

Would I ever be able to struggle over ice to reach such perfection, to ascend hitherto unclimbed peaks? To gain a vantage point from which I could look down and make sense of the bewildering vastness of life? Whenever my parents took us hill walking in the Dales, I imagined I was trekking in remote and untouched places. So much of Britain was concrete and tarmac, even then. I didn't realise that others had felt the same until I found this verse by Shelley in one of my schoolbooks:

'This ride was my delight. I love all waste
And solitary places; where we taste
The pleasure of believing what we see
Is boundless, as we wish our souls to be.'

*

Two years later we moved back south to Beaconsfield, a commuter village in Buckinghamshire. The yearning for mountains disappeared into cold storage. By the age of fourteen, I was desperately seeking the meaning of life in a nutshell. Who could possibly believe in a personal God who intervened in human affairs? And, if not, how could I continue to swear the Girl Guides' vow to God and the Queen?

'Don't worry,' our leader said, dispatching me to the local clergyman. 'He'll be able to help.'

'Please do come in,' he said, with a broad smile. We had never met before. My parents were most definitely not Anglican. My atheist father descended from nonconformist Protestants; my mother occasionally revealed a mystical streak. They didn't attend church or chapel but packed me off to Sunday school at the Methodists, or the Baptists, depending on where we were living. All in the interests of moral education.

The vicar sat me down next to a small teak table. 'Help yourself to a couple of chocolate biscuits, Mary,' he said, pointing to a blue Chinese dish. 'I hear you are having a spot of trouble with God. That's not uncommon, you know. It'll probably just pass. Don't worry about it. But do come round again any time you would like to discuss something.'

The following day I discovered Radhakrishnan's *The Hindu View of Life* in the Religion section of the school library. Its version of Hinduism was a humane and mystical agnosticism – just what I was seeking.

CHAPTER 2

2005 SHANTA CALLS UP THE PAST

I LOOKED BACK UP THE ROCKY TRACK TO THE SEMI-CIRCULAR cliffs of the Ajanta Gorge. The cave's gaping mouth marked the entrance to the ancient frescoes. Halfway down, Shanta's head and face bobbed above the sides of a sedan chair carried by four porters. She wasn't doing badly for an eighty-two-year-old who'd already suffered several heart attacks. I closed my eyes for a moment and waited for them to catch up. The tender face of the Bodhisattva swam back into view. More than sixteen hundred years old and the paintings could still make my eyes well up.

We didn't talk much on the bus back to the rickshaw stand. The skin on my face tightened in the dry heat, and my eyelids sagged. I'd hardly slept on the sleeper to Jalgaon the night before. The manager at the Fardapur INTC Guest House greeted us like old friends. Our unopened bags sat exactly where we'd dumped them early that morning. A leisurely cold shower and a change of *selwar-kameez* soon revived me. I wandered out into the shady garden and plonked myself in a cane armchair. Shanta was already sipping sweet tea and nibbling hot *pakoras*. Myna birds and bulbuls fluttered on rose bushes. I could hear a *koel* singing non-stop. No wonder it was called 'the Indian Nightingale'. What more could anyone want?

'Mary, I'm thinking that we've not talked at all since you stepped off the plane yesterday morning. And it's more than a year since we met in London, when I was visiting the family. You have only one week with me before you move on from Mumbai to Bangalore, and all you do is fall asleep.'

I smiled. Shanta was always one to get up and go, in-between bouts of illness. 'Look. I'm wide awake now,' I said. 'So what have you and your group of feminist writers been up to lately?'

'I've gone back to translating. At the moment I'm working on Toni Morrison's *Beloved*. What a wonderful book that is. Somebody had to produce a Marathi version.'

Shanta wasn't wasting her retirement back in Mumbai after years of dreary maths teaching in a secondary modern school in Southall.

'And this is for you,' she said, pulling out a slim volume. 'I've translated a long poem called *Ajanta*, by Mahanore, a Marathi poet from this area. How I cried when I first read it. It's about the love of a Victorian soldier/artist and a local tribal girl in the 1840s. The British Government commissioned Robert Gill to paint copies of the frescoes. He spent decades in a hut at the foot of the cliffs. The girl moved in with him. Her relatives couldn't keep them apart. After she became pregnant, they dragged her out and burnt her alive while Gill was working in the caves. He was heartbroken. Local Sufi ascetics were the only people who agreed to perform her funeral rites.

'Mahanore was out walking, looking for new water sources, and bumped into a small monument in the undergrowth. The inscription said:

'To the memory of my beloved Paru
Who died on 23rd May 1856.
Robert Gill.'

'But who on earth was Paru? Mahanore asked the local tribal people. They told him the whole story. That was what inspired him to compose this poem. He cleaned and polished the stone. Every year on the 23rd of May, he, and a few friends, place flowers there.'

'But I thought the tribal people were more easy-going than caste Hindus about such relationships,' I said. 'And are you sure he hadn't just taken advantage of the young girl who cooked for him?'

'Definitely not,' Shanta said. 'You've become so cynical nowadays, Mary. Paru loved the frescoes and showed him how to mix paints from local leaves and stones so that he could reproduce the original colours. It was true love, across religion, race, class and caste.

'Gill's paintings were a sensation in London. Tragedy struck again when they were destroyed in a fire. He was heartbroken a second time. He returned to India and spent the rest of his life as a recluse in the forest. Somebody constructed a memorial to him. And one of the village gates still carries his name. I've translated the poem because I want English people to know this story. Tomorrow we'll go to the village and I'll show you Paru's monument. We can visit Mahanore's farm at the same time.

'But I've been doing all the talking, Mary. What about you? Gill had a job. He came in the army as a major. You came at the age of twenty-one in 1963 to study Indian Philosophy for two years at the Hindu University of Banaras. You didn't have to do that. You came long before the overland trips at the end of the 1960s, or the minibuses in the 1970s. Whatever led you down this path? Our youngsters are all trying to get out as fast as they can. And what happened in those two years to create your life-long fascination for India?'

'That's a long story, Shanta. Maybe it was a similar impulse. To see another world. To walk through open doors. It changed me for ever. And the worst thing was that I didn't know anyone to discuss it with when I got back to England. I was so lucky to meet you eighteen months later. You were like a mother figure.'

'If forty years and more doesn't count as a love affair, I don't know what does, Mary. Anyway, you're looking sleepy again. I've been meaning for some time to suggest you write about it. I admit that I don't always enjoy British travel writing. Not so amusing for us as for most of you. Too voyeuristic. I expect you know what I'm talking about. Might you be able to hold up the traveller to scrutiny as well as the people observed?'

I leaned back and gazed through a clump of banana trees. Perhaps I should. There'd been so much death and dying lately with people vanishing into puffs of smoke and the past disappearing at speed like a train into a tunnel. And I still had all my letters in a box on top of the wardrobe.

'I suppose I shouldn't be surprised if a mother figure gives marching orders to her child, should I? And you've never ceased to be curious about the antics of the British, have you, Shanta? But it was a long time ago, only fifteen years after Indian Independence. Things are very different now. Who would have thought that Indian corporations would one day buy up British companies and that Britain would go the way of all former empires?'

'That doesn't matter, Mary. It was the beginning of a new post-colonial world. Or was it? It seemed so to us. Just get on with it.'

CHAPTER 3

1956–63 THE WAY LIES AHEAD

A N ANGLO-FRENCH COALITION INVADED EGYPT IN 1956.
'I can't believe this,' my father said. 'Anyone would think we were still in the nineteenth century.'

'Is there no human progress?' my mother asked.

Dreams of solidarity with anti-imperial movements now loomed larger than my childhood visions of Asia, though, of course, I still had to unravel the meaning of life. The study of literature on its own would not be enough, so in 1960 I embarked on a degree course in English Literature with Philosophy at Nottingham University.

In my copy of W.H. Auden's *The Enchafèd Flood: the Iconography of the Romantic Imagination* (one of the books on my course list), I underlined key sentences in his description of sea and desert symbolism: 'the search for possibility and the escape from necessity', and 'the flight from finite repetition to infinite novelty'. Auden believed such aspirations belonged in the past. His book was published in 1951, in the shadow of the Second World War. A decade later, the delights and dangers of romantic yearning had crept back. My brother, Richard, was reading Thoreau and Whitman, and dreaming of a smallholding in the Scottish islands or the Canadian wilderness.

Rowena Farr's *Seal Morning (1957)*, a tale of life in a remote part of the Scottish Highlands, offered me the same promise of self-sufficiency.

Halfway through my first year, a student from Bangkok sat next to me one lunch time in the refectory. We discussed Buddhism over cups of lukewarm, instant coffee. On the eve of her departure for Thailand, she presented a book of Buddhist teachings. Could that provide the ever-elusive composure? Only in the third year did my dream of visiting Asia revive. Sarah, a woman on my course, asked, 'Have you heard about the Commonwealth Scholarship Scheme for postgraduate study? You could go to India.' What magic words. Tibet was still closed; India would surely be the next best thing – albeit teeming, tropical plains instead of empty, frozen mountains.

My student friends dreamed of socialist Utopias in a bright new world. India was the last place they wanted to go. Who would choose to spend two years in a hot, unhealthy region, impoverished by several hundred years of British colonialism? But it was on their radar. India and Tibet were in the air young people breathed. We weren't all looking for the safe dreariness of a job in the public services, or industry. It wasn't as if you needed to slave for years to keep the wolf from the door, as our grandparents had done. Wolves didn't prowl anymore in welfare-state Britain.

The Commonwealth Scholarship Scheme to send British students to South Asia had begun with one student, only two years earlier. I filled in all the forms, opting to study for an MA in Indian Philosophy and Religion at Banaras Hindu University. All I knew about Banaras was that it was an ancient city on the banks of the river Ganges, and a major religious centre for Hindus.

'I'd understand Mary wanting to go to India if you had army connections,' Mrs Howarth, our next-door neighbour, said to my mother, when they were both hanging out washing. 'But to study in an Indian university, for heaven's sake!'

'She can think what she likes, Mary,' my mother said that evening. 'I'm not surprised you want to go to India. Your grandfather and his best friend trained to do missionary work in China when they were your age. The friend went ahead but was murdered a few weeks later in the Boxer uprising. The locals were protesting about western interference. Your grandfather hastily cancelled his plans.'

'That was fortunate for me.'

My mother smiled wanly. 'The only adventure he was ever to know took place in the trenches of France. And his sister, your great-aunt, turned to Roman Catholicism as a teenager, and got herself to a French convent. She nursed with the nuns behind enemy lines during the First World War.

'I had my dreams, too, Mary. I wanted to train as a nurse and join the mounted nursing service in the Canadian Rockies.'

I don't think my mother had ever ridden a horse except on the beach at Southend.

'Your godmother nursed in India during the war. She sent the blue embroidered bedspread, with the red temple design, when you were born. Don't you remember, the one that used to lie on your bed? Afterwards she joined the "flying nurses" in the Australian outback.'

So was it only single women who found adventure?

My father grew up with tales of seafaring relatives but, for him, it was the rational scientist who was the explorer, cutting new paths through the undergrowth of ignorance, fearlessly disregarding narrow convention and vested interests. Knowledge was what mattered.

My parents' contrasting visions battled it out over the dinner table. My secular father, with his trim beard and newspaper, sat at one end, demolishing the shibboleths of past tradition.

'You're ignoring the evidence, Winifred,' he would protest, quoting chapter and verse.

My mother, opposite him, rehearsed the attractions of remote and traditional lifestyles, especially of the Hebridean islands. 'You've no soul, Edgar,' she would say. My brother and I watched from the side-lines, and sometimes jumped into the fray. Food would go cold as one of us stormed out.

*

My interview for the scholarship took place in the Headquarters of the Association of Commonwealth Universities in London. A porter in a dark uniform ushered me into a Victorian room with a blue Persian carpet and plaster mouldings around the ceiling. A dozen middle-aged men were arrayed on the far side of a polished mahogany table. The chairman gestured towards the solitary chair near me. He introduced the members of the panel – a mixture of professors and ex-Indian colonial officers.

'So, you want to study philosophy in Banaras?' He raised his eyebrows. 'You enjoy philosophy, do you?'

'Oh, yes. It makes me think. But I want to move beyond Western philosophy.'

'Have you read any books of Indian philosophy?' asked a tall man in a brown tweed jacket and bow tie.

'I've read Radhakrishnan's *The Hindu View of Life*, and several *Upanishads*. I found their approach very rational.'

'Do you not think it will be difficult for you to adjust to India?' someone else asked.

'I'm sure I will manage all right.'

The trace of a smile flitted across his face.

'Do you think you might write a book on India?' asked a man with a large curling moustache.

It had never entered my head that I might write a book. I didn't want to tell a lie. But then how was I to know the future? I fidgeted with the sleeve of my cardigan.

'I think I might.'

Anything was possible. The India of my imagining was a vast slumbering giant, ready to heave into action at any time, with larger-than-life figures like Gandhi.

Four other British students were about to launch into a similar period of postgraduate study or research: Economics in Poona, Painting in Calcutta, History and Economic Planning in Delhi, and Education in Ceylon. The 1960s were the highpoint of the programme. India seemed to offer something we were seeking, though we would have been hard put to say what.

'So, you're not going there to help the poor and suffering?' my doctor said, as she plunged in the needle for my final cholera vaccination.

I avoided her eyes.

Academics, too, often did not see the point of studying in another culture; nor do they, even today. Recent research into the attitudes of British university administrators towards North-South student travel met with the blunt question:

'Why would British students want to study in developing country institutions and why would British institutions want to send them?'

How little did they know... and how mistaken they were.

CHAPTER 4

1963 THE JOURNEY

THE JOURNEY TO INDIA BEGAN THE DAY AFTER MY GRADUATION ceremony. At last the future was opening up. I hadn't flown on a plane before. The Air India crew in their white shirts and dark trousers smiled indulgently as I stepped up the gangway in my new, mid-thigh dress. 'Wear cotton and dress modestly' was the only advice I'd been given before leaving for the sub-continent. A matronly woman from Delhi sat next to me. Her pale blue sari of flimsy voile fluttered around her hips.

'So, you are going to India to study philosophy? Very nice. Very nice indeed. Very ancient philosophy. Banaras a very holy place. I never had opportunity to see it.' She looked at my heavy denim frock. 'You'll be needing something cooler than that.'

She wasn't the first South Asian I'd spoken to, though in the early 1960s few were to be seen in Britain outside the cities. Once, when I was fifteen and travelling home from London by train, a middle-aged Indian man sat down opposite me.

I must be friendly, I thought. 'Where are you from?' I asked.

He blushed and inclined his head. 'I hail from South India. I do advanced training in nursing at Amersham Hospital for two years. I have been in your good country for one year.'

'And how do you find it?'

'Very nice but I have never entered the house of any English person. I very much want to enter an English house. I can see you are from a good family. Can you take me to meet your parents?'

'Oh… well, yes,' I said, gripping the strap of my handbag. 'When would you like to come?'

'Very good. You take me straightaway.'

We descended from the train at Beaconsfield. The ten-minute walk home into our little side road took an eternity. What would my mother make of this? We rarely received visitors. The door opened.

'Mum, this is Mr Naik. We met on the train. He wanted to meet an English family.'

My mother smiled as if this were a routine occurrence. Why had I worried so much? Mr Naik stayed an hour, drank tea, and departed happily to resume his train journey. I never saw him again.

In the following year, two Sikh naval officers in their late twenties would sometimes visit. My parents had met them on an organised walking holiday. Inderjit and Nindi were studying at a naval college in Devon. They wore suits and looked athletic, a bit like my father, who was very dark for an Englishman, and occasionally mistaken for an Indian. On the second occasion they arrived at our house on motorbikes, with a tiny boy in a turban as a pillion passenger – the day after the one arranged. Luckily some of the left-over cakes and sandwiches were still in the larder. Two months later one of them sent me a card from Egypt, signed, 'Yours'. I had never before received a card signed that way. Could he be in love with me?

And then, at university, a Punjabi man had engaged me in conversation at the bus stop.

'We go for coffee,' he said.

So I went.

'I have a degree from my country,' he continued. 'But here I have to work in a factory. You people know nothing about India. We have our own Shakespeare – Kalidasa. Please to read his play, *Shakuntala*. Now let us take a taxi to my house.'

I made an excuse and bolted. A week later I found a copy of *Shakuntala* in the library.

*

The sun was flaming over the horizon as the plane touched down in Delhi. The rush of hot air when I stepped out onto the gangway hit me like an unexpected opening of an oven. I traipsed after the other passengers. The woman sitting next to me on the plane showed me the luggage collection point and the taxi queue.

I staggered out through the crowd and found a driver standing beside a rusty car.

'Other airport?' I asked.

'Very good, memsahib.'

He bundled my baggage onto the roof and set off at a great pace. Televisions were not common in the early 1960s and I had not grown up with images of Asian cities. I stared through the window, too tired to register much. We accelerated towards a mass of people, dogs and rickshaws. All went flying as my cab approached, honking continuously, sometimes on the left, sometimes on the right. Shacks of canvas and corrugated iron lined the road. Men stood in their underwear soaping themselves, next to pumps, or crouched by taps, ladling water from buckets over their shoulders. Others relaxed on rope beds. Behind, bloomed luxuriant green trees, yet dust swirled all around. An unfamiliar sickly sweet smell rushed in through the open windows. To cap it all, my driver kept leaning out and peering up to check my luggage.

No sign of any other foreigners on the plane to Banaras. How small and fragile it looked in comparison with the one from London. Halfway down the runway it screeched to a halt and returned to base, where we were unloaded onto another plane. This one managed to take off. It circled for some time, before we were told that 'owing to weather conditions' we would once again have to return to our starting point. The passengers grumbled but didn't seem too concerned and chatted quietly in a foreign language. The third attempt succeeded.

'No need to worry. Indian pilots are very good,' a stewardess said, as she handed me an orange boiled sweet. 'Not like some countries where pilots too proud to turn back if weather not good, or some other problem.'

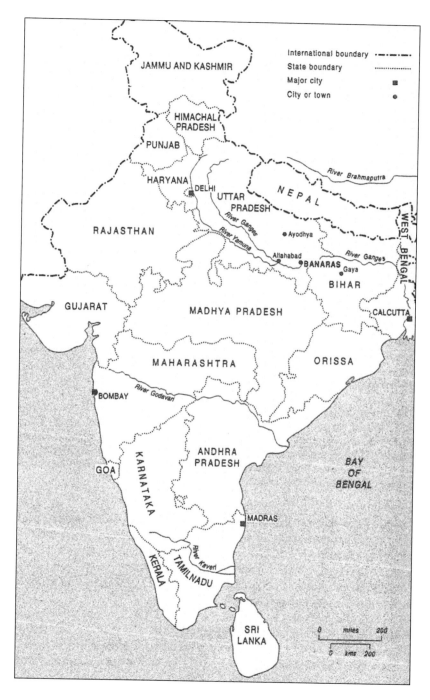

Map of India

CHAPTER 5

1963 FIRST ENCOUNTER WITH THE CITY OF BANARAS (VARANASI)

I STEPPED DOWN INTO A DARK AND DESERTED AIRPORT. ODD that nobody from the university was there to meet me. After all, I was being funded by the Indian Government with a generous top-up from the British Council. I followed everyone onto the airline's bus. They looked at me with interest.

'Here, take my address, if there is anything you need.'

'Mr Shukla at the City Bank will help you.'

'I can get you books for learning Hindi,' said a policeman sitting behind me.

'I already know a few words,' I said, reeling off the equivalents of *hallo, thank you, goodbye, where, how much.*

'Wonderful. Listen, she knows Hindi. Very good.'

We drove into the forecourt of the Clarks Hotel. Porters mobbed us, vying for the privilege of carrying my bags. The other passengers proceeded into the palatial dining room. Turbaned waiters in uniform guided them to tables with starched white tablecloths. I had hardly any rupees left after the taxi in Delhi. How could I afford a meal in a place like this?

'Not to worry,' said a large man in a dark suit from the bus. 'You just go ahead and take food.'

Several waiters and customers from adjoining tables joined in, a chorus of voices urging me to eat.

'How can I? I haven't changed any money,' I said. This was before the advent of credit cards.

People turned their chairs round to look.

'I'm not hungry. A few biscuits will be enough.'

'A few biscuits! The girl will get ill,' someone said.

The prospect of hunger was not my main concern after all the meals on the plane. I was more worried about how I would get to the International Students Hostel in the dark. The Banaras Hindu University campus was on the far outskirts of the city.

'I'm a travel agent,' said a burly man. 'You come. I'll get you a taxi.'

The gateway to Banaras Hindu University

He looked kind so I followed him to a car near the hotel gate. All I wanted was to lie down and go to sleep somewhere. Anywhere. What bliss to lean back against the fraying seat. The taxi jolted. I half-opened my eyes. Spacious avenues narrowed into winding alleyways. Small pools of light in the gloom – paraffin lamps on street-side stalls. Figures milling around as if in a fairground. Goats flashing out of our way.

We drove through an imposing arched gateway into the university – a pocket of tropical forest. Huge trees, luxuriant ferns, and long grass separated flat-roofed colleges, painted soft pink. I breathed in the sweet, fresh air. But what was the loud clicking and croaking rising from the ground?

The taxi pulled up and the driver got out to make enquiries. Nobody seemed to know anything about me. Surely somebody must. We continued to a single-storied, white-washed building. After what felt like a long time, a middle-aged man emerged in his pyjamas, running his hands through his tousled hair. Was it so late that he was already in bed? My watch was still showing English time. After a lengthy talk, and much waving of hands, he called another man from inside the house and directed him to sit next to the driver. Two unknown men in the front of the car. And I had no idea what they were saying.

We arrived at a large bungalow and the driver unloaded my case. I pulled out my last ten rupees – just enough to pay the fare. The other passenger produced a large brass key and opened the enormous padlock on the door. He switched on the light. I sleep-walked into a concrete-floored room, furnished with a wooden bed and a small table. Wire mesh and metal bars protected windows with shutters. A wooden towel rack stood on the right next to a row of hooks for clothes. I dumped my handbag on one of the shelves cut into the thick, white-washed walls. But what was this – a fireplace without a chimney? And a twig broom? The holder of the key was rigging up a mosquito net. 'Bathroom,' he said, pointing to the back of the building. And then he and the taxi driver vanished.

I tiptoed out to the unlit area behind. Clouds of moths brushed my face. I stumbled on the edge of a hole. A tap dripping somewhere but no sign of anything like a bathroom. I returned to my room and collapsed onto my bed. Within minutes, I felt the most tremendous heaving in my bowels. I could only get as far as a large black metal rubbish bin near the door. And that, I am afraid, was how I spent my first evening as a student of philosophy in India.

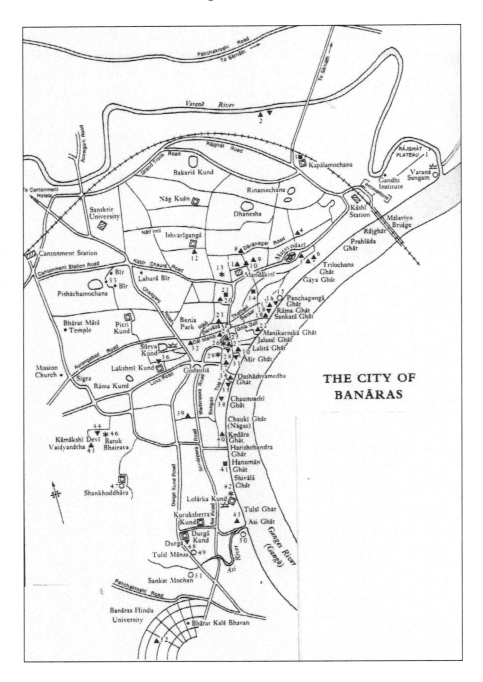

City of Banaras/Varanasi

CHAPTER 6

1963 EARLY DAYS IN INDIA

I WOKE EARLY IN THE MORNING AND UNBOLTED THE SHUTTERS. A blaze of greenery and colour greeted me, a cottage garden, overflowing with unfamiliar shrubs. Scents of jasmine and rose wafted in through the window. Beyond the track, grassland and tall trees stretched into the distance. I stepped out onto the veranda. The outlines of trees and buildings were clear and distinct, as though edged with fine pencil. A large notice at the gate announced: 'The Women's Annexe to the International Students Hostel'. The desecrated metal bin had vanished. Perhaps that incident was just a nightmare.

An open side door led into a walled courtyard with a washing line at the back. Facing me was a small concrete-floored room with a bucket and tap. Water trickled out along an open channel.

'Good morning.' An East Asian woman, perhaps ten years older than me, was standing quietly in the corner, holding a brass jug. Her hair was tied in a low bun, with a white flower tucked behind one ear. She was wearing loose trousers and a smock.

'Welcome,' she said, bowing slightly. 'My name is Sujata. I come from Bali and I study for a PhD in Indian Philosophy, at Indology College.'

I found myself bending forward. 'I'm Mary, from England.'

Almost immediately, a chubby girl, aged about seventeen, peered round a door and bounced out.

'Hallo. Hallo. Me, Chun. From Bangkok. I study Pharmacy. Where you from?'

Before I had time to reply, a European woman with rosy skin, and very dark hair and eyes, emerged from another room.

'You must be Mary. I'm Ann Wilson and this is my husband, Jim.' She gestured towards a wiry, fair-haired man who had followed her out. 'We're from New Zealand. You look exhausted.' Ann and Jim were several years older than me.

The women were all wearing baggy Indian trousers and long loose tops.

'Come right in. I'll make some toast,' said Ann, drawing us inside.

We perched on the edge of a rope bed while she toasted bread on an electric ring. It was black round the edges but soft in the centre. I munched ravenously.

'Like you, Mary, I've come to study philosophy,' Jim said, 'but I'm also a mountaineer and have climbed with Edmund Hillary. That's partly why I opted to do my PhD here. I can spend all the vacations in Nepal. It's not far by plane. Our friends at home are all outdoor types. We've more in common with them than with your average academic. Of course, I'm interested in philosophy as well. The examiner of my MA thesis was amazed that I could write thousands of words, weighing up different theological arguments, only to conclude that they were all evenly balanced.' Jim roared with laughter. 'There's never just one way of looking at things. That's why I want to study Indian thought.'

I smiled. These were kindred spirits. And kind as well.

Ann finished making toast and added her bit. 'I felt anxious about coming,' she said. 'After all, he has his climbing and his philosophy. I'm a nurse, but if I took a job, I wouldn't be able to go with him to the expedition base camps in Nepal. So I occupy myself with painting. I carry pastels everywhere. There's so much to look at. I've already exhibited once in Kathmandu.'

Sujata sat at the end of the bed, straight-backed and motionless. She spoke only when Ann and Jim were sipping tea.

'My government sent me here to study *Shakti* philosophy,' she said. 'We have forgotten the ancient teachings in my country. Now we need to find them again. But first it was necessary for me to learn English. That took a long time. But it's good. I don't like to stay in my country and be a housewife.'

That sounded like me.

'I practical person, not like you all,' laughed Chun. 'I work very hard, then will have pharmacy shop in Bangkok and earn lots of money.'

These four would shepherd me through my first bewildered days, for this was long before the advent of the *Lonely Planet Guides* in 1973.

Ann showed me the squat toilet. 'Just be careful you don't fall in.'

They all smiled. 'It depends on your leg proportions,' she said.

Chun explained how to bathe by crouching on the floor of the washroom and ladling water from a bucket over my shoulders.

'If you don't want to cook – and I definitely didn't, hardly knew how to – you must go for meals to the main hostel,' Ann said. 'That's ten minutes' walk away. Sujata cooks for herself. We usually go over there. But first you need something for your diarrhoea and your mosquito bites. Look, you're covered in them.' She rushed into action. 'Now come and meet Dudhnath.'

The annexe servant cringed and smiled.

'I get fan for you, memsahib, and clean room very good,' he said.

I hated being called memsahib, and I didn't want a servant, but hadn't the energy to resist, and I liked his face.

We all went in again for another cup of tea.

'The campus is one of the largest in the world,' Jim said. 'It occupies the land of twenty-four villages, three square miles. The villagers now provide the service work force.'

Ann handed me a roll of toilet paper. 'You mustn't drink the tap water,' she said. 'And don't eat ice-cream or salad.'

Don't eat anything, perhaps?

A chorus of voices now chimed in.

'Be careful to avoid rabid dogs.'

But how would I recognise them?

'Get your letters franked in the post office or the stamps will be removed... And check sandals for scorpions before you put them on.'

My mouth dropped open. I wasn't expecting this. Britain, for a brief historical interlude, was enjoying an unprecedented low rate of crime and sickness, and my parents had instilled a trusting attitude towards foreigners, and foreign places.

*

'Patriotism is good, but not nationalism,' my mother had often said. 'I'll never forget one occasion in the war, Mary. We were glued to the hospital windows, watching a stricken plane spiralling downwards. I thought I was going to be sick. Some of the nurses cheered. Then they realised it was a British pilot, not a German, who was burning to death in the cockpit.'

My parents were both active in UNA, the Association for supporters of the work of the United Nations. And in the 1930s they had belonged to the internationally minded Commonwealth Party, sometimes referred to as "communists in bowler hats". The party manifesto advocated a welfare state, as well as the nationalisation of all land, a commonality of wealth – unthinkable as that now seems. As a toddler, I handed out leaflets from my pushchair, clutching my two pretty dolls, one black and one white.

*

That evening I opened the little booklet, recently ordered from the London Institute of Tropical Health and Hygiene, the newest edition of the colonial-era manual, *For People Proceeding to the Tropics*. The first page was not helpful. 'In the event of a cholera outbreak, commandeer the largest cricket field in the vicinity, dig several trenches of twenty feet in length, and shepherd the populace into it as expeditiously as possible.'

The following morning, I set off by rickshaw for the State Bank of India – the only place in Banaras to cash travellers' cheques. A stream of young males were cycling into the campus as I was heading out towards the gates. They rode two abreast, or two on a bike. Their dark, bright eyes turned in unison to look at me. Some shouted and pointed at my exposed calves. I tucked my dress under my knees but

Photo of author

couldn't help staring back. They wore ironed white shirts, and their hair was cut short, not like the long-haired and unkempt students at home. Those on foot sauntered with their arms around one another.

As we passed out of the campus, the air became hotter and dustier. I breathed shallowly, in an attempt to block out the stench of sewage. The rickshaw wheeled and manoeuvred like a small motorboat, cutting its way through a sea of people and cycles. I pulled the hood up against the heat of the sun and held tightly to the side as we bumped and lurched our way forward. An hour later we broke away from the current and turned into a quiet backwater where a spacious garden housed an imposing building – the State Bank of India.

'Memsahib. You go,' said the rickshaw man.

A white-haired sentry, whose bones stuck out from under his crumpled khaki uniform, was gripping a rusty rifle as I stepped into the cathedral-like building. Small windows in enclosed counters around the sides opened onto different sections, each with a queue of men. I couldn't see any women – anywhere. I inched forward. The queues revolved to face me. I shrivelled, and froze centre-stage, as a thousand eyes bored into me. Sweat was trickling from my face onto my denim dress.

A young bank official caught my attention and beckoned me over to the safety of the foreign exchange section.

'Can I help you?' he asked.

I pulled out my book of travellers' cheques and signed the forms he was pushing towards me.

'And now your passport, please,' he said.

'My passport? I didn't know it was needed.' Tears leaked out from under my glasses. I would have to endure that nerve-wracking journey all over again.

He waited, his large eyes softening. Ashamed, I ran out to my rickshaw. He followed me.

'Please come and take tea,' he said. 'My name is Toofan.'

I followed him, like an automaton, to a scruffy tent at the back, with benches and tables. He ordered tea and roasted peanuts. How calm he was.

The next day, I ventured into the city again for a second attempt to cash my travellers' cheques. This time I accomplished my mission. I could buy the necessary extras like an electric ring to make tea and coffee.

Sujata took me to a nearby tailor to be kitted out in local garments to avert the gazes of leering students. I still admired their thick glossy hair and gleaming skin, but now averted my eyes as they passed.

'The tailor should not touch your body when he measures you,' Sujata said. 'I am here so he will behave properly. Men in this place are very bad, especially for the foreign women. And for you it is worst. They think you live like in Hollywood films.'

On the way back, we passed Chun. 'Have you eaten?' she shouted. That was her normal greeting.

'No, have you?' I yelled back.

A bicycle for getting around the University, with its scattered buildings, was another essential. Tree-lined avenues were gloomy in the evenings. The bike was to be assembled on the spot, though it wasn't ready when I arrived at the arranged time.

'Dear Miss, please not angry. I very busy. Now I work double quick. We want you be happy,' the shopkeeper said, smiling up at me.

I plonked myself on a metal stool, under a canvas tarpaulin. Maybe this wasn't so bad. I could watch the world passing by. Giggling college girls wandered along, holding hands. The bike was heavy and old-fashioned, with Sturmey-Archer gears. That evening I rode it to the main hostel, passing peacocks and parrots.

A few days later, I was cycling slowly through the campus. A crowd of male students were riding towards me. They stared hard, laughing and smiling. Women hardly ever cycled in Banaras at that time. As I approached, they fanned out across the road. It would be good fun to force me to dismount, perhaps put the British Empire in its place. I was determined to keep going. It wasn't for nothing that I had memorised that stirring Tennyson poem about the 'six hundred of the Light Brigade' riding into their valley of death in the Crimea. Wasn't there a line from somewhere that 'Britons would rather die than be dishonoured'?

I focused my eyes on the student directly in front of me and kept riding slowly ahead. He kept riding, too, with his eyes fixed on me. The two bikes collided with a loud crash. Both of us tipped sideways. I yelled at him. Would he attack me? But he and his friends scattered in all directions. What cowards, I thought, as I stood there shaking, proudly holding my damaged bike. Why hadn't they stood their ground like men? But it wasn't the Crimea. They knew they were in the wrong. And all I had was a few scratches.

It was something to write home about. By now I was beginning to construct my own collection of stories, all calculated to reassure my parents. I deluged them with letters. It was almost impossible to make phone calls to Britain from Banaras at that time. In one letter, dated 15th July 1963, I wrote:

'Extraordinary birds and animals abound. I rush over to pat a scruffy mongrel in true English fashion and discover it's a jackal or hyena.'

That must have been embroidered for effect. It couldn't possibly have been anything other than a dog.

'Today the New Zealanders saw a rat under the bed. Ann chased it with a broom and the only thing Jim could find heavy enough to kill it with was a Fowler's *Modern English Usage*, combined with a carving knife.'

I had only just learnt that Jim was an ordained clergyman.

'Yesterday narrowly escaped death from a rampaging bull which had trapped me in a narrow alleyway.'

Yes, it was a narrow alleyway, and the bull did have large horns, and was in a hurry. But all I had to do was retreat down a side lane.

The letter of 8th August maintained the pitch.

'I have been hearing alarming tales about bandits on trains. Please buy insurance for any permanent injury which makes me unable to earn my living. It needn't cover death. That would be of no use to me.'

*

A week later, Jim suggested an early morning trip. 'It's time you went to see the sun rising over the Ganges, Mary, since that's what this place is all about. Do you know that the city is on the west side of a huge curve in the river, so it's a natural amphitheatre, facing the rising sun? It's not surprising that it's become a religious centre where Hindus hope to die.'

We set off by rickshaw, with Jim perched on the hood behind us. Rows of sick and deformed beggars lined dark, narrow lanes, spattered with cow dung and piled with rubbish. The alley led down to the stepped bank. A sliver of sun had edged above the horizon, but the river was no more than a swirling, murky backcloth to a mass of forlorn humanity. We wandered along the bank for a few minutes but turned back when we reached high piles of logs stacked at the side of the cremation grounds.

A letter home included a few additions: 'Women sometimes fling themselves onto the funeral pyres to be with dead husbands, although this is now illegal. About thirty people die of smallpox every week and the bodies are thrown into the river. Sometimes you see corpses floating by if you are in a boat.'

These last comments must have been parroted from longer-established foreigners. I never once saw a corpse in the Ganges. Nor had there been any recorded case of a woman committing *sati* in the city, for many, many years, though ancient memorial *sati* stones remained down by the river.

There was so much I couldn't make sense of. Why did the men walk hand in hand? We puzzled over such things in the Women's Annexe. And why were there wet red patches on the road? Was it blood from menstruating cattle, or from patients in an advanced stage of T.B.? How were we to know it was betel-nut juice?

Two weeks later, the rains began. The roads emptied. People stayed at home regardless of office opening hours. The few people on the street carried large, black umbrellas – even men in loin cloths. No sign of any waterproofs even when the rain came down like a waterfall.

The humidity flattened me. As a letter home said:

'Today I couldn't settle to anything. I flopped onto my bed, watching the lizards running up and down the walls. When I got up, I was crackling with irritation, could not remember what I had intended to do, and tripped over a sandal. Then it was time to wash my face and cycle over for a meal. Study is out of the question. I'm often down with diarrhoea. So is everyone else. A hundred girls in the Women's Hostel are sick with fever every day, apparently.'

Sweat trickled down my face and legs, except when I was sitting right below my ceiling fan. I would lie under it, staring up at the huge contraption, whirring and clanking like some monstrous bird. What would happen if it fell off onto my head?

And now my bedding smelt mouldy. 'Why is that?' I asked Sujata.

She was rearranging pots on her window ledge. Her expression and movements were crafted like a work of art. I often consulted her. She always knew what to do.

'It's because you don't hang it outside in the sun.'

I would never be able to attain her serenity.

CHAPTER 7

2006 CONVERSATION WITH SHANTA CONTINUES BY EMAIL

January 30th. Mumbai

Very happy that you're writing at last, Mary. I've read everything you've sent. I sometimes feel uncomfortable when you talk of India as a place for adventure. It's just home for us. Of course, you were only twenty-one. And I had my fantasies, too. Not to mention wanting to go to England, my magical land of streets paved with golden possibilities.

March 10th. Manchester

Dear Shanta. Re-reading the letters to my parents has been a shock. I hadn't remembered how negative my feelings were in the first months. I hope you agree I should carry on with my warts-and-all account. My warts, I mean. India's warts are hardly likely to be cleaned from the record, are they?

March 11ᵗʰ. Mumbai

I think I can rely on you to show India's warts, Mary.

The bicycle incident perhaps was only "Eve teasing" spiced with "foreign girl". But you were right to stand up to them.

March 12ᵗʰ. Manchester

I might have expected your comments on the bicycle incident – you, with your cronies rewriting the Ramayana from a feminist point of view. Maybe to the students it was just "Eve-teasing". To me, it was "stick to your guns" and "we British don't show fear". Perhaps that was because I grew up with a brother, and lots of books on heroic adventures in foreign lands. See attachments.

Love Mary

PART II
THE FIRST YEAR 1963–4

CHAPTER 8

1963 HOSTEL FOR INTERNATIONAL STUDENTS

'Y OU GO FIRST,' ANN SAID, NUDGING ME INTO THE DINING room of the main Hostel for International Students. The buzz paused. A sea of curious male faces turned towards me. Ann conducted me from one table to the next. 'This is Mary. She has just arrived from England to study philosophy in the Indology College.'

Blonde Americans on short-term English teaching schemes sat near the entrance, their bulky bodies threatening to spill out of folding metal chairs. They leaned back, arms and legs spread around, sharing jokes. 'Hi, Mary. Welcome to the International Hostel.'

Three Europeans, nearby, hunched forward, arguing as if the future of the world depended on their opinions. Eberhart, a heavily built German lecturer in his late twenties, and with the beginnings of a bald patch, grinned. 'You might as well go back home,' he said, 'if you're hoping to find oriental wisdom in this place.'

I flinched. And laughed.

The dark-haired Polish Sanskritist in the next seat frowned, and elbowed him in the ribs, while pushing a dollop of brown vegetable curry to the side of his plate.

He lifted his head. 'Ignore him. I'm Chris. And in case you are interested, I'm studying ancient Indian drama and aesthetic theory. And I've found many insights here.'

Eberhart smiled. From the other side of the table, a tall blonde Danish linguist looked up and nodded. He wore a red scarf around his shaved head, like a rickshaw driver. He stood up to get a glass of water, and padded, barefoot, across the room.

'He likes to be called Prem Chand, after a famous Hindi novelist,' Ann whispered, as we moved along. 'He wandered all over the Rajasthani desert in the hottest part of the summer. The police arrested him on suspicion of being a Chinese spy. They couldn't think of any other explanation for such odd behaviour. Chinese troops had recently poured across the Himalayan frontier.'

What an exciting new world I'd arrived in. My interest in India didn't seem so odd here.

Halfway along the room, students of emigrant Indian ancestry chatted together, along with a round-faced African.

'Hi, Mary. I'm Ram from Guyana. This chap is from Mauritius, and he's from Kenya. You won't be remembering all our names yet. Francis here is from Uganda.' They smiled and resumed their conversation.

'They feel more at ease here than in the hostels for Indians,' Ann said, as we proceeded further.

Three Nepali students sat nearby. They waved. And, across from them, at a long trestle table, a contingent of more than a dozen South-East Asians turned to acknowledge me. Mainly Laotians and Thais. Half were wearing ochre robes.

'The monks are Thais,' Ann said afterwards. 'They're only monks while they are studying. That's their custom.'

On the last table, two older Japanese men bowed their heads as we approached, and, duty done, lifted their soup bowls back to their mouths. They were well-established scholars of philosophy and ancient languages. Most of the other non-Europeans were studying scientific and technical subjects.

These were the people I was to spend the next two years with.

*

Between 1961 and 1988, India awarded almost two hundred Commonwealth Scholarships to students from Asia and Africa. By the early 1990s, thirteen thousand were studying in India. Few equivalent institutions of higher education existed at home and it was much cheaper to study in India than in the West. Increasing poverty in Africa reduced the number to five thousand by the end of the decade. That coincided with cuts in educational aid. Western governments no longer calculated any political benefit in funding scholarships for Africans after the collapse of the Soviet Union.

*

Ann and I helped ourselves to full plates at the serving hatch. I looked down at the goat meat curry. Not many bones but lots of greasy gristle. Hot and spicy. My throat flared into a cough. Not boring, though, like the yellow pumpkin curry. That was the only vegetable on offer for the first few weeks. The new monsoon vegetables hadn't ripened yet. Breakfast was limp cornflakes in lukewarm boiled milk. But I could manage. Better than struggling to cook in my room on a kerosene stove, or on my unreliable electric ring.

The Thais would squeeze into the tiny kitchen with raw ingredients to make additional dishes, rice and stir-fried vegetables for breakfast, lunch and dinner. 'No problem,' said the cook, sweat running down his face. He slaved away, seven days a week, in the heat of the plains, while his family struggled on without him in their hill village.

The students in the hostel all ate meat, including the Indians from overseas. Yet the Hindu University of Banaras, founded in the early twentieth century by conservative North Indian Brahmans and their upper caste supporters, was a bastion of evangelising vegetarianism. An exception was made for us. Local students who wanted meat had to venture into the city or wait until they returned home.

'A foreign Sanskritist, staying in one of the Indian hostels, once smuggled in two boiled eggs,' Eberhart said. 'The Warden threw him out.'

'Only last year, two Thais tried to catch tasty frogs one night, behind our hostel. Some Brahman students noticed and beat them up. You have to be careful,' said a veteran Cambodian.

Not a likely risk for me.

A local student, met later, saw it differently. 'You foreign people have no discipline. You eat anything, dirty things like frogs and pigs and sheep. You know what disgusting things pigs eat? And you let it cross your lips. What to say of eating holy mother cow?'

'I don't eat frog,' I said, hoping to gain a smidgeon of virtue.

'No matter. What difference?'

Everyone in the hostel complained about the food, and the cook, and much else, including the materialistic attitudes of the local people and the aggression of the crowds.

'It's even worse for me,' said Francis, the Ugandan.

Eberhart put it more strongly. 'Whatever made anyone think India is a spiritual place? All they ever want to know about Europe is how much I earned and how much my watch cost. Those inspiring Indian philosophies I read about in Germany have disappeared without trace.'

Why was he always so cynical? Surely not everyone in Banaras was like that?

*

We often sat with students from a similar cultural background. The Western students sometimes divided into two, Anglo-Saxons on one table, and Continentals on another. I was the only British student for most of the time. Where did I belong in this system of divisions?

One evening, I joined a group of South-East Asians. The conversation turned to the smells of the city.

'I don't like going into a lecture hall full of Indians,' Chun said. 'The smell of milk is too strong.'

'But I can't smell anything.'

'Of course not. You Europeans also smell a bit milky.'

'I don't know about that,' said an American from the far end of the table. 'But I do know that when I was doing a semester in a UK university, I always tried to sit near an open window. I reckoned those guys didn't shower much.'

*

Visitors occasionally punctuated the daily routine of the dining room. A rotund Sri Lankan Buddhist monk would sometimes shuffle in to join us at the evening meal. He always sat on his own and rarely spoke, so we knew nothing about him. This all changed when a bearded physics lecturer arrived from London for a few months.

'This monk,' he said, 'is an untutored genius – a natural scientist, surrounded by a sea of superstition. He has taken apart a radio and built his own crystal set, using a toothbrush holder. He has also designed a fan, which doubles as a clock that wakes him in the morning with a knock on the head. I am going to write an article about him.'

I could have done with a morning knock on the head. Everybody else, it seemed, got up at around five o'clock. After three years as an undergraduate in Britain, it was hard enough to wake at seven. But however sluggish I felt, I always enjoyed the first moment of day, opening my eyes and looking out of the window at a green world, bathed in golden light.

In late July a middle-aged Indian academic engineer, domiciled in Canada, turned up for a week. He joined my table but at the end of the meal quickly excused himself and left. An argument broke out among the Western students.

'Why doesn't he come back here and try to do something for his country, instead of making money abroad? It's because of selfish people like him that India never advances.'

Only one voice spoke up in his defence. 'Every human being has the right to better his own life,' said Eberhart.

*

Foreign scholars have visited the sub-continent throughout history. Nobody thought it odd to study there before the growth of nineteenth-century European racism, and its transformation, in the 1930s, into the new idea that some societies and economies are immature and backward. Alexander the Great took scribes from Greece to record information on local sciences, medicine and engineering. In the first millennium students travelled from China and other parts of Asia to study at the University of Nalanda, particularly statecraft and Buddhist philosophy. Later on, Arab scholars wrote detailed notes on social customs and ideas.

Once power shifted westwards, the up and coming European states instructed their scholars to learn what they could from India. Jesuit missionaries in the sixteenth and seventeenth centuries gathered scientific and mathematical knowledge. This became a dangerous, even heretical, activity, at times. British scholar-administrators arrived in the following two hundred years. Their interests ranged well beyond commercial and military needs. They gradually ceased to acknowledge their sources as their power and confidence grew.

*

A few weeks after my arrival, an American student of my own age turned up to share my small room. Becky was tiny and perky.

'I'm here to study North Indian music,' she said. 'I've already done modules on the music of China, Thailand, Malaysia and the Maori people. The world is so wonderful, so many varieties and I love most of them. I guess my life won't be long enough to explore them all.'

Like everyone else, Becky rapidly succumbed to diarrhoea. As I wrote to my parents:

'Now it is my turn to scurry around. We are squashed into one room in which I have to cook soups for a bed-ridden woman, who is vomiting, and on a fluids-only diet. Leprosy will be the next thing I suppose' – outrageous exaggeration – 'and Ann is down with hepatitis.'

This was a blow for my family. The presence of a nurse from New Zealand had allayed many of their fears. Life outside the hostel had its tensions, too, as I revealed in a letter tossed off at speed.

'I don't mind if people stare at me but it is infuriating when they laugh and point. Sometimes I feel a blind hatred for all Indians, but it's confusing, as I also find something very attractive about both the men and women. I have hardly spoken to any real locals, apart from the servants, and a few shopkeepers, and I haven't entered the home of any Indian. It looks as if it's going to be almost impossible to form friendships, except with a few Westernised people. In 1958, serious riots erupted when the university hospital committed itself to Western medicine. Students were in the forefront of the resistance. My ideas of cultural exchange are fading away.

'All the marriages here are arranged. Even professors make loud lamentations when girls are born to their wives. The women are not much more than graceful breeding machines. Maybe this is why prostitution and homosexuality are rife in the city. The culture is so different from ours. Even when people speak English, it's impossible to know whether you've really understood.' The letter ended with the pronouncement that 'the Indian mind is completely beyond me'.

My parents wrote back, advising me to 'make allowances for a "backward" country'.

This was awful. Not the response I wanted. But I hadn't been thinking about their reaction. Just pouring out my discomforts on paper. I responded with an indignant defence of India. Hadn't modernisation led us to lose many good things? And what did Dad mean when he said that Christianity is a more forward-looking religion? How could any religion be forward-looking? And he, an atheist, in any case.

By the end of July I was getting desperate because my trunk, containing all my books and clothes, hadn't arrived. I'd assumed it would turn up on the doorstep, just as happened in England, when you went off to university. I hadn't realised that I needed to have the receipt with me. Nor did I remember the name of the agent. It all seemed so long ago since I'd left. Time had expanded like a piece of infinitely stretchable elastic. I'd written to my parents to ring my old landlady to ask for the name of the agency near the main station. And then, in the heat and muddle and all that, I lost their reply with the name in it. The embassy in Delhi had informed me that the trunk would take six months to one year to arrive. I would have to go to Calcutta to collect it.

How would I be able to cope once lectures started? I could barely cope with the practicalities of daily life.

CHAPTER 9

COLLEGE OF INDOLOGY

LECTURES BEGAN AT LAST, MORE THAN THREE WEEKS LATE. I walked into a handsome pink building constructed in the early 1900s in neo-Indo-Saracenic style. High ceilings cooled the lecture rooms. An angular young English man, perhaps in his late twenties, was waiting in the corridor outside the lecture room.

'Are you looking for the MA class in Indian Philosophy and Religion – English medium?'

I nodded.

'So you must be Mary. There are only two of us. I'm Nigel. I am preparing for my Christian mission work in India.'

That was a disappointment. I quizzed him while we waited in the corridor for the second-year class to finish.

'Nigel, what made you interested in Indian philosophy?' I asked.

'Oh, I'm not actually interested in it. But I need to know about it, so I can be more effective.'

'But how do you know you will still prefer Christianity, once you have completed the course?'

'I just know.' He smiled.

How could anyone have such certainty?

The College of Indology

The second-year lecture finished and two plump-cheeked Bengali girls in saris came out through the door. Could they really be as young as they looked? They bowed. We smiled and introduced ourselves, and all stood silently, wondering what to say next. I took a deep breath.

'What made you interested in Indian philosophy?' I asked.

'We want to learn about the time when India was great.'

And what were my motives? They didn't ask. Well, of course, I was seeking wisdom, wasn't I?

Our first lecture was given by Dr Mishra, the Master of the university temple, a scholar with a gentle smile. Unlike his colleagues, he wore traditional dress: a *dhoti* and *kurta,* and a white skull cap. He was also happier to chat.

'Please to tell me what you know about Indian religion,' he asked me.

'I've read a few books on Indian philosophy.'

'Ah, but that is of no use on its own. That is only first stage. You need to learn Sanskrit, and practise renunciation.'

But what was I to renounce? I only had a few clothes, and a couple of books. My trunk had renounced itself.

'Let us leave that for now,' he said. 'Today I give you historic summary of interpretations of the sacred Vedic texts, especially the *Upanishads*.'

First came the *Advaita Vedanta* theories. These insisted on the unity of the *atman*-self and the *Brahman*-universal. But were they talking about a shared biophysical substratum, or a desired state of consciousness? And were the philosophers who *rejected* the Vedas denying the claimed unity of underlying being, or only their opponents' know-all conviction? I so much wanted to find the Truth, with a capital T. As an undergraduate, I had spent months mulling over the arguments for and against the existence of God as propounded by Western philosophers. Not that I was looking for a guru, as foreigners in India at that time often were. I had to work it out for myself. That was the Baptist heritage from my family; no baptism until you were old enough to make a personal choice.

Europe was still wobbling at the tail-end of the old religious world. You might be an atheist or agnostic, but you were not indifferent, and you only made jokes about the wilder fringes of the Christian brotherhood. Hence my atheist father would later disapprove strongly of Salman Rushdie, for his irreverent playfulness with the Quran.

In our second week, the College of Indology organised a 'Felicitations' programme in honour of the new Principal. A speaker gave 'thanks to the gods for having given us a man like this'.

My philosophy professor, N.K. Devaraj, gaunt and bespectacled, stood up. He expressed his regrets that another, named, man had not applied for the office of Principal. Not that he knew anything to the disadvantage of the man in whose honour this was all being held, but offices always fall to those who enjoy position. He quoted Acton's view that power corrupts and ended by saying that he hoped this man would not be corrupted. He sat down, and two girl students placed flower chains round the new Principal's neck. Milky tea and sticky white sweets awaited us on a long trestle table.

That was a daring speech.

'He is not popular with the Brahmans,' Jim, my neighbour from New Zealand, informed me at dinner that evening. Jim was a PhD student, so he knew more of departmental gossip than I did.

'Do you know that he thinks Plato's *Republic* is equal in value to the earliest Hindu Vedic scriptures? He accuses Banaras of resisting all spiritual reformers.'

In Dr Mishra's third lecture he summarised different views of the nature of Brahman.

'I wish I could be sure whether God existed,' I confided at the end.

Nigel wasn't present.

'I don't know why you worry about it so much,' he replied. 'Those arguments miss the point. The real issue is the meaning of words – the meaning of the word "God".'

I stared at him. What on earth was he talking about?

Some of the other tutors simply relayed their lecture notes and then disappeared. They didn't always turn up. Yet attendance at seventy-five percent of lectures was a requirement for sitting the final exam. This worried us, particularly Nigel, until we found we only had to attend on seventy-five percent of the occasions when the lecturer and one student were present. Even that was hard enough. I would often nod off in the afternoon. The working day was still organised in terms of the British clock, without any siesta.

I plodded on through the recommended books. Though not in Sanskrit, they could not be considered lightweight. My arms ached, and the seams of my new blue and orange, hand-woven shoulder bag soon gave way. I wrote notes in the little pink exercise books on sale in the bazaar. The names of some of the East European and South Indian authors were impossible to pronounce. Names like Theodore Stcherbatsky. My struggle to make sense of his two volumes on *Buddhist Logic* pushed the problem of God onto a back burner. How could I worry about God when I didn't know what basic words meant? Any hope of pre-digested answers to difficult questions evaporated. Debates among Christians, as I remembered them, now looked infantile.

A month after the start of the course, I fired off a letter of complaint to the Commonwealth Scholarship Secretary in London. I protested about compulsory lectures, in poor English and of low standard, in the heat of the day, and complained that it was only exam-oriented, with no written work and little scope for discussion. It was just the Western system of lectures at its worst, I ranted, much inferior to the ancient Indian educational system, with its public debates. I received a polite, but firm, reply. They were sorry to hear of my difficulties, but these were some of the problems to which I would have to adapt myself, and any complaints were an internal matter to be settled between myself and the department.

In late August, Dr Mishra let slip that he favoured a *Visistadvaita* interpretation of the Vedic *Upanishads.*

'We stress unity but think Divinity can also be viewed as separate from the world.'

'In that case I'm surprised you aren't more negative about your arch-enemies, the Buddhists. They showed little respect for anyone who affirmed the truth of the *Upanishads.*'

Was I sounding impolite?

'Non-believers,' Dr Mishra said, 'are mistaken rather than sinful. Perhaps you are confusing philosophy with theology?'

But surely even a philosopher would want to challenge a viewpoint he didn't agree with? I definitely would. His easy-going approach reminded me of some of the ancient rationalists I was reading.

'You mustn't take words too literally, Mary,' he said after his next lecture. 'Words are metaphors. Our philosophers always insist that the texts and teachings are no more than branches pointing to the moon. They should never be mistaken for the moon itself.'

I struggled to get my head around all these different views. I hadn't known about the wide variety of intellectual thought in Indian tradition.

'Indians are so materialistic,' Eberhart said, for the umpteenth time, at dinner in the hostel that evening. 'I thought I was coming to a country of mystics.'

'But why on earth did you expect them all to be spiritual? My lecturer was telling us today about the ancient schools of materialist philosophy. Their books were later destroyed but critics in other schools often referred to them. And what do you mean by the word "spiritual"? There doesn't seem to be a Sanskrit equivalent.'

Eberhart smiled.

Why did everyone always smile when I expressed an opinion?

One afternoon in the middle of September, Dr Mishra raised the issue of the relationship between faith and reason.

'Religion and philosophy are not divorced here as they are in the West,' he said. 'We use rational thought to help us find out how to live – how to find peace. To do this we need to know what is real, and what is true. Egoism is irrational. We think your modern analytic philosophers have odd ideas. Why is it necessary for philosophy to be disconnected from questions about the best way to live?'

I remembered how, only a year before, as an undergraduate, I had encountered A.J. Ayer's famously dismissive remark, 'Indian philosophy? What philosophy?' He was one of those analytic philosophers who showed contempt for big questions about the nature of reality, and for anything that smacked of religion, preferring to focus on the logical implications of conventional grammar. Someone should have sent him Stcherbatsky's *Buddhist Logic*, I thought wearily.

'And your Christian writers in the nineteenth century,' Dr Mishra continued with increasing heat, 'made the opposite complaint.'

An elderly *peon* shuffled in to top up the water in the earthenware pitcher in the corner of the room.

'They said the problem with India is that its philosophy is divorced from religious and ethical questions. How can you people hold such contradictory ideas?'

'Christian missionaries and analytic philosophers aren't the same sort of people,' I said, 'any more than *Yogacara* and *Advaitin* thinkers were.'

'Of course not.' Dr Mishra smiled and relaxed back into his chair.

My classmate, Nigel, didn't argue with our lecturers. He already knew what to think.

Dr Mishra sent us off to the well-stocked library to read more about the different schools of Indian thought. They all included numerous subdivisions, with objections and counter-objections, in a never-ending cascade. The philosophers wrangled endlessly over types of knowing, theories of error and the nature of causation and perception. Multiple, alternative definitions of core terms were dissected, along with the variable consequences of each. According to one school of logic, the *Nyayika*, philosophic debate is unsound, unless it follows fourteen rules. I wasn't sure that I wanted to know them. It was hard enough without any rules.

How strange that these thinkers of the first millennium, and even earlier, had thought so hard about what constitutes a reliable source of knowledge. That was one of their favourite topics, as was the nature of consciousness. Does it presuppose a knowing subject or even a waking state? This was long before Descartes, the seventeenth-century French philosopher known for his work on those issues. And could I remain awake as the afternoon wore on?

Where was the intuition-induced sedation of the rational mind that the logical positivists had accused Indians of? More likely, these philosophers were part of a strategy to grind down the opponent until he shouted, 'Leave me alone. I agree with everything you say.' I pitied the thinkers who'd faced the onslaught of Buddhists like Nagarjuna. An alpha male intellectual of the second century AD/ACE, probably from South India, he demolished theorists from all sides. T.R.V. Murti, the Professor of Philosophy in the adjacent Arts College, had written much about him in his internationally influential book on Madhyamika Buddhism.

What I didn't know then was that the passion in those historic disputes was partly rooted in the Buddhist rejection of the underpinnings of the social status quo. So all that nit-picking subtlety wasn't the same as the arguments of mediaeval European intellectuals about how many angels could sit on a pinhead. More was at stake, and many ancient Indian philosophers emphasised reasoning, rarely seeming greatly inhibited by dogmatic reference to the founding texts.

The problem of knowing the world as it is, rather than as it appears to be, was another core topic debated by all the classical thinkers. Dr Tripathi told us the story of the rope mistaken for a snake, or vice versa. How is one to distinguish them and establish the criteria for knowledge? A new twist on this theme was related to me later, by another Commonwealth Scholar, who, before setting off for India, had been given helpful tips at the Commonwealth Universities headquarters in London.

'You must remember,' the director had said, 'that India may seem like a snake at first, but when you get used to it, you will find it is only a rope.'

I struggled over other recurring metaphors. What was the relation of a wave to the sea, and was it the same as the relation of a pot to clay? And could I ever get my head around the idea that I might be no more than a fleeting wave in the ocean?

But it was hard to link any of this intellectual culture to the ordinary people I saw as I roamed around the city, though I often noticed men in heated debate, sitting on the raised ledges above the streets.

We progressed to Hindu myths and legends. How odd that they would sometimes go into reverse, as if they refused to take themselves seriously. Gods were not sacrosanct, but could face correction, or even humiliation, if they were over-arrogant. The path of renunciation was to be followed, but renunciation, too, was to be renounced, if any hint of self-satisfaction emerged. And, according to some writers, a moment of goodwill could outweigh neglect of all the teachings and authorities. Sometimes this was probably the interpolation of a later reformer, but often it seemed more like awareness that a story is, after all, only a story.

Myths were one thing. What I could not bring myself to show any interest in was Hindu rituals. Fortunately, my lecturers ignored them. It was only the ideas of India I wanted. Priestly ceremonies were reminiscent of the mindless superstition of the bad, old European

Staff and students at the College of Indology with Sujata on the front left

past, still found in Roman and Anglican Christianity, not something my family had any truck with. I couldn't see what connection they had with the high-flown debates of the philosophers.

Meanwhile I stumbled on with my head down, still sweet twenty-one, trying to make sense of it all, while, outside, the towering white monsoon clouds scudded overhead in the bright blue sky.

Dr Mishra was happy to do no more than lead me into the intricacies of Indian thought. The other members of the two philosophy departments also wanted to show that early Indian texts had anticipated later European thinkers. That was a major theme in Professor Murti's book. Constant references to Hegel and Hume littered the pages, as though the Indian philosophers would only be deemed worthy of study if shown to resemble, and predate, well-known Western thinkers. Wasn't that over-defensive? Why didn't they attempt to move debates forward, or to contextualise them? Why did they need to do this? The stature of the intellectual giants of early India was now so obvious.

'They feel inferior because of our higher standard of living, and our science,' Jim said one evening. 'They've been to the West and seen what it's like. That's why they don't invite us to their homes.'

But what had standards of living got to do with intellectual confidence?

A week later, Sujata took me for afternoon tea with the Head of the Hindi department, in his large house down a mesh of alleyways in the centre of the city. Hidden from the clamour of the streets, it wrapped itself around a closed courtyard, with pomegranate trees, and flowering creepers climbing up the balconies. The bare, white-washed walls were a soothing relief after the surfeit of pattern in 1960s British houses, with their patterned carpets, patterned wallpaper and patterned curtains. Uncluttered by ornaments, the house's minimalism exuded grace and peace. Sitting on mats, we ate hot spinach *pakoras*. Our host's wife served us, standing unobtrusively in the background, while he attended to us with courtesy and charm. No sense of inferiority in this house. It was me who was anxious. Supposing I absentmindedly ate with my left hand?

But why, I wondered, sitting on my flat roof, early next morning, were so many Indians overawed by European wealth and power? Non-elite groups in Britain faced the same psychological problem. They escaped some of the damaging effects by developing alternative value systems. It didn't matter to the Puritans if they had less money, or lower status, than the Anglican landowners. They were the people who were going to get into the Kingdom of Heaven. Couldn't Indians be similarly resistant to Western opinions? Of course, some could. Only later would I see that the solace of egalitarian ethical visions, or detached historical analysis, was not an option for many of the Indian elites. The running sore of national stigma could only be soothed by retreat to the short-term comfort of a glorious image of the past.

Philosophy wasn't the only subject offered in the College of Indology. Students also pursued courses in history and archaeology, and in the languages and literatures of the ancient, pre-Islamic, subcontinent. But why was Indology the study only of India's *remote* past? The word "Indology" was odd in other ways. I couldn't imagine foreign students going to Britain to study "British-ology", or "British Civilisation" – even if we put aside Gandhi's famous quip, 'British civilisation? That would be a good idea.'

CHAPTER 10

2006 CONVERSATION WITH SHANTA CONTINUES BY EMAIL

March 20th. Mumbai

Mary, I encouraged you to be frank, because I wanted to hear how you felt at the time, even if it sometimes makes me cringe. Of course I have known my share of negative feelings, too, in Britain. But you were naïve to expect to make friends so quickly. Why should Indians be less prejudiced to foreigners than you people?

Students may have been progressive in 1960s Europe, but not in the 1980s. They were too busy then trying to get jobs. Things go in cycles, Mary. My generation could never imagine that prosperous Indians would again start to glorify widows who die on their husband's funeral pyres. Campaigns against sati, by our ancestors, led the British rulers to ban it as long ago as 1829.

March 25th. Manchester

I knew hardly anything of India at that stage, Shanta. Other British students in India experienced a deeper initial immersion. They stayed in Indian hostels, or with families, and mixed only with Indians.

March 26th. Mumbai

And, Mary, going back to your comments on your lecturers. I think it's difficult for an English person to imagine the impact of several hundred years of British domination. Indian self-respect wouldn't have suffered so much if the resentment and contempt for the alien culture hadn't been mixed up with admiration.

March 27th. Manchester

I stand rebuked. But don't you think there's anything in what I've said, Shanta? Isn't possession of a nuclear bomb today another salve? I admit that the so-called British bomb, not really British anymore, is also just a status symbol, a pacifier, to soothe the pain of loss of empire. But hardly anyone I know is in favour of it.

At that stage of my life I hadn't experienced the excitement of meeting cosmopolitan Indian intellectuals, people at home in several cultures, and confident enough to carve out a non-defensive path of their own. They are the unintended beneficiaries of an imperial bequest. The British inheritors of the main estate have been stunted by self-imposed segregation at the high table.

Anyway, I attach more chapters. If it weren't for you, I'd never get this stuff down. Hope you're finding things to say in your new newspaper column. Love, Mary

CHAPTER 11

1963 BRANCHING OUT

B Y THE END OF AUGUST, DOMESTIC LIFE WAS EASING. I NO longer wobbled when I sat on the squat toilet; I now found it more comfortable than the sit-up-and-beg, Western type. Major difficulties like the absence of custard were at last resolved. Ann and Jim managed to get their gramophone to work, so we celebrated by buying a tin of custard powder and a packet of sugar from the food shop in the Lanka parade near the university gates. That was where enterprising Sikhs sold items desperately craved by foreigners, including tasteless tinned cheese. Extra milk was provided by the man who came in the morning with a pail on his cycle handlebars. We spent a Sunday afternoon eating pots of the sweet sauce that we hadn't tasted since we left home.

'What food do you miss most?' Ann asked, as she spooned the last of the custard into her mouth.

'Cheese and salad… crusty bread… bacon… and bread and butter puddings. And wouldn't it be nice if they had fridges so you could eat crunchy cornflakes with cold milk?'

'It wouldn't be the same. It's the humidity makes the flakes soft. I don't know why they hang on to those English dishes. They're not suitable for this climate.'

'They think that's what we want,' Jim said. 'Anyway, Mary, it's a full moon tonight so why don't you join us to see it rise above the river? Eberhart's coming too.'

The water level was dropping dramatically now that the heavy rains had finished. We hired a rowing boat at the Dasasamedh Ghat and drifted past temples still half-submerged, stacked one upon another, steeples rearing upwards. The lights of candles and kerosene lamps dotted the steps. A fresh breeze cooled my face. I gazed up at the moon; its impassive face looked down at me.

Daytime excursions also appealed more as the humidity declined. The following Saturday, after lectures finished, Becky and I set off to explore the rural area between the campus and the Ganges. We cycled away from the city along a mud lane behind the university wall. Green countryside opened out on every side – fields of sugarcane and corn, with occasional shrines and small straw shelters perched on legs. A sharp turn revealed the whole sweep of the vast river, the city gleaming white along the curve of the bank to our left. Ahead, the honey-coloured palace of the Maharaja lay across the water. A couple of boats, with large sails like Chinese junks, glided past.

We stepped down from our cycles. Two young boys with short sticks were hanging around, keeping half an eye on wandering goats. A couple of men stood in the river, oblivious of us. They filled their little brass bowls with water and sprinkled it in the four directions. A younger man waded up to his chest in a side channel, dragging along a fishing net. Images of Old Testament stories came to mind. I pictured Ruth, or David playing his harp while he guarded his sheep. How peaceful it was to be away from the harassment of the city.

That evening, Becky took me into the centre to my first music recital. We arrived at a modest house down a back alley. Jasmine and marigolds lay heaped in front of the lead musician, the famous *shehnai* player, Bismillah Khan. Incense smoke spiralled towards the ceiling. Squashed in a corner against a wall, I struggled to sit cross-legged. The pain in my legs lessened as the haunting melodies drew me out of my body. The men in the audience – and they were mainly men – waved and sighed, even groaned at times, crying out with appreciation. Nobody stared at us. They were far away, lost in another world.

'Do you understand our music?' someone asked me afterwards.

I mumbled something. I didn't know that music required understanding.

Recitals were no more than the tip of the music iceberg. Wherever I went, radios and loudspeakers blared out film songs or devotional verses. Groups of villagers sang as they walked, or rode by cart, to the early morning vegetable market.

Our next musical outing arrived three days later. A midnight trip into the city for 'The Night of the Courtesans'. The rickshaw took a circuitous route to avoid the bamboo platforms erected in the central streets. A lone woman stood on each one, her face glittering with ornaments and make-up. Men thronged and ogled. The first song struck out into the night air. It stilled all chatter and brought tears to my eyes. Thunderous applause followed the closing line. Another woman, though prettier, wasn't musically up to scratch. The crowd spat obscenities.

*

In mid-September, Toofan, the bank official who'd taken pity on me in the foreign exchange section, called round. I'd met him a couple of times when withdrawing cash from my account. He was wearing drainpipe trousers and a nylon shirt.

'*Namaste*, Mary,' he said, draping himself against the edge of the veranda. 'I wish to invite you to one of our movies. *Godan* is based on the classic novel by the Hindi writer, Prem Chand. You have come here to learn about India. This will teach you something of the hardships of village life.'

This was unexpected – and a bit exciting. I hesitated for a moment.

'I like to meet the foreigners and show them places,' he said. 'It is not so difficult for me. I studied at an English-medium school, the

View of river Ganges

Theosophical College. And my parents had English friends in Calcutta in the 1930s and 40s, when my father worked for an American company. They were open-minded, not like the Brahmans in this city.'

Young men packed the courtyard in front of the cinema. My elbows moved outwards and forward on autopilot to create a protective shield, but Toofan pushed his way ahead, and the crowd parted without incident. We sat among families, up in the gallery. The Hindi film was grim, at least the bits I could follow.

Competition for rickshaws home resembled an auction mart. Who would offer the most? Perhaps we did; fifteen minutes later we were comfortably ensconced, with the hood up, and our driver pedalling furiously away from the noise and lights, plunging us into the darkness of deserted narrow lanes. Occasional passing cycle bells and flickering kerosene lights punctuated the tranquillity. We sat in silence until we reached the cooler air of the campus.

I stepped down outside my hostel, turning aside to adjust my shawl. When I looked up, I saw three men emerging from the bushes, closing in on us. They ignored me and surrounded Toofan. Angry voices pierced the silence. They hustled him back the way we had come. The rickshaw turned and followed them. What had happened? It was so difficult to know what was going on in this place. It didn't seem real. As if I was watching a film. I walked slowly into the hostel annexe.

Two days later, a note arrived. It said: 'They threatened me if I didn't hand over a good sum of money. Of course I refused, so they took me to the main gate where the Proctor told me not to associate with a foreign woman student. After some argument, he agreed I could meet you outside the walls of the campus.'

Sujata supplemented the message with her own interpretation. 'The Proctor is responsible for your safety but not if you choose to expose yourself to the dangers of the city. It is considered immoral if an unmarried woman goes out on her own with a man she is not related to. You should not go with him, Mary.'

I stared at her. The next day, two university officials came round.

'You must not see this man. Your name will be spoiled. All Banaras will regard it as a scandal.'

Was this the tolerant India everyone was always talking about? I resolved there and then to abandon my resolution to adapt to Indian customs. Wasn't it a matter of principle to be free to follow my inclinations provided they didn't infringe any higher moral law? And I wanted to see him again. Three days later I heard a knock on the outside entrance.

'Can you believe it?' Sujata whispered, putting her head around my door. 'The Warden himself has come to see you. This is serious, Mary.'

'You must not go out with the man from the bank,' the Warden said.

I listened but puzzled over it after he had gone. Banaras was free in so many ways. Where else could a man – and only a man, I think – saunter down a major street, naked and coated in ashes, with long matted hair? And did the local female students never go out, I wondered?

An outing with local female students soon materialised. Becky's music teacher, Miss Nalini, called round with an invitation. She was a tiny, precise woman, with her hair in a tight bun, a well-respected classical singer.

'Next week,' she said, 'we celebrate a public holiday to remember Gandhiji's birthday. The girls from the music and psychology departments will be visiting waterfalls in the hills near Mirzapur. We will be most happy if you join us. Please to reach the Women's Hostel by 5.15 in the morning. A bus will be waiting.'

I had already peered through the huge gates of the Women's College Hostel. Girls of my age were rocking on swings.

It wasn't easy getting to the meeting place so early, but somehow we managed. Only a couple of students were there on time. To crown it all, the coach didn't turn up for an hour, and didn't move off until everybody had arrived – three hours later. Nobody else seemed to be irritated by the delay. Becky practised her flute. The others chatted. I was fuming. They wore their best silk saris, with gold necklaces and bracelets. Becky and I had put on our worst clothes in case of mud and rock scrambling. They were giggling with excitement and blowing soap bubbles.

The coach reached the river, with its massive tumbled rocks and chain of waterfalls, at mid-day. We stood around waiting for instructions until a lecturer gesticulated frantically.

'You please come this way. Not by the river. Now we are finding that the boys from the metallurgy department have come to this same place. Very unfortunate it is, but how is one to know these things?'

The plan to bathe in saris was crossed off the programme. The staff spent the day rounding us up. We couldn't walk anywhere – couldn't explore the rocks nearby or savour the peace.

'Is it true,' a girl called Indira asked me, 'that British people use paper, not water, to clean themselves after toilet?'

I had faced this once before. 'Yes,' I said. 'They think it is better for the hand to stay clean.'

She wrinkled her nose. 'How is it possible to clean the body properly without water? Of course we clean our hands too.'

Might it be better to use both?

Three lecturers erected a brocade canopy and organised tea-making beneath it. They lit a wood fire and boiled up water with milk, tea and sugar. We drank from unglazed pottery cups and tossed them into the bushes afterwards. What a strange thing to do. The Indian students ate cold spiced vegetables and deep-fried round breads from little metal boxes. We struggled with our dry sandwiches made with sliced, white bread bought from the Sikh shopkeepers near the University. At six, we set off for the four-hour journey back.

The women students were younger than us, often graduating at nineteen. None of them wanted to discuss Indian philosophy, or even political issues. The American students in our hostel seemed almost as alien. Four Fulbright Scholars had just arrived from Michigan to teach English, now that the weather had cooled. Bigger than anyone else, and with more expansive hand gestures, they occupied space, and carried on with business as usual, gradually reshaping everything to fit their own way of life. Expensive meals at the Clarks Hotel, with all the other Americans, were a regular feature, and life was made tolerable by peanut butter from the Sikh store. How could butter be made of peanuts?

Six more soon arrived for a year of study: four women and two men, though 'girls' and 'boys' were the words we used. 'Women' and 'men' were boring, older people, settled in jobs with mortgages. The Americans had completed a six-week orientation course before arrival, but after two days one of them returned home. In the States he had been studying the Vedic texts of ancient India. Adjustment to the present was difficult. Three days later, another two transferred to Delhi. They 'couldn't take anymore'.

'It was the same last year,' Eberhart said. 'Except that they were accompanied by a woman psychologist, investigating cross-cultural adaptability. After a few days she crumbled with dysentery and flew back.'

We all made jokes about the Americans. Only Becky was spared. But it was easier for us. We weren't used to such a high standard of living. And I was accustomed to hiking in the Scottish Highlands, staying in simple youth hostels.

As Becky said, 'In the States we know nothing about hygiene, we don't need to. Everything is automated, so it would never occur to anyone to think about the problem of washing crockery and clothes in the same sink.'

Ants would appear within minutes if a few crumbs were left lying around. At night it was the turn of the rats. My small electric heater, on which I had started boiling water for tea, broke down almost every day. I had to twiddle the wires or shake it. Everything felt damp to the touch and sometimes I got a mild electric shock. As if that wasn't enough, the electricity would often fade out. Fevers and dysentery continued to trouble us, though the monsoon was almost over.

Were we like pampered infants who couldn't survive without the whole supportive public health infrastructure of an industrialised state? Perhaps that was what Gandhi meant when he wrote that people should be self-reliant, and that we cease to be adaptable if we become too specialised, or too dependent on unnecessary stuff. Not that the unnecessary stuff in my trunk showed any sign of arriving. I needed to learn more about the Gandhian movement.

I also needed to study Hindi more systematically. My attempts to teach myself from the old-fashioned grammar books available in the city had proved unsuccessful. Sujata put me in touch with a teacher willing to see me once a week. Padma lived nearby on campus and gave individual tuition in her bungalow. She was in her early thirties with a young child at home. She opened the door without smiling. At the end of my first lesson she asked, 'So what are your experiences here in the International Hostel?'

'The main problem is the food. The meat is tough, and the cornflakes are soggy and limp, and we have pumpkin day after day.'

Padma at once began to tell me about her bad experiences in England when her husband was a medical student.

'You complain about the food in your hostel here. You think it was easy being vegetarian there? Usually all we got was mashed potato, a tomato and a lettuce leaf, sometimes with a caterpillar as well, even in the hospital canteen. You talk of your, what you call, your limp cornflakes. We had our limp lettuce. How I dreamt of my mother's hot *rotis* and *sabzi*.

'And people often gave us lectures on the follies of arranged marriage. Someone once said to me, "What a bad mother you are if you can even consider arranging a marriage for your daughter."' Padma looked down at Sunita, her six-year-old, who was wrapping herself around her knee and gazing up in puzzlement as she heard the note of rising indignation in her mother's voice.

'As if your system of family life is anything to admire. Where is the respect and self-sacrifice for others? You people think India is just at an earlier stage of development. English people can't see that it is a completely different, autonomous civilisation. And they don't know anything about India. We know so much about Britain.'

Padma was in full flow by now. It was all terrible. It was true, but what could I do? When I got back to my room that evening, I fired off another letter to my parents, denouncing English arrogance and narrow-mindedness.

*

Towards the end of term, I made my first trip outside the city, south, to the state of Madhya Pradesh, to the famed temples of Khajuraho, with their sculptures dating from AD/ACE 900–1100. Ann and Jim had joined up with the visiting physics lecturer from London to hire a car from Clarks Hotel.

'It shouldn't be boring,' Jim said. 'There could be tigers or bandits.'

'I try to fit in as many overseas lecture tours as I can,' the physicist said. 'It's unusual in my college but I'm not the only one. I have a colleague who researches Zoroastrians in Iran. She drives a van, cloaked in a *burka*, as though heavily pregnant, fitted out with a tape-recorder and camera. Women not dressed in such a way run a risk of being beaten or killed in riots.'

I gazed up at him. The world was unfurling like a giant flower, revealing endless possibilities. When would I have the opportunity to accomplish such exciting acts of heroism? The hardships of our journey, though, were more to be endured than conquered: two hundred and seventy miles of narrow roads, with a driver who had never been required to have a driving licence. We manoeuvred around, and hurtled past, buffalo carts, cows, sleeping dogs and goats. Clumps of women, weaving baskets, would suddenly appear in the middle of stretches of otherwise deserted road. 'Slowly, slowly please,' Ann implored. I gripped the window frame and closed my eyes. Our driver accelerated whenever he saw a pigeon. He got two, squeezed on the brakes, and leaped out to bag them for his evening meal.

Hooting persistently, with animals fleeing in all directions, we left the plains and climbed up onto a plateau with scrubby vegetation. Camels stretched up to eat leaves from dusty trees. The precipitous descent took us past waterfalls in steep wooded gorges. Elephants strolled by the roadside, and monkeys and parrots balanced on branches.

'Must go very fast,' our driver said. 'Many bandits here in this jungle.'

A cluster of Jain temples among wooded hills and grassland awaited us at the bottom. The car jerked to a halt and we all climbed out. What a relief. Monks sat cross-legged outside their cells and images of meditating yogis stood inside the shrines. An eagle balanced on one pinnacle. In the distance buffalo bells tinkled.

We stretched our limbs for a few minutes before preparing to set off again. An elderly monk beckoned. He approached, and with a gracious bow, presented us with handfuls of exquisitely scented jasmine petals. How I longed to prolong the loveliness of the moment. Should I remain here and give up studying? Yet we turned away, and by evening I was sitting in Khajuraho, like some Victorian official, sipping lemon tea on the veranda of a *Dak* bungalow, the government guesthouse.

Breakfast the following morning was *rotis* and fried eggs. We walked across the grass towards the temples. A sprinkling of Asian and Western voyeurs were already hard at work, peering up earnestly at erotic sculptures. I spent more time behind bushes relieving myself than contemplating the sculptors' representations of the permeability of body boundaries. Hardly anybody boiled drinking water. It smacked of colonialism. And nobody drank bottled water – I don't know if it even existed. And this was long before the advent of the ultra-violet water purifiers that prosperous urban Indians now use.

CHAPTER 12

BANARAS: RESIDENT EUROPEANS AND ANGLOPHILES

'HAVE A LOOK AT THIS,' ANN SAID ONE DAY, AS WE MUNCHED toast. She pushed a battered paperback towards me. 'Jim found it at the airport.'

It was a novel, *The Necklace of Kali*, by Robert Towers, published only three years earlier. I took it away to read. Most of the characters were American. Jim had underlined a piece spoken by Martin, its only Briton.

'My theory is that the earth's crust is thinner in India than anywhere else in the world. And at Banaras there is an actual puncture, a sort of crater leading all the way down. Banaras will triumph over the refrigerator... its insatiable darkness will swallow and suck in the rest of the world. London and Paris and New York and Moscow are all built on the foundations of Banaras. It is the oldest city in the world, and it will outlive the rest.'

Jim had pencilled 'rubbish' in the margin.

That was a relief. I read on.

'Then Martin's... friend realised he was drunk.'

Banaras had succeeded in sucking in one larger-than-life figure, Allen Ginsberg – but the American Beat poet walked willingly into the city of sun worship, drawn by its promise of light, and by the prospect of difference from the now despised social order of industrial society. He rented a room near the river front at the end of 1962 and left the city two months before I arrived. This was a new kind of white man. 'He was the American with long dark hair and beard, like a wild man, like one of our *tantric* holy men, a bit dangerous maybe, always wanting drugs and sex,' said a bookseller in the city centre.

Ginsberg heralded the post-war rejection of the deferential conventions of the old American and European class systems, now made possible by growing prosperity and social mobility. Personal experience and fulfilment could now be the goal, as well as the yardstick. Individuals had to construct themselves from scratch – that at least, was what the writings of the French existentialists seemed to be claiming. And Nietzsche's earlier emphasis on self-assertion suddenly made complete sense. But "Beat" philosophy was more than this, according to Jack Kerouac. It involved a search for a beatific vision, as well as a state of exalted exhaustion. Ann Charters, in her introduction to Kerouac's 1955 version of *On the Road*, pointed out that:

'Kerouac was never able to convince his critics that the Beat generation was basically a religious generation, that the characters in the book were actually on a quest and the specific object of that quest was spiritual.'

Not that I knew much of this at the time. Most of us who travelled to study in India during the 1960s were considerably less flamboyant than Ginsberg, but we shared his elevation of individual freedom and experience to a transcendent value. And, for some of us, that chimed in, paradoxically, with the older, subversive, Puritan emphasis on personal independence. So, too, did Ginsberg's anti-elitist rebelliousness. That was why foreign art students in India at that time often opted to study street art as well as the great works of the classical past.

Ginsberg may have been a one-off, but Miss Lewis, the first long-term Western resident I met, was another foreigner in love with the idea of India's difference. Miss Nalini took Becky and me to her home at the far end of the parade of shops outside the university. We entered through a large gateway in the high wall behind a fabric store. The flat was part of a single-storied, cream-coloured building, circling a walled garden.

Miss Lewis was aged about sixty, and wearing flowery English clothes, with a skirt that ended well below the knees. She welcomed us into her small living room. Curtains of bright, hand-woven textiles matched cushions sprinkled on cane chairs – quite unlike homes in Britain at the time, or in Banaras, where guests usually sat on wooden beds or mats on the floor, except for those with Western aspirations, who used plastic or wooden chairs, with unobtrusive functional cushions and curtains.

'I am Irish, not English,' she insisted in a very Southern English accent. Her face was inflamed with eczema and she continually brushed her right cheek with her hand. Placing a pan of water on a kerosene stove to make tea, she explained how she had come to India.

'It was all to do with a great Indian philosopher named Mallik. I met him at Oxford. He was a wonderful man. Many people think he is the most original thinker of the last two thousand years. He died five years ago.' She dabbed her eyes. 'I had promised that I would take his body to be burnt in Banaras and would maintain the memorial trust founded to publish his works. After his death I felt it was time to make my life in India so I left England by plane, with only a suitcase, and the body in a coffin, putting whatever money I had into the trust. I now live on a few pounds a month. The distinguished philosopher, Professor Murti, met me at the airport and had the foresight to bring a set of tools for opening the coffin, so that the body could be removed for cremation. Imagine a philosopher being so practical. He was so kind.'

Her eyes filled with tears. How honoured I felt to be in the presence of someone who had participated in such solemn events.

'After a few weeks,' she continued, 'I began to look for somewhere to make my home. It was not easy. The landlord demanded a letter from my father, giving permission for me to live in a flat on my own. But he had died twenty years earlier.'

A month later, Becky and I visited her again. She recounted more tales about her life. It was the first of many such occasions. Ann and Jim were less willing to provide an audience.

'I excelled in my maths degree,' she said, as she poured tea into a fine china cup, 'but by the terms of my scholarship contract I was bound to teach for a few years. I couldn't bear the thought of that so, on the day of my graduation, I fled from Ireland to France. I lived there for three years on a pittance, learning the language, and then moved around Europe, acquiring German and Norwegian in the process. Returning to my remote village in Donegal, I heard from my old principal about a job with Bovril, in milk chemistry. I rapidly taught myself the subject and was soon manager of a factory in Devon, in charge of two hundred women and four hundred men. There I lived in the lap of luxury, tended by the local squires, eating cream, and riding horses.'

We managed to extricate ourselves after a couple of hours and get back to the rickshaw we'd kept waiting outside. Becky wanted to deliver a letter to one of her friends, so we continued to the city centre, to the Godaulia crossing.

'It's all very well for Miss Lewis to see Banaras as the source of all wisdom,' I said. 'She doesn't get harassed all the time.' How could I be open to what was around me while I had to expend so much energy walling myself off from the onslaught of male eyes? For fleeting moments, I could, and that was when the city put out its tendrils and wrapped me in its web. My mind would reel back for a moment from the merry-go-round of sensation, attempting to retain control, dizzied, until it yielded once more to the seesaw of delight and nausea. Consciousness of myself would slip away as I was swept along by the crowd welling up against the sari shops and shrines.

Becky laughed. I peered out from under the safety of our rickshaw hood and savoured the sights: mature women of extraordinary grace in silks and gold, sailing like ships in calm waters through that eddying mass of humanity; small boys shouting with excitement as they cut down their rivals' kites with glass-impregnated strings and raced to bag their trophies; tangled piles of sleek-skinned, large-eyed babies resting their heads on soft-haired goats by door steps; emaciated old men; ragged lean-to shops thrown up out of tin and canvas; and, above all the agitation of the crowd, the lines of flat-roofed buildings, with carved balconies and crumbling ornamentation – here a collapsed house, there a new one going up with its rickety scaffolding, sun filtering through trees growing out of temples. There was no end to the sights of Banaras streets.

*

Allen Ginsberg and Miss Lewis represented one face of European attraction to India. Another was displayed by Professor Bashworth, an elderly Englishman, based in the Mining Department, who had stayed on after Independence in 1947. Twice a week he gave dinners for amenable Western students. All new arrivals from the homeland were invited to his large home in the campus. My turn came round a month after my arrival. Ann, Jim and Eberhart had already eaten there many times. Professor Bashworth was a heavily built man, dressed in a well-ironed bush shirt and linen trousers. A servant in uniform led us from the veranda into a spacious living room furnished with ornate mahogany chairs and a large table covered with a starched white cloth. After the canteen fare at the International Hostel, the professor's food was lavish: quail and guinea fowl, roast potatoes, savoury bread sauce, and delectable trifles and bread pudding – proper English food. We fell upon it like half-starved waifs, but there was a price to pay.

'I am an international expert on steel, you know, here under British Council auspices. But I get lonely without company from home. I've known a few people in my time. Lord Dudley used to ask me what I thought about the Indian situation. And I knew George the Fifth, too.

I can't tell you the details of what we talked about, of course. We had a whisky or two together. We used to get a lot of good gin, too.'

The Professor tried to ply us with drinks – but wasn't this prohibited in Banaras? In any case I came from a Methodist/Baptist background and had not tasted gin before. What an unpleasant, burning sensation. The Professor showed us cuttings of newspapers, with photographs of himself, standing beside maharajas and other bigwigs.

'I'm a lay reader in the Church of England. I came out here to do my little bit to help Indians.'

I looked round at his palatial house with his eight servants.

'Why don't you come again in two days' time? But of course, if you get bored with an old fogey like me you can make excuses to not come.'

'I'm not going there again,' I said to Becky. 'I don't care how good his food is.' Americans were never invited.

The prospect of meeting additional colonial relics soon arose again courtesy of a temporary visitor to the hostel. Terry looked Indian but had the mannerisms and accent of a Londoner.

'He was adopted by an English family,' Ann said.

Terry was to preach the sermon on the coming Sunday in the local Anglican Church. It was situated on the far side of the city near the Clark's Hotel where I had first arrived, in the Cantonment, where the British colonial army had once been stationed. It looked just like an English parish church. I had not been to any place of religion in Britain for some years, and the Anglicans were off the radar, but in India it was okay to try anything once.

'Are you sure you want to go?' Becky asked.

The church showed no concession to Indian tastes. Once in the pulpit, Terry's cheerful modesty metamorphosed into threats about hellfire and damnation. After the rituals came to an end, a charming couple, the Simlas, introduced themselves and invited us to join the lunch they had arranged for Terry at their large bungalow further along the road. An American student standing nearby came along too.

Mr Simla was Chief Inspector of Police in Banaras. His house was furnished in the British style and we sat at a table for lunch. It was worth enduring the threats of damnation to eat this, I thought, as Mrs Simla served mounds of lamb *biriani* onto my plate.

'We are Christians, so we follow Western customs and don't give dowry,' Mr Simla said. 'But it is very difficult to be a moral person here. There is dreadful corruption among the police. It would be easy for me to make thousands of rupees. Every day I get letters threatening murder, but nothing ever happens.'

'Really?' I looked up, wide-eyed.

'You needn't worry about walking around. A European girl here is much safer than an Indian one. Everyone knows six hundred police would be out looking for her if anything happened.'

This was comforting, if strange.

'Not long ago an Indian girl was kidnapped and held for fourteen days, to be sold as a wife. Luckily the police found her in time.'

It was like listening to a story on the radio. Was I becoming part of a story?

CHAPTER 13

AUTUMN VACATION: THE RAM LILA AND A GANDHIAN COMMUNITY

'YOU COULD SPEND THE ONE-MONTH AUTUMN VACATION AT A Gandhian community for village girls in the Himalayan foothills,' Miss Lewis said when I next called in. 'It's a farm and school combined. And you need a change after three months of the monsoon.'

A chance to learn more about my hero.

'I'll do all the bookings as it's your first train journey. And I'll come with you to the station. But you mustn't set off until you've seen the start of the Ram Lila street theatre this week. The performances continue for twenty-nine days.'

Overnight, makeshift stages appeared everywhere. Becky and I wandered down an alley that opened into a square. Elaborately dressed figures stood motionless on a platform. A storyteller on the ground below recited verses in a rising and falling tone, alternating with words and gestures from the actors above. Drummers and flautists, seated at the side, occasionally launched into action, and an intermittent bell indicated when interest was moving from the actors back to the narrator. It was more like a pageant than the performances

Ramnagar Palace

we knew. As we drew nearer, the whole audience revolved silently to look at us, but then, just as swiftly, resumed their concentration. We sat down cross-legged on the ground with everyone else.

After ten minutes, Rama, Sita and Lakshman were banished to the forest. They stepped off the stage and walked along the road, carrying bows and arrows. We followed with the crowd until they reached a raised stone platform, part of a small temple, where a long-haired ascetic in orange robes was waiting. They conferred with him and then all disappeared behind an orange sheet, held up by two men.

'He is teaching them the Vedas in a cave,' a woman nearby said.

The audience wasn't at all irritated by this and waited for ten minutes while a man in ordinary clothes moved around the stage, fanning away the insects. Nobody seemed to feel this damaged the dramatic illusion. Of course, it was play. Why pretend otherwise?

'We must see the Ram Lila sponsored by the Maharaja across the river in Ramnagar before you go to the hills,' Becky said in the rickshaw home. 'That's the largest and most impressive of the performances in Banaras.' Becky was based at the East-West Centre at Honolulu, so she knew all these things. The following day we boarded a small ferry with a handful of foreigners. We disembarked at the palace and climbed onto an elephant. Swaying like a boat at sea, we followed in the Maharaja's procession.

Vast crowds congregated in a huge open space. A fair stretched in all directions, with vendors carrying trays on their heads, selling balloons and toys, sweets and fruit. Families from neighbouring villages had camped wherever they found a spot, their brass cooking vessels stacked on mats. They roasted peanuts over open fires or baked small savoury wheat cakes in hot ashes. Thousands of ascetics milled around. Some reclined naked, dusted all over with a greenish, luminous powder, and with hair long enough to sit on. I shuddered when I met the intensity of their eyes. They looked sub-human.

*

I was ready now to set off for the Ashram. Miss Lewis met me outside the Sikh store. Our rickshaw halted near the station at the edge of a dense mass of people. She beckoned to one of the porters and showed him a slip of paper with the compartment details on it. He slung my bags onto his shoulder and carved a way through for us. I looked up at the sign on the compartment.

'This can't be right. It's First Class.'

'You will have to change trains at Lucknow,' Miss Lewis said, without pausing. 'I have arranged for Professor Niggam to meet you there and see you are all right. He knows your compartment number.' And, having installed me in my seat, she was gone.

The only other person in the Ladies' Compartment was a middle-aged woman dressed in white. She was asleep when I boarded and still asleep when I departed a few hours later. For all I know she might still be asleep.

Hawkers moved up and down the platform with their brass urns of tea and little baked clay cups, books, snacks and fruits – along with anything else you could think of. Small boys with cheeky faces thrust baskets of dry roasted peanuts in their shells temptingly close.

Shouts and snatches of song blended with the hissing of the steam engine. Porters rushed backwards and forwards, followed by anxious passengers.

At Lucknow I clambered down to find an elderly man positioned outside my door. He bowed and led me out of the station. 'I think the first thing we need to do,' he said with a smile, 'is buy you woollen blankets and socks.'

I hadn't thought to bring warm clothes to India. Our mission accomplished, Professor Niggam took me out for a meal, before settling me on the night train to Kathgodam.

Two elderly women were already snuggled up inside enormous bedding rolls in my compartment. What huge bolts and bars there were on the windows and door – and how strange that Professor Niggam was checking that nobody was hiding in the attached toilet. My travelling companions knew little English and didn't want to talk, so I curled up in my blankets and soon fell asleep.

Six hundred miles later, we arrived just in time to catch the morning bus for the sixty-mile ride on a hairpin-bend road, up seven thousand feet to Nainital, an old British hill station, often referred to as Little England. The town squatted in a claustrophobic valley, wrapped in a cold grey mist, with characterless modern shopping parades. Boats cruised busily around a dark lake. I stood alone outside the bus station in my baggy *selwar* trousers and loose *kurta*, staring at groups of Indian girls sauntering past in tight trousers and fashionable European tops.

A moment later another of Miss Lewis's friends turned up. He conducted me briskly to the Hotel Metropole, the best in town, where he had booked me in for two nights, as instructed. In the foyer he spoke a few words to the proprietors, bowed, and disappeared without saying another word.

I ordered an omelette and fried rice in the almost empty dining room. The hotel prices were exorbitant by Banaras standards. A middle-aged couple and a young man walked in and sat down at the nearest table. They leaned across to shake hands and introduced themselves.

That was nice.

'We are from Bengal. I am a professor of politics in Delhi and my son here is a member of the Indian Administrative Service.'

The son laughed when he heard I was studying Indian philosophy. 'What on earth are you doing that for? It's just a lot of old rubbish.'

His father nodded in agreement.

I stiffened. 'Have you read any of it?' I asked. I didn't want to be rude, but this reminded me of prejudiced European philosophers like A.J. Ayer.

He admitted he hadn't.

'I know some of it does seem to be rubbish, but there is magnificent stuff as well. How can you dismiss it when you've never looked at it? Why don't you try Dasgupta's four volumes, *The History of Indian Philosophy*?' I paused for breath.

The young man froze. His mother pursed her lips and asked the waiter to bring a plate of *pakoras*. There was a moment's silence and then the professor smiled at me.

'The trouble is, Miss Mary,' he said, 'that old philosophy was simply a means to justify the whole damn Brahmanical framework of caste society. Those philosophers might have been as clever as anything. But what can they offer us now?'

'Well, why not try some works by the mediaeval Buddhist philosophers? They weren't defending the status quo. And...' as I saw him frowning, 'I don't mean the older, devotional writings. I mean the argumentative treatises by people like Nagarjuna and Asvaghosa. They're the ones I like most.' Must stop now, I thought.

We ate our fruit in custard without speaking. How could Indians think like that? But maybe I had been dazzled by Sankara's intellectual brilliance. And maybe that kind of spiritual elitism does encourage acceptance of the social order. I choked on a piece of banana.

The proprietor led me to a large, colonial-style bedroom with faded wallpaper and beige floral curtains and cushion covers. I shivered under the skimpy eiderdown. One night of this was more than enough, so the next morning I boarded a bus to continue my journey.

It clanked its way uphill and soon we were out into open country, passing through Almora, a ridge town with breezy vistas. I descended at Kausani, a small village with a few shops. The sky was light and clear, with a panoramic view across the valleys to the high Himalayas. Their dark solidity, and the pinnacled white wall of cloud floating high above, blocked the horizon. But no, that wasn't cloud. It was the snow and ice of Trisul and Nanda Devi. Here, at last, was the vision that had drawn me to India.

Before I had time to ask anyone the way, two women at the bus stop pointed in the direction I must go. I walked along a narrow path through neat terraced fields, with a backdrop of dark green forest. A woman, probably in her thirties, was waiting for me at the door of Lakshmi Ashram. Radha Bhatt drew me in with a warm smile. Next to her, stood a fair-haired Scot, a few years older than me. 'I've been living and working here for some years,' Bill explained. 'Radha first entered the community as a child, but now she handles most of the management.'

Radha took my hand and led me into a long rectangular room without any furniture. She sat me down on a mat and served me rice and *daal* with vegetables on a large brass plate. Bill told me something about the history of the community.

'Lakshmi Ashram was founded in 1940 by an English woman, now known as Sarala Devi. She left Britain to join Gandhi in his struggle to free India from the British. Girls from all over this region of the hills come to live here and have a free education. We teach them literacy and numeracy, spinning, weaving and other traditional crafts, hygiene and improved farming methods, along with Gandhian social and political principles. They also work in the fields, and with the animals, to make their own food, clothing and bedding, though the land is too hilly and rocky to provide all that is needed, even with the sale of their woven blankets. A few older destitute women also live with us.'

I finished eating.

'Come,' said Radha. 'I take you to meet Sarala Deviji.' We walked up a stony track towards a small hut. 'Nowadays she stays alone here. She reads her books, and she spins cotton.'

Sarala Devi was small and serious, dressed in white, hand-woven Indian clothes, with her hair pulled back in a plain bun.

'You are very welcome here,' she said, extending her hand. 'Come and sit next to me. We enjoy having guests like you and we want more people to learn about Gandhi's principles. Gandhi taught us to aim for self-sufficiency. That is why we make gas from cow dung. He thought reliance on merchants puts us at risk of their greed. He wanted us to return to traditional methods of spinning and weaving cotton cloth. Indians had switched to wearing imported Lancashire textiles.

'But tell me more about what you are doing in Banaras. Do you think the philosophy you are studying will have any practical effects on society?'

I hesitated. The old lady chuckled. 'We can't always know the consequences of our actions, Mary, but I am sure you will be fine.'

I told her a bit about my courses. She listened intently.

'I am going to rest now,' she said after a few minutes. 'Radha will take you back.'

On the way down, the fourth adult member of the community introduced himself. He was a local man, with a matted mass of hair and beard, a bit like an ascetic. His gimlet eyes and angular frame disconcerted me.

'How does a spiritual person like you manage to live in an unspiritual country like England?' he asked.

I stared at him. Did he think that he and I were both in the same kind of superior group? And what did he know about England?

It was a relief to turn my attention back to Radha. She led me down to the main building and showed me the space on the floor where I would sleep on a hand-woven rug. Bill explained how he had come to Kausani.

'I travelled overland to India after leaving university, intending to go on to Australia. Once in Calcutta, I searched for a job to fund the next leg of my journey, but all I could find was English teaching in an elite school. That wasn't what I was looking for, but I stuck it out for some months, until I heard about this place. I've decided to stay on in India.'

The girls crowded round us. They were aged from five to twenty and gleamed with health and life, their cheeks rosy with the mountain air.

'What is your name? What country you are from? You like India? Where is your husband?'

They showed me around the buildings, including the library, and the fields bounded by forest. Real countryside at last. Maybe I could go for some long walks.

Our days followed a routine. We rose soon after dawn and I joined the girls in their daily tasks: collecting firewood, digging in stony fields, shovelling dung out of the cattle shed. My shoulders ached. What a feeble townie I was. Taking the cows out to graze was the daily reward. We strolled through the pine forest, listening for the sound of cowbells. Sometimes we sat on a fallen trunk – but not for long. Soon the cows would scatter and move off again and have to be rounded up.

We cooked in turns, collectively. The lentils had to be picked through to remove stones, vegetables to be peeled and chopped. Wheat grains had to be ground into flour on a heavy stone quern, ready for kneading into *rotis*.

I was free to do what I wanted while the girls were studying. Sometimes I sat outside in the fresh, cool air, reading Tolkien's *The Lord of the Rings* – an unexpected find in the library.

One afternoon, I wandered into the forest, following a small track that dropped down towards a wooden house, set by a tumbling stream among low hills. An English-looking woman in a floral dress was pruning roses in the front garden. A man of South Indian appearance was moving pots around. He smiled at me.

'You must be yet another one from Lakshmi Ashram,' the woman said.

I winced.

'We're missionaries. This is my husband. He's from Madras.'

'Aren't you lucky to live in such a lovely place,' I said, looking around.

'Lucky? I wouldn't stay here for another day, if it weren't for the Lord Jesus. I'd be back at home.'

I gulped. Was she insane? Did the Lord Jesus give such specific instructions, and was her marriage part of the divine plan? I snatched a look at her husband, but his face showed nothing. I excused myself and slowly retraced my steps uphill into the pine-needle-carpeted peace of the forest.

A message was waiting for me from a couple I'd chatted to on the bus up from Nainital, inviting me to join them for breakfast at six o'clock the next morning, at the nearby government rest house. They had booked in for a month. It was the first time anyone had invited me for breakfast. We sat on the terrace looking across at the Himalayas, eating *parathas* and fried eggs.

By now I was wondering if I ought to become a vegetarian permanently. Ought I to give away most of my possessions when I

Sarala Devi at Lakshmi Ashram

returned to Britain? How awful that I had travelled First Class on the train. The adults in the ashram believed so strongly in self-sufficiency that sometimes they dispensed with the bus and walked to the station – a hike of several days. They didn't purchase anything except for soap, or occasional stamps. That was why, on my return train journey to Banaras, I travelled Third Class, squeezed in with all the crowds.

No charge was made for staying at the ashram though a donation was customary. The community could not survive without extra cash income. Bill suggested an acceptable amount. It seemed paltry.

'I'd like to give more,' I said.

'Money is the easy part,' he said. 'It's people and labour we want.'

Did this mean I should give up my studies and do something practical?

CHAPTER 14

2006 CONVERSATION WITH SHANTA CONTINUES BY EMAIL

April 30th. Mumbai

Mary,

It was your stomach problems and the monsoon that gave you such a jaundiced view in July and August.

I like your account of the musical life of Banaras. But your description of the picnic sounds a bit unfriendly. They weren't nature worshippers as you seemed to be. For them, part of the pleasure was being with people, not getting away from them. Could that be why you have so much loneliness in the West?

May 2nd. Manchester

Of course I have a different view of Banaras now, Shanta. I was amazed to find the phrase 'awful little streets' in one of my letters.

Love, Mary

June 25th. Mumbai

Mary,

Your Lakshmi Ashram people perhaps were later involved in the Chipko movement, hugging trees to protect them from timber merchants?

June 26th. Manchester

Yes, they were. They must have had a major impact in that region, in their own quiet way. At the end of her life Sarala Devi went to Central India where, along with others, she persuaded bandits, hidden in forested gorges, to give up their weapons.

See attachments. Love, Mary.

CHAPTER 15

1963 RETURN TO THE CITY OF CEREMONY, TEMPLES AND MOSQUES

'WE'VE BEEN INVITED TO A WEDDING,' ANN INFORMED ME, the day after I got back. 'Why don't you come too? Nobody will mind. We're going to the groom's house this evening.'

I was beginning to love the informality of Banaras life.

'Ceremonies have already been going on for a week,' Jim said, as we eased our way into the packed courtyard.

The young groom sat centre-stage on an embroidered silk rug. He was wearing a Western suit, along with a skull cap, a silver, star-shaped brooch on its front, and a white feather on top. A portly man was twining gold thread and flower garlands around his neck while a priest marked his forehead twice with coloured powder. An elderly woman wandered through the crowd, holding a small silver dish. She paused in front of me and dabbed scented paste on the back of my hand.

Ten minutes later, relatives ushered the groom out onto a horse garlanded with paper chains and flowers. A crowd of men swept us along after him. Women and children followed. We wound through narrow streets in which we had to walk single file, picking our way through mud and dung, and around cows and goats. High buildings rose sheer on both sides. The groom's father sported a long beard, like an Old Testament patriarch. His mother carried a candle; her forehead sparkled with gems and red paste. At last we reached the bride's house.

'He hasn't seen her yet,' someone said.

The bride's parents stood on the threshold of their house at the top of a flight of deep stone steps. Her mother's face and hair were partly covered by the end of her sari. This was like something from *The Arabian Nights*. She stretched out an arm in welcome, offering the groom a coconut as he began to mount the steps. But why was she trying to grab his nose with her left hand? He ducked back at once, seeming not too surprised, protecting his face with a handkerchief, while still attempting to take hold of the coconut. I think he succeeded, but it was hard for us to see over the heads of the crowd. The procession began to surge up the steps.

'It's nine-thirty already,' Jim said. 'Time to get over to the annual Music Conference. It's nearby in an open field. We don't want to miss Ravi Shankar on the sitar. We can always come back to the wedding later.'

Ravi Shankar was playing in a huge tent. He was warming up.

'Performances by India's leading musicians will continue for over sixteen hours,' a man in a suit, next to us, said. 'Shopkeepers have pulled down their shutters, and office workers have taken casual leave.'

People wandered in and out of the perfumed tent, munched *pakoras*, or dozed with their feet on empty chairs. Yet when the music built up to a moving sequence, they lifted up their heads and listened with rapt absorption.

At half-past two in the morning, we returned to the wedding. It was difficult to find our way back through the deserted network of passages leading off in all directions. Twice, I nearly tripped over sleeping dogs. We passed figures sitting cross-legged, wrapped in shawls, asleep on ledges above us. Nobody objected to us wandering in and out of the bride's house, so we stayed for a few hours. She sat next to the groom in the centre of the gathering, heavily veiled in a blaze of scarlet silk and glittering gold. At last her mother lifted the veil. We three were almost as tense with expectation as the couple. Everyone else looked relaxed. They'd seen it all before. A faint shadow of disappointment crossed the groom's face.

*

Another kind of wedding soon followed. An American student in the International Hostel invited me to the nuptials of old school friends.

'They've been travelling around India for several years and want to marry here in the holy city.'

We crowded into a small hall. The bride's T-shirt revealed every curve. She drew a diaphanous veil over her face.

'We've found a priest who will do it for us,' she whispered.

Every few minutes she pushed aside the veil to puff at a cigarette and then pulled it across again, lowering her head in a pantomime of modesty.

I gaped. What would Indians think? I had never seen a woman smoking in Banaras. Only occasionally an elderly low-caste woman. I looked round at the handful of Indians in the room. Their faces said nothing.

Marriage in the West was a challenge often thrown at me.

'You people have no morality or discipline. Here, if a girl is seen with a boy more than once, we think she is spoiled,' a lecturer explained. 'It would be difficult for her to get married. That is why girls sit apart in lectures. Not like the West where everyone gets divorced.'

I winced. What would they think about the different men who'd accompanied me to historic buildings in the city? And, anyway, it wasn't true that everyone in the West divorced. I knew of only two cases.

Weddings were usually held in private homes, but much ritual took place in public spaces. Wayside shrines perched in the roots of banyan trees in almost every street and square. Their images of deceased local saints, and strong men, spilled out all around. Offerings of fruit and coins lay at their feet. In hidden alleyways I sometimes passed exquisite sculptures, half covered in lengths of fabric, with incense sticks poking out of the folds. Irregularly shaped lumps of stone, smeared with red powder, poked out of the most unlikely corners: anywhere someone felt a source of special power emerging, almost like a spring breaking through from underground.

These bore not the slightest resemblance to anything I thought of as religion. I still harboured clear ideas about God, even if I didn't believe he existed. God, surely, must be a lawgiver, or a glorified role model, a means of bolstering social and moral codes – not a lump of stone smeared red? Shouldn't an icon of divinity have a face of beauty and compassion? Mass-produced posters showing plump gods, with rosy cheeks and benign smiles, were possibly all right – though they looked more like film stars – but not bloodthirsty images of Kali and Shiva. I'd forgotten the Christian image of a tortured Christ, racked with pain.

I often wandered into temples or hovered on the fringes of ritual activity. Participants sometimes beckoned me to move closer. But some spaces were definitely off-limits. I knew better than to attempt to enter the most sacred Vishvanath temple. That was about to change.

At the beginning of November, a British Commonwealth Scholar from Delhi arrived for a few days, with his wife, Vicky. She was wearing a tailored Western dress and her hair was stylishly cut. Not like us, with our long hair. Hairdressers for women did not exist in Banaras at that time. Tony was well-groomed, in a linen shirt, and trousers.

'You're wearing Indian clothes,' Vicky exclaimed.

Tony was doing a PhD, researching Economic Planning and the Five-Year Plans for which India had become famous.

'Isn't India great,' Vicky enthused.

'And isn't the Commonwealth Scholarship Scheme great, too,' I said. 'It's such a wonderful opportunity for us to learn from other parts of the world.'

'Of course it is,' Tony said, 'but you do realise, don't you, why the British Government puts money into a programme like this?'

'I suppose it's to show the new sense of mutual respect?'

'It's more instrumental than that, Mary. Geo-politics, I'm afraid. The ultimate aim is to cement links among the English-speaking classes of the former British Empire, and to protect a large trading community. They hope the Commonwealth will prevent the spread of socialist ideas, and the growing power and aggression of the Soviet Union.'

'Really? Surely governments don't calculate ahead like that. As if it's all a game of chess?'

'I'm afraid so. But where are you going to take us, Mary? We're very keen to visit the famous Vishvanath temple.'

I hesitated. None of the foreigners from the International Hostel had ever managed to get inside. Entry was restricted to Hindus. It would be a shame to disappoint my guests. And it would be an exciting challenge.

A saffron-robed *saddhu* stopped us at the entrance. 'Hindus only,' he said.

'I am a Hindu,' I responded. After all, I did sometimes feel I was.

He pointed to a little shop next door. The proprietor beckoned us in and served tea on a tray. Perhaps I could match local styles of ornate courtesy. Could I charm them into allowing us into the temple?

'I cannot express the profound depths of my gratitude,' I said. 'We shall remember your kindness in all the years to come. Hinduism embraces all the religions of the world and extends its arms to welcome all who yearn for the infinite.'

Tony did his bit too. 'We know that Christianity originated in India before it spread across to Palestine.'

'You go in,' somebody said.

Our strategies had paid off. We removed our shoes, deposited our bags, and, with scarves draped over chests, and flowers in hand, entered. We hesitated near the door. Worshippers pushed past, intent on getting closer to the image of the *lingam*. We followed, copying what they did. We bowed before the central shrine. Priests chanted in the inner sanctum, swaying with total concentration. But the temple was noisy and dirty, with a multitude of untidy statues jostling for attention. A priest smeared red paste on our foreheads. Another placed garlands around our necks and gave us each a small leaf plate holding two milk sweets from the offerings to Shiva. Mine looked slimy. Squeezing past a cow, I sneaked into a side shrine and reoffered them to another god.

We didn't know the correct etiquette. What if we blundered? 'Let's get out,' I muttered. Tony and Vicky turned at once and headed for the entrance. We stood outside for a moment, deflated. It was something of a coup to have got in, a story to tell when we returned to the safety of the hostel. But had we done something to be ashamed of?

It was impossible for me to relate what I'd seen to the relics of my Protestant Christian notions of the religious life. Maybe the English word 'religion' was not applicable in another culture? And was it even useful in Britain?

The shopkeeper stepped forward and bowed. 'I believe there is a man out there expecting a rupee or so,' he said.

Was this a bribe? Or was it that, like children, we didn't know the basic rules and had to be instructed? But perhaps they understood us more than we understood them. Were they just playing along with us?

By now, Vicky had fallen head over heels in love with Banaras.

'It's just like a Spanish city. Tony, why don't we leave Delhi and transfer here? Can't you telegram London now?'

Tony raised his eyebrows. 'Most definitely not. I need the intellectual stimulus of the capital if I am to have an academic career. Delhi has outstanding economists who are part of the international world – study groups with people like Nehru.'

How strange, to let career ambitions determine your life. Experience and learning was what mattered.

Tony and Vicky returned to Delhi as planned.

*

I often passed mosques when I walked through the city. They catered for the third of its residents who are Muslims. I admired their graceful architecture but remained outside. Going to Hindu temples was what Western foreign students in India mostly did; mosques didn't have the same fascination. Perhaps their solemnity made us apprehensive. And we were looking for something different. Islam was too similar to Protestant Christianity. We hadn't gone to India to find what we already had at home.

'Mary', Eberhart said one Monday morning, at breakfast in the hostel. 'Would you like to visit the Panchgunga Mosque? It's one of the more striking buildings in the city, standing on the high escarpment near the river front.'

I had only ever floated past it in a small boat.

'I can take you there today if you like.'

I sat side-saddle on the back of his scooter. Women never rode astride; the locals thought it indecent. At the Godaulia crossing, we forged our way through a mass of men, some with young women close behind, darting glances here and there. We wove in and out of rickshaws and bullock carts, avoiding idling camels and buffalos. Cars weren't a problem; it was rare to see one. The mosque was easily found. Its minarets soared above everything.

We entrusted the scooter to a shopkeeper selling brass pots and made our way through the lanes towards the imposing gateway. Mounds of rubbish lined a high wall but didn't smell bad now the weather was drier. I took off my sandals and draped my *tuni* over my head. Eberhart pulled a small scarf out of his pocket. The place was deserted and locked outside the fixed hours for congregational worship, unlike the major Hindu temples, where people wandered in and out all the time. We poked around for a while before we found a grizzled doorkeeper, dozing at the back. He produced an enormous, rusty key. With a loud clang, the huge door into the main hall swung open. The curves of the roof shot heavenwards. White-washed walls

Panchgunga Ghat

swept away distractions. It was peaceful and austere. A place I could recognise as religious by the standards of my own culture. We stood in silence before stepping out again to gaze across the Ganges.

'Look at that smoke,' Eberhart said, pointing further downstream. 'It's coming from the cremation grounds over there. We can go and look at the half-burned bodies, if you like, see the dogs nosing around.'

I frowned and he laughed. Why were foreigners in Banaras always going on about corpses? Was it because death was hidden away at home?

'Let's go and have an iced coffee at the Quality restaurant,' he said.

We headed for the family table at the back.

'I don't get the feeling, Mary, that you've read much about the city. Do you know why it's always been a magnet for outsiders?'

Something to do with sun worship, I thought.

'It's also to do with the trade in luxury goods. The main route north crosses this huge river just here. That's why the site has been continuously occupied for so long. It's been urban for more than two and a half thousand years.'

The snacks arrived. 'It's a pleasure to eat with you, Mary,' Eberhart said. 'You really do like your food – not like most women, who only pick at it in a ladylike manner. Just look at you, wolfing down that *pakora*. You must have an iron will to have turned down Professor Bashworth's invitations to dinner.' He smiled. 'But why don't you treat yourself to some of the lovely silk scarves sold here? I know you can afford them. That one you're wearing is torn and faded.'

I pulled the end towards me and peered at it. Was it really? Students in the hostel were always giving me advice or trying to educate me. I didn't really mind. They were older and had been in Banaras for longer. I made a mental note to go shopping for a new scarf.

A week later, I peered into a much more modest Muslim place of worship, a shrine in Nagwa, not far from the university. Men and women were streaming around a pavilion enclosing tombs draped in green and black. Narrow strips of cloth hung from trees at the back. Incense wafted around. Worshippers placed their hands on the graves and offered milk-based sweets and bottles of water. The custodian of the shrine in turn offered them newly sanctified sweets. Nobody chatted or looked around; their focus was complete.

'Whose tombs are they?' I asked someone hanging around outside. 'They're for Yakub Shahid and his two followers,' he said. 'He was a strong man, a fighter. A saint.'

But these devotees weren't just Muslims. Half of them looked like Hindus.

'The Hindu and Muslim educated classes would not approve of what was going on there,' Sujata commented afterwards. 'But the common people find comfort and strength wherever they can. They often prefer to worship in humble shrines like that, rather than in the large historic temples and mosques.'

I hadn't gone to India to find a religion. But Western students often dragged me along to temples and festivals. Descriptions of outings to religious places made for lively letters home. Students from South-East Asia had no interest whatsoever in Hindu ceremonies. They focused on passing their exams or having fun with their friends.

Sujata was an exception. The government of Bali had sent her as part of its programme to refashion Hindu practices. Indonesian national policymakers now insisted that all citizens believe in God and subscribe to an officially recognised 'world religion'. They were attempting to contain hard-line Muslim demands for an Islamic state, while also accommodating the new global view that civilised people belong to labelled religions. Customary beliefs and practices that mixed Hindu and Islamic traditions with rural animism were no longer acceptable. Yet few Balinese knew anything about Hindu scriptures or philosophy. Sujata was to do her bit.

She often celebrated sunrise on the bank of the Ganges. I tagged along to enjoy the loveliness of the hour. We set out early before the sun popped up at five o'clock. The rickshaw clattered through the deserted main streets, until we reached the lanes through which people were hurrying to arrive in time for a dawn bath. Sujata placed her flowers on one of the steps at the edge and raised her arms to salute the sun. She bowed and murmured Sanskrit verses as she scattered her offerings in the water. I cast in my flowers, too, but couldn't bring myself to perform any rituals.

We would climb back up the steep steps and walk into the main market, that was just opening up, sidestepping mangy dogs and cows, and squeezing in past the stalls. Bullock cart drivers coming in from the villages cursed and shouted and threw sticks to drive away the dogs, but still they got their wheels stuck in the ruts. Village women, with heavy loads of fish and vegetables on their heads – and straight-backed, with a walk to shame the models of Paris – elbowed their way in and uncovered their baskets ready to catch the first trade. Sujata haggled for what she needed. By seven, we had finished shopping. We pushed our way out into the street, where we met the smell of fried *puris*, and smoke from the newly lit cooking fires.

On the way back to the university campus, we called in at the Durga temple. We left our food baskets outside with the man selling garlands, so as not to be harassed by the monkeys inside. The scent of marigolds and incense greeted us as we entered. Sujata rang the bell

The Durga Temple

hanging from a rope before making her offerings. When we came out, we often found a few of our fruits missing. The flower man always blamed the monkeys.

We sat in silence on the way home, companionably squeezed into the rickshaw, as it scudded through the cool and fragrant air of morning.

Anti-ritualist sceptic though I remained, I could not for ever resist the appeal of all icons. Nandi, the sacred bull, protector of the entrance to the temples of Shiva, gazed at me through large peaceful eyes. His solidity reassured. There he always was. I would stroke his marble flank when I brushed past in the lanes. And classic images of the serene meditating Buddha would pull me to a halt and draw me forwards. They sat in the museum at Sarnath, the village a few miles outside Banaras, where the Buddha had preached his first sermon.

Buddhist thought featured prominently in my course, but Buddhist practice had died out in India almost a thousand years earlier. The Buddhist merchants and kings who had bankrolled its institutions lost the wealth they had derived from India's maritime trade with south-east Asia. That had now fallen into the hands of Arab traders.

Power within the sub-continent shifted back to Brahmans with their land-based wealth.

This led the urban artisans who, centuries earlier, had abandoned Brahmanical ideas in favour of less hierarchical Buddhist teachings, to switch their allegiance to the new Islamic cultures brought by Turkish-speaking rulers from Central Asia. Ancient Buddhist ruins still lay scattered in corners of the older Muslim weaver neighbourhoods in the north of the city. The only practising Buddhists in the 1960s were the new Tibetan refugees. The stigmatised castes had not yet begun their mass conversions.

It was time for another visit to Sarnath. The long and bumpy rickshaw ride was the price to be paid for the pleasures to follow. I ambled in the deer park surrounding the modern Buddhist temple, built by overseas Asian funds, and chatted with Tibetan monks congregated around the tea shops, and near the ancient reliquary *stupa*. They didn't ogle or stare at women. Was that something to do with Buddhism, or was it Tibetan culture, or something else?

As usual, I made my way to the large bathing tank at the deserted Someswara temple, hidden away at the back of the village. It only came to life on festival days when the god touched down. That was true of many Muslim, as well as Hindu shrines. Perhaps deities and saints were like wandering chieftains. I sat alone on the steps. Kites wheeled and swooped above the trees. A deep peace flooded through me.

At the end of November, the world beyond the city of temples and mosques – even beyond India – broke through into our consciousness. John F. Kennedy, President of the USA, was shot. All shops and schools closed for a day of mourning. Small groups of Indian students sobbed in the streets. A male engineering student, a friend of Ann and Jim, was too distressed to sit for his physics exam. Kennedy was like Gandhi, he said, a friend of India, and a martyr to ideas of racial equality. He was the only leader who sent weapons to India when the Chinese attacked. He'd been our hope for the future.

The Indian students were different from us, from all the foreigners in the International Hostel. The men quoted Shelley and Keats as if they expected to woo a woman in a rose arbour, rather than in an arranged marriage. Ann and Jim showed me a letter from another friend, Sangwan, an engineering graduate who had just returned home to Delhi to train as a pilot. He was one of the most down-to-earth people they had met in Banaras, able to put up shelves and repair broken gadgets.

'My golden student days will always remain fresh in my mind, as the perfume of a morning flower.'

Nor were the Indian students as independent as most of us. Toofan remained in Banaras with his mother on the instructions of his older brother in Calcutta. The family worried that she would be lonely. He wanted to invite me home for a meal but had to wait for her permission. She was away for an extended stay with relatives. After her letter arrived, he spent a whole day cooking a grand feast. Unfortunately, his invitation never reached me.

'I was so angry,' he said later. 'I waited two hours for you in the centre of the city and then I went home and threw away all the food in a rage.'

What a waste, I thought. But people were different here – more emotional, perhaps.

CHAPTER 16

TRIBAL VILLAGES AND CHRISTMAS CELEBRATIONS

THE UNIVERSITY WAS OFTEN CLOSED, AND IT WASN'T ALWAYS *un*official. India is a secular state, with Bank Holidays for the festivals of all religious traditions. This includes a week off at Christmas.

A letter arrived from Sarala Devi:

'Bill, and Manilal, a local community worker, will be passing through Banaras on their way to tribal villages in the Vindhya hills, on the border between Uttar and Madhya Pradesh,' she wrote. 'They will be checking how War on Want donations have been spent. And trying to find out what is needed in the future. Why don't you join them, Mary? You would learn more about rural India.'

My friends from the Gandhian movement wanted me to leave my ivory tower. Perhaps they would try to persuade me to abandon my course.

I met them in the home of a long-time supporter of the ashram, the Principal of the Girls' Theosophical School, Mrs Lila Sharma. She was wearing a plain white cotton sari. The spacious living room with its bare stone floors, white walls, wooden shutters, and handful of wooden chairs, reflected her calmness. She introduced Manilal, a married man, a few years older than Bill.

A painting of Jesus hung on the wall in front of me.

'Are you a Christian?' I asked.

'Gandhi respected all religions,' she said. 'Look, on the wall around the corner hangs a picture of the Lord Buddha.'

The peacefulness of the room deepened as she spoke about her educational work.

'Theosophy, you may not know, Mary, is an international movement that began in Europe, under the influence of Asian religious ideas, both Hindu and Buddhist, but then found itself more at home back in India.'

Mrs Sharma handed us boxes of fried *puris* and spiced vegetables for our journey and packed us off to the station in a rickshaw. We arrived in Mirzapur a few hours later. My companions deposited me on the steps of a shop selling the local, hand-woven *khadi* cloth promoted by Gandhi, and disappeared, to make arrangements for the next stage. A wizened little man, bare-chested, and wearing a gleaming white *dhoti*, ran up to me with sparrow-like steps.

'Ah, Miss Mary,' he cried, 'I am trying to arrange a jeep for you.'

I didn't want to travel in a jeep. I wanted to travel like ordinary people – but how could anyone resist his sparkling eyes and impish expression?

'My hermitage is near your villages,' he explained.

A bystander gestured towards him. 'Babaji is a Jain monk, aged over eighty.'

'Fate brought me here to your good presence,' Babaji said.

He stayed with us for the next hundred miles of our bus journey, watching over us like a mother hen, always calling out to anyone in a jeep, trying to wangle a lift. His servant, a solid, bovine-looking man, shadowed him, carrying a large basket covered with a cotton cloth. Babaji lived on food donations, accepting only fruit, nuts and milk. These all ended up in the basket. He even had a jar of Horlicks in there. Whenever we flagged, he would rummage around and fish out something tasty like oranges and nuts. On one occasion, when we were sitting with drooping heads in a broken-down bus, he pulled out a small tin of milk.

'You see, daughter Mary, I'm squeezing a little lemon into it, and see, now, it has turned into curds,' he said, holding up the pot triumphantly. 'Now please to get out of the bus and sit down on that tree trunk.'

How could I possibly refuse his commands?

We drove through land almost as dry as desert, passing lines of camels weighed down with quarry stone. After two hours, the road fizzled out and the bus came to a halt. We set off on a twelve-mile walk along a forest track. Babaji did not move at ordinary speed. He would run ahead and then dance around, waiting for us to catch up. Occasionally, he burst into a loud clatter of laughter that seemed out of character, and might have been frightening, had it come from anyone else. We passed occasional tribesmen walking alone, with long pointed spears to defend themselves against bears. One man carried a bow and arrows, slung over his shoulder.

Wattle fencing protected Sehra, our first village. Stunted cattle were tethered outside. A group of men, all extremely short, moved a panel aside and drew us in. Small, single-room huts of dried mud stood separately in their own allotments of crops. We stood in a doorway. Inside, a stove and a few utensils of sun-baked pottery rested by the wall on the smooth earth floor. Everything was spotless, both inside and outside. The huts were uncluttered by furniture. Nothing needed dusting or polishing; no need to worry about finger marks on walls, or spillage on white tablecloths, the bane of English domestic life at that time. A couple of homes consisted only of roofs on poles, with fronds of banana leaves dangling down for a semblance of privacy. They would have blown away in a strong monsoon wind.

Bill pointed out a newly dug well, forty-five feet deep. 'In the summer they used to walk miles to dig through sand to find water,' he said. 'Tribal villages are much cleaner than the ones down in the plains. They use ash from fires to clean themselves.'

We sat down on a mat outside the Headman's home. An elderly woman offered us balls of compressed molasses, and rice with unspiced, boiled leaf vegetables, a supplement enjoyed only in winter. A circle of villagers watched us eat. Babaji sat cross-legged on the earth outside another hut, munching with intense concentration, his toothless gums moving rapidly back and forwards. He paused for a moment to call out the names of gods or goddesses, glanced around with his eagle-like eyes to check we were all right, and fired a few questions at us, before lowering his head again to focus on the business in hand. As soon as he had finished, he leaped up, bobbed up and down on the spot crying out 'Rama, Rama, Rama,' and then, turning his back to me, relieved himself in the ditch.

A young man lit a huge, blazing fire. We moved across to sit round it, huddled together for warmth.

'Every year,' Bill said, 'someone who doesn't own a shawl or blanket stands too close to the fire and gets severely burnt.'

Manilal talked about the lives of the villagers.

'They make everything they use: millstones, pottery, baskets, mats and wooden farm implements like linseed oil presses.'

That sounded like self-sufficiency.

'Nowadays they can no longer produce all the food they need because some of their land has been taken by urban people from the plains. They have to labour on those same fields for the absentee landowners. But the people they hate most are the government forest officials who prevent them from collecting their traditional fuel and timber.'

Bill broke in. 'The British were the first to treat forests as government property instead of common land.'

I flinched.

'It didn't change after Independence, under the pretext of protecting forest resources – though nobody plants any replacements. Only a rich man can secure a permit to cut timber. The villagers have to collect firewood from the wasteland. They carry enormous loads on a yoke of bamboo slung over one shoulder. They sell it to urban merchants fourteen miles away, who then sell it on for three times what they have paid. Yet these tribal people have to pay six times the normal rate per kilo for rice.'

'And in some villages,' Manilal continued, 'people are so poor now that they survive for six months of the year on roots from scrubland.'

So their poverty didn't lie in their lack of furniture and gadgets – that's just simple living – but in their lack of secure supplies of food and fuel. And it was exploitation and injustice that lay at the root of their problems.

The light of the fire flickered on the circle of earnest faces.

Babaji sparked into life. He talked to the villagers about Gandhi, and the new work being done by Vinoba Bhave to encourage people to give up individual plots, and to hold them in common. They should stand together against moneylenders and not sell off land to pay debts. Then he sighed and said in English, 'It's all anger and pride and lust. Those are the three you have to subdue. That's what it all means.'

That night we slept comfortably on straw in the Headman's hut. He had one brass pot alongside the earthenware. Babaji's voice woke me at four o'clock in the morning.

'Wake up, sister Mary. Attend to your nature calls.'

Fifteen minutes later we set off for our next village. We filed along a path through dense forest until we emerged into a clearing. Babaji tore off his garments, leaving on only his loin cloth, shouting, 'Look at the beautiful sunshine, take your free dose of Vitamin D.'

I took it gladly, though without removing my clothes.

Two bulls were fighting in the lane by the house where we spent the second night. Babaji rushed towards them, shouting in Hindi, until they broke away from one another.

'Did you know he was imprisoned with Gandhiji for three years?' Manilal asked me. 'Recently he went on hunger strike, sitting on top of a government dam, because they weren't paying the farmers the promised compensation. He stayed there until the situation was remedied.'

On the third day, we stayed at Babaji's forest hermitage near Rainbari. Four poles supported a bamboo and thatch sloping roof, without any walls. A brush of fine peacock feathers hung from the roof so that he could sweep the earth free of insects that he might crush when he lay down to sleep.

'See, Mary,' he said. 'I am getting these fields levelled to prevent erosion. And here are our vegetable gardens and fruit trees. We are starting an irrigation system.'

He fed us guavas and curd and then turned to the villagers sitting in a circle at his feet and put them through their catechism. No meat, no alcohol (they had taken the pledge), live as a family, avoid moneylenders. 'The rate of interest is 75%', he said, turning aside to speak to me. 'Until recently the people round this village were serfs, tied to the landowners.'

In the morning we set off for the sixteen-mile walk back towards a road. We passed nomadic basket weavers near Meodi, another of the villages overseen by Babaji. Blue linseed flowers brightened small fields of grain and pulses. We took the mandatory drink from the village well to verify our lack of caste consciousness.

'What will the villagers do with the War on Want money?' I asked Bill.

'They will buy blankets. That's what they need most.'

'But blankets aren't permanent. Wouldn't something else be of more long-term value, like improved seeds?'

'Life isn't permanent,' Bill said. 'We need to reduce their suffering in the present.'

The world was an ocean of suffering. And I was doing nothing.

A jeep was waiting for us when we reached the bus stop. Babaji had succeeded at last. Five minutes later, we passed an abandoned village.

'Debts made them flee back to the jungle,' Manilal said. 'Sometimes they get into such severe debt that they disappear and start again somewhere else, if they can find a patch of uncultivated land on the edge of the forest, but that is becoming more difficult.'

The driver insisted we visit the Rihand Dam, built by the USA, but at the cost of the most fertile land in the area. I didn't want to see a great mass of ugly concrete. And Manilal had said the families that used to farm in the fertile valley before it was flooded now went short of wheat. Nor, once we got there, did I like the stilted ornamental gardens. I would rather have spent the time in a forest clearing, with the sun filtering through the leaves. Our new hosts were disappointed by my lack of enthusiasm.

'I prefer natural places, not concrete,' I said.

'Natural is anywhere and everywhere,' an engineer standing nearby said. 'Why you people like the backward things in India? This is our future. This is what India can do now.'

I looked down at the crumbling earth.

*

During my absence, Becky had returned to the USA. I would have missed her more, but soon got caught up in the turmoil over the planned Christmas party for the International Hostel servants. Preparations for a great meal had begun while I was away but had broken down when the Thai monks refused to have anything to do with it. They claimed that Christians were trying to take over. My absence meant I wasn't tainted with these accusations.

'Christmas customs have nothing to do with Christianity,' I said. 'They're just folk traditions, like appeasing the spirits in Buddhism.'

Fist fights, a Nepali student told me, had broken out a few years earlier over similar issues. For all I knew, the European students had started the arrangements without discussing anything with the others.

A mixed group divided up the tasks. A couple of students opted to create decorations with flower garlands and evergreen branches. My responsibility was to buy clothing, shawls, blankets and sweaters, ready for presentation on the great day. As if that wasn't enough, I also had to purchase twelve coloured bags for the children, and to fill them with sweets and nuts, combs, ribbons, balloons, kites, flutes and fireworks.

Working out the number of servants wasn't easy. We thought we had sixteen, but some had several names. Had they been counted twice? New names and faces materialised. We'd forgotten about the gardeners and occasional maintenance men. Should they be included? Did a few hours a month, or even a year, qualify – and what about the regular rickshaw men who waited outside?

On Christmas Eve, a few of us gathered privately to play records and sing carols. A newly arrived American served a traditional Christmas Eve drink of rum nog. I made Scottish pancakes on my electric ring, and Eberhart produced mustard and *wurst* from home. Then, atheists as we mostly were, we trundled over to midnight mass at the nearby Catholic chapel.

On the great day, everyone piled into the hostel. The servants sat nervously at the tables, as instructed. We served them roast chicken and potatoes. All passed happily and without incident. Even some Thai monks joined in. One of them presented me with the *Selected Works of Lenin*. It came from the heavily subsidised Soviet bookshop just outside the university. Perhaps the cheapest thing he could find.

Other Christmas events followed, including a slap-up traditional meal, cooked by Miss Lewis. How surprising that such an elevated and high-minded lady could turn out great food. I did not join Ann, Jim and Eberhart for the feast in Professor Bashworth's house. A New Year's meal with Ann and Jim was another pooling of treats from home. Tinned sauerkraut and beef from Germany, ham from England and cakes from New Zealand. I kept a nervous eye on the door while I ate the beef. We played records of Joan Baez's anti-war songs.

Parcels from England were always welcome, though I felt uncomfortable, having to ask my parents to send so many things. Everyone I knew wanted something from England. The latest request from Sujata was Hugo's booklet on learning German. That turned up in my Christmas parcel. It was even more awkward when people asked me to find them jobs in England. I wasn't confident that I knew how to get one for myself. But I passed on all requests to my parents. Their letters had developed a subdued tone, not like mine, with their regular accounts of near-death experiences, interspersed with political ranting and moral hectoring.

'Poverty is the fault of the world economic system, propped up by the West. Donations are not enough. We must get rid of most of our possessions. We must do something to change the world system, though I don't know yet how we should start.'

CHAPTER 17

1964 FESTIVALS, FUN AND THE CYCLE OF THE SEASONS

I SHIVERED IN JANUARY AT FIFTEEN DEGREES CENTIGRADE. Neither rooms nor water were heated. Buildings were designed for hot weather; winter was only a brief interlude. The dark green glass panels in the wooden shutters softened the glare of sunshine but excluded light. We had to keep them open if we wanted to read. My parents sent woollen bloomers for me to wear under my baggy cotton trousers. I had to pay a fortune in import duties. India was protecting its textile industries. The locals were much hardier than us, continuing to shower with cold water soon after their early morning cup of tea. We dragged full buckets into the sun to warm up and showered later.

The winter eased, but did not eliminate, my health problems. The doctors said my stomach trouble might be due to a change of diet, perhaps an absence of yeast. I don't think they knew. Someone suggested an *Ayurvedic* physician but added that he could only speak Sanskrit. Constipation was a far-off dream. A Thai student was hospitalised. My friend, Chun, spent hours carrying thermoses of tea and cooked rice. The hospital did not provide food for patients.

On free mornings, I sat on our flat roof, reading in the pale yellow light, enjoying the rich greens of the vegetation. In the afternoons, I sometimes walked in the *Ayurvedic* herb gardens, always on full alert, in case of ogling, or threatening, male students. Glorious sunsets trailed across the sky most evenings.

Early in the New Year, the newspapers announced a lunar eclipse. Six thousand people, they said, had already converged on the banks of the Ganges. The rituals were to avert personal danger from such an inauspicious event.

Sujata and I found somewhere to sit on one of the steps leading down to the river. She dusted off a fine layer of sand. A family of middle-aged South Indians unpacked bags nearby on a patch of level ground. The women wore blue and red silk saris, embroidered with gold thread. They pitched a tent and stowed their bags and bundles neatly inside, before spreading mats on the earth, and lighting charcoal in a cooking pot. This was travelling light – a bit like us on the Aldermaston marches. But these pilgrims weren't young.

A letter from Mrs Lila Sharma was waiting for me when we got back. 'Please join us tomorrow, Mary,' she wrote, 'at the annual conference of the Theosophical Society.'

Delegates had arrived from all over the world. An elderly Englishwoman stood near the door, wearing a full skirt that trailed the ground. Speakers pontificated on the nature of the Cosmos and the Divine principle. The audience clapped and nodded. How could they be so certain about such things?

In a quiet moment, Mrs Sharma talked about her family.

'For two years my husband was imprisoned by the British for anti-colonial activities. They hung him from his wrists for several hours. Luckily, he didn't suffer serious damage, but many people were permanently disabled.'

I looked up in horror and bowed my head in shame. She said nothing.

Other shadows occasionally insinuated their way into our fun-filled life of colour and festivity. Letters from Britain hinted at grim events in India not reported in our newspapers. We read only of passing riots in Calcutta. Whispered rumours of anti-Muslim massacres circulated behind closed doors.

Spring brought the *Saraswati Puja* festival in honour of the goddess of learning and music. Students donned yellow clothes and joined processions filing through the streets to one of her hastily assembled shrines. *Saraswati* would improve their results, if only they could attract her attention. I had hardly given the exams a thought. That wasn't why I'd come to India. But I went along all the same. Sujata lent me a lemon shawl. The goddess was wearing a yellow sari. Offerings of books and musical instruments lay in piles at her feet. She smiled benignly from her pedestal. Her warmth lightened my spirit. I couldn't help smiling back.

None of these events prepared me for the scale of the annual *Magh Mela* festival at the confluence of the two major rivers, the Ganges and Yamuna, near Allahabad. The potency of this sacred spot intensifies dramatically with the conjuncture of the stars on this occasion. True believers can hope for a sudden onset of good fortune. I needed that too.

Six of us from the hostel arrived at the Varanasi station. 'No ticket for Allahabad without cholera inoculation,' shouted a large notice. Only two of our certificates were up to date. Jim worked his way to the front of the queue, brandished his valid document, and asked for three tickets to cover his whole 'family'. That worked wonders, so Eberhart did the same. Inoculation was contagious, it seemed.

Men in the queue helped friends with problems. One approached the counter wearing a hat and returned a few minutes later with the same certificate but minus the hat. He rejoined his friends, brandishing another ticket. Others were less fortunate, perhaps because more shabbily dressed, or unable to speak English. In Allahabad, officials yanked families out of bullock carts and forcibly inoculated them.

Rows of beggars lined the approach to a featureless expanse of sand, across which hundreds of thousands of people wandered. Fences, erected by the army, directed our movements and marked out the ground in squares. Tents, assigned to pilgrims from different regions and castes, sported identifying pennants, like a painting of a mediaeval battlefield. Down by the river, worshippers leaped off a floating pontoon bridge, or haggled over the cost of hiring a boat for a ritual bath off a sandbank. But there weren't any ancient temples or eighteenth-century palaces soaring above long flights of steps.

Among all those millions of pilgrims, it was astonishing – except that nothing was astonishing anymore – to meet Toofan. He and a friend were sitting on a borrowed motorbike, wearing black leather jackets and woollen military caps.

'But I thought you said you couldn't obtain a certificate, so how did you get here?' I asked.

'Well, it was a big worry for us with three military checkpoints,' Toofan said. 'A young officer stopped us at the first one. "What's the harm?" I said to him. "Why not just let us through this one?" "Okay," the officer said, "just this one, but you'll never get through the next two." We slowed down at the second barrier, waving a piece of paper in the air, yelling out that we'd got a permit. Then we roared through the third checkpoint on full throttle. The police stood to attention and saluted. They must have thought we were army officers. All you need is the right manner.'

I laughed. He had the manner all right.

'Let's meet on Tuesday at eight o'clock for an early morning row,' he said. 'The river's much lower now.'

The boat wasn't ready when we arrived. We sat down on the top of the steps at Dasasamedh Ghat. A man was painting blue elephants on the front wall of a house while children in the street chased hoops. Old women, walking home from the vegetable market, tossed outer leaves to animals loitering at the sides of the lane.

We drifted in the sun. Monasteries and temples flowed past. His thick hair hardly stirred in the breeze. And we swam, fully dressed, in the cleaner water on the far side of the river. It was warm now that the temperature had risen. Breakfast was *samosas*, sitting on the sand. The sun soon dried my *selwar-kameez*. I looked at him out of the corner of my eye. He was only nineteen. I was only twenty-one. I'd never before met such a good-looking man, with so much grace and poise.

I followed him, single file, back towards the main road. He paused next to an open workshop where men and young boys were embroidering fabric with gold and silver thread. They sat cross-legged on the floor, in poor light, with their noses just a few inches above threads stretched taut on wooden frames. I peered forward across an open drainage channel, thinking I might see decorations for wealthy Indian homes. But no: these were blazer badges for the RAF, and for Rugby, the British public school.

'It takes one day to make a badge. One of moderate quality costs fifteen rupees to buy, but the craftsmen get no more than sixty to seventy rupees a month,' my friend said. 'That isn't enough for two full meals a day. They can work only as long as their eyesight keeps going.'

Someone was growing rich on their labour. And chubby-faced schoolboys in Britain were not paying a fair price for their badges.

*

In February the Women's Annexe closed and we all transferred to the Multi-Purpose Flats. They were nearer the main hostel. Sujata and I now shared a two-room flat with kitchen, bathroom and veranda. What luxury but more difficult for my flatmate – especially when I cooked for myself.

'Mary,' she would say, 'you've burnt the pans again. How am I going to prepare my food? We'll have to leave the door open to remove the smell.'

Sujata's room rapidly developed the beauty of a shrine, with delicate drapes on the walls, and decorated matting covering the concrete floor. Incense floated around her images and paintings. But before long, our peace was disturbed by an unwanted visitor: a super-sized rat. Sujata's belief in non-violence was more developed than mine so she would not allow me to kill it with a trap. We were to catch it manually and then take it away to open fields, where it might settle down to a cleaner, more rural life. My task was to chase it with our twig broom, driving it into the metal waste bin she was holding.

We locked ourselves and the rat into the cupboard-like kitchen and started our military campaign. He sprang through the air, eluding all my swipes. Didn't rat bites give awful diseases? At last we got the monster into the bin and covered it with a wooden plank, ready for Sujata to carry to the other side of the campus in the early morning. Heavy weights would, hopefully, stop it being shaken off. All night I could hear banging. At six o'clock Sujata got up and carried the box for a mile before freeing the wretched animal. Would it return? Was Gandhi right to think that violence was never justified?

The engineering students faced grimmer problems. Their courses were speeded up in response to the demand for army technicians to counter the Chinese invasion. The University reduced their holidays and brought forward their final exams to March instead of April. One student couldn't take the pressure and drowned himself in the Ganges.

*

My first *Holi* festival, marking the onset of summer, arrived in early March. By now the hot weather had crept up on us again. For five hours a day the temperature was well up in the nineties.

'For one or two days, all caste and status restrictions – all Law and Order – will disappear,' Eberhart warned me. 'Nobody is immune from being sprayed and smeared with red paint: not the chief magistrate, nor employers, nor the high priest, nor the Vice-Chancellor. Anybody can be rolled on the ground, or pulled out of vehicles, and drenched in colour. All shops and offices will close. Whatever happens, you are supposed to take it in good spirits.'

'Families with unmarried daughters store enough food for a siege,' Ann said.

'Anything is possible after the midnight fireworks and bonfires of leaves marking the death of winter and the old year,' added Sujata.

It sounded interesting. In the morning we locked all doors and shutters. I peered through chinks in the frames. Roaring crowds of men, sixty or seventy strong, with matted red hair and crimson faces and clothes, raced across the open ground in front of the hostel. Processions and drummers streamed past the window on the other side. How exciting. But alarming, too, when loud crashes shook our outer door. Later in the morning, bored with being stuck inside, I nipped out for five minutes, disguised, effectively, I hoped, as a man, to see how Ann and Jim were getting on. I looked up the stairs. A figure, all encrusted with red paint, hair, face, clothes. He looked down at me. The whites of his eyes and teeth flashed. I shuddered. Then rushed back into my room, banging the door behind me. As I wrote later in a letter home:

'He was like a savage tribesman. We stood against the door for five minutes, while he tried to push it open. The papers the next day reported that *Holi* revellers in Delhi had been arrested for spraying red colours on unwilling onlookers. That's unthinkable in Banaras. Here, even the police are not immune. Someone unpopular, or even an unlucky passer-by, can face buckets of cow's urine. Women stay indoors, though in the Women's Hostel, with its huge walled compound and armed sentries, the girls enjoy *Holi*. In private homes, children and adults throw colour in courtyards and gardens.

'After lunch, the wildness subsided, and men went home to shower and put on new clothes. In the evening, they wandered the streets, embracing friends, and dabbing a touch of perfume on their foreheads. One American student dared to go out and came back reeking.'

As the temperature went up, so, too, did my irritability and fatigue. My letters from England sometimes arrived in an outer envelope. They'd been opened. I didn't have enough energy to investigate. That would have involved a ten-hour wait in the main post office. As I said in another letter:

'I have tried everything I can think of in government offices, quiet, amiable patience, only possible in a state of extreme physical exhaustion, or cool superciliousness and bored indifference. Sometimes I pull out a huge book, and thermos flask, and seat myself in a chair in front of the chief clerk, periodically smiling ostentatiously to indicate that I am enjoying myself, and not in the least annoyed about being kept waiting. Usually I am much less cool than that, sweating, rushing out, with tears of frustration starting out from under my sunglasses, raging back on my bicycle, even more aware than usual of the horrid leers. Thank goodness I don't understand obscene Hindi. Then I toss for ages on my bed, contorted with rage. Even an ordinary parcel has to be stitched up in cloth.

'Indian students endure whatever comes. They don't have the same consciousness of what we call our rights. Sujata goes straight to the Vice-Chancellor when she dislikes anything, so she has become the most feared student in the university, she tells me. Jim's bulldozer approach has made him enemies. Ann said he's often on the verge of a fist fight. But after a few years foreigners become resigned to the frustrations.'

By mid-March, the temperature was 105 degrees Fahrenheit in the afternoon and, even at eight in the evening, remained around ninety-five. Trees blossomed into gorgeous colours and the city took on a more Middle-Eastern appearance. The earth dried to a whitish shade and the streets emptied in the all-obliterating heat. Men wore towels around their heads. If I had to go out in the middle of the day, I covered my face and hair with something soft and loose. Everyone smeared scent on the back of their hands and lit joss sticks inside. We walked barefoot around the flats. After all, I'd done it in London once.

Early morning outings lightened the day. I often woke before dawn and took a rickshaw to the *ghats*. A few stars and a faint moon still lingered. We sped along the empty lanes, passing people sleeping outside, on roofs, or on the raised ledges above the streets. I sat for a couple of hours in a corner, on one of the flights of steps at Shivala Ghat. Nobody stared at that time of day. Worshippers focused on their own concerns, bathing, praying, changing clothes, combing, oiling, massaging. The men busied themselves with whisker-trimming and shaving, and the children laughed and splashed in the water before mothers soaped and towelled them. Boys swam with all but the tip of their heads submerged. Older men washed loin cloths and *dhotis*, beating them on stones, or chanted, motionless in prayer, standing in water up to their chests. Children held up their mothers' saris to dry.

The morning temperature soon rose above one hundred degrees. Heat intensified the rich scents of flowers. At ten o'clock we closed our shutters to keep out the light and poured water on the wash-room floor so that cooler air would filter through to the rest of the flat. After lunch we slept for an hour. We delayed shopping until seven o'clock in the evening. It was difficult to find vegetables other than pumpkin. Sujata showed me how to soak lentils overnight. After a day or two, they sprouted. She fried them or ate them in a salad.

'When the summer proper comes,' she said, 'we will have to keep all the floors wet and hang up mats soaked in water to cool the hot winds and make them smell sweet.'

Could the summer proper possibly be worse than this?

*

The end of term was approaching. Prem Chand, the tall, thin, very blonde Danish linguist, who liked visiting deserts during the summer, thought there was time for a quick outing before the heat ruled out everything except a trip to the mountains. On the last Sunday of March, I joined him, along with the two short, plump, Japanese students, for a day trip to Jaunpur. How would we get on together? One of the Japanese was so scholarly that he rarely spoke. He was translating ancient Chinese versions of Indian texts, back into what he presumed to have been the missing Sanskrit originals. On one occasion I had offered him a cup of tea in my room, but he had refused it.

'There is no pleasure in drinking from a cup like this,' he said, smiling, with his eyes lowered.

Our destination was home to the oldest mosques in India, built by Sharqi sultans of Turko-Afghan descent. The crumbling ruins lay silent and abandoned in scattered fields. We washed our feet before entering one of the mosques, and wandered around, followed by twenty men who watched every movement we made. They were especially curious about me.

'She is married to all of you?' one man asked.

In the end, to shut them up, Prem Chand said I was his wife. A little later, a burly shopkeeper approached.

'You are most welcome to take my horse and cart. It is needed to see all the buildings. Very far, they are.'

On our return from the next stint of mosque visits, he fed us *parathas* in his front room, while the crowd waited outside. Later, in the afternoon, we ate fried salty snacks in a field, seated in the shade of a wall, admiring other monuments from a distance. Our followers sat down alongside us. One young man got up and walked over to the neighbouring field. He returned with a handful of tomatoes. He could see we were struggling with the heat.

On the slow train back, I was jammed between bodies, swaying as one, to the pulse of the pounding wheels. The parched white smell of a desiccated land blew in through the barred windows. A vast and shapeless sky stretched above. In the distance, small, bent figures in the fields merged with the flaking earth. The all-pervading heat softened and soothed, smoothed away fidgety thought. I slipped in and out of sleep. Villages were brown anthills, earthen mounds come from the soil, soon to pass back again. The seasons rolled round remorselessly. The crumbled ruins of empires came and went.

I surfaced to hear Prem Chand singing the Pakistani national anthem. Passengers in the compartment laughed uneasily. How could he do such a thing?

*

Three days later, the exams started.

'Be sure to prepare your answers,' Dr Tripathi said.

'But I must have got the general drift by now.'

'General drift is not enough. Details are a must,' he said, frowning.

Somehow, I couldn't feel too worried. This wasn't what I'd come to India for. But, yes, the exams were more factual and specific than I was expecting. The Indian students were well-prepared; they had memorised their answers in advance.

CHAPTER 18

2006 CONVERSATION WITH SHANTA CONTINUES BY EMAIL

July 15ᵗʰ. Mumbai

Thanks again, Mary. A lot to read. Glad you enjoyed so many festivals, even if you weren't gaining all the philosophical insights you'd hoped for.

I've picked up my Narmada Dam campaigning again. Have been busy going by jeep into the forest area to interview tribal women for a piece I'm writing.

July 16ᵗʰ. Manchester

Don't overdo the jeep trips, Shanta. You're not as young as you were.

You won't be surprised when I say that the fun of festivals in India left a permanent mark. Not that it could change my attitude to ceremonies that had the logo of religion written all over them.

August 10th. Mumbai

The problem, Mary, is that you people are like Muslims. You take beliefs more literally than we Hindus do. I know you don't consider yourself a Christian anymore but you are, as far as we are concerned. You were born in a Christian country.

I'm surprised you didn't know about the perils of going barefoot. Hookworms, and all that.

CHAPTER 19

1964 THE HIMALAYAS AT LAST: NEPAL

'W E'RE GOING TO NEPAL AT THE END OF THE MONTH,' ANN said, the evening after exams finished. 'Why don't you join us? Jim and Edmund Hillary will be attempting an unclimbed peak, Tamserku. It's supposed to be technically more difficult than Everest.'

This was too good to be true. I was itching to get closer to the Himalayas. I rushed around getting ready.

The plane shot off into the heavens. Within an hour we would reach the land of my dreams. Maybe this would be my doorway to adventure. Odd that my childhood books on the Himalayas never mentioned women. The only adventurous women I could remember reading about were unmarried missionaries: Mildred Cable crossing the Gobi Desert, and Gladys Aylward, the London parlour maid, who walked children to safety a hundred miles across China. Ian Burgess's account of her feat in his book *The Small Woman* sat on my shelf in England. Surely life as a missionary couldn't be the only way to escape being a housewife and mother enclosed in a house? Couldn't it be possible to live adventurously with a tall, dark handsome man at one's side, but as his comrade, not as his housekeeper?

The *Dhammapada* sat unopened on my lap.

As we touched down in Kathmandu, flames spurted from under the wing of the plane. Nobody looked worried. I closed my eyes and breathed deeply.

The city centre exuded green fragrance. We unloaded our bags in front of a three-storeyed wooden house, with a pitched roof, and carved balconies extending over the street. A porter was waiting near the front door to update my friends on their trekking arrangements.

'Our team will have a spare Sherpa,' Ann said afterwards. 'Why don't you trek with him? You could go directly north to Gosainkund. It's a Hindu pilgrimage destination. You'd reach high ground much sooner than if you accompany us eastwards, through malarial valleys, for several weeks. You'll only be twenty miles from the Tibetan border.'

Perfect! Especially as I couldn't spend more than a month in Nepal. I had arranged to meet Sujata in Kashmir, and also wanted to return briefly to Lakshmi Ashram. Sarala Devi had written saying I would be welcome any time, for as long as I wanted.

Jim introduced me to my Sherpa guide, Ang Pemba, a man in his late thirties, who had climbed on Everest several times. Dorje was his young assistant. They were short and stocky, and looked tough enough for anything I would be doing. Both wore Western trekking clothes. Ang Pemba beamed at me and Dorje smiled shyly. I relaxed. Hopefully it wouldn't matter that they knew only a few words of English.

First I had to get a permit to go trekking in a border area close to Chinese Tibet. I hired a bike and cycled all over the town, looking for the right government office. The officials wore tight, white trousers, with long, high-necked smocks, and pillbox hats pulled well forward. They moved with feline grace, much slimmer than most Indian clerks.

Expensively dressed Westerners, looking bored and languid, meandered around near the foreign embassies. It was hard to believe that thirteen years earlier, Nepal had been closed to outsiders, with only one British military representative stationed in the country. On my way back to the Guest House I passed the British Council offices. It would be good to have a chat with some fellow nationals after such a long time. I hadn't expected the gravel-lined drive to lead to such a palatial building.

'Yes?' asked the young woman in a linen suit with pearls, looking with disapproval at my crumpled sarong.

What should I say? 'I'd like to meet some English people' didn't seem such a good idea now.

'Do you have a library?' I asked, fidgeting with my glass bangles.

'Round the corner, on the left, though it's not meant for people like you.'

I avoided her eyes and slunk through the glass doors. Ten minutes later I fled.

Ann and Jim sorted out my financial arrangements and guided me in my purchases, including sufficient food for a three-week trek. I dashed round looking at Hindu and Buddhist temples, while we waited for the necessary documents. Mine was ready a few days later. It stated that I must keep a distance of twenty-five miles from the northern border, but added that the 'Ministry of Foreign Affairs would appreciate any such courtesy and assistance as I might stand in need of, by the Anchaladhish, Bada Hakim, Gauda and Goswara check-posts, and local people concerned.'

Maps weren't available in Nepal at that time and I had only the haziest idea of our planned route but was happy to rely on Ang Pemba. A tailor in Banaras had stitched me a Punjabi woman's outfit in heavy handloom cloth. Baggy trousers with a drawstring are all right in fine cotton but this made me look decidedly pregnant. Had my family banished me to the far corners of the earth, to hide the shame of an illegitimate birth? Ann and Jim added two long-sleeved men's woollen vests. I already had woollen socks and plimsolls. On top of my tunic, I wore a heavy shawl. Waterproofs and tent were not needed as it wouldn't rain or snow in the summer. My bedding was of a higher standard: a second-hand sleeping bag that had been on Everest, donated to a Sherpa, and sold off in the bazaar.

Ready for trekking in Nepal

Ann and Jim's team departed a few minutes before we did. I panicked.

'Tell me some Sherpa words,' I called out to them, as they went through the main door. I tried to think of expressions that might be needed in an environment without lavatories. 'How can I say, "Wait a minute, while I go behind a rock"?'

'*Ek chin* is one minute,' shouted Jim, as he disappeared from sight. And that was all I knew of their language when I set off into the mountains with two Sherpa men.

A horse-drawn cart transported us to the edge of the valley to start trekking in the direction of Helambu. In 1964 few roads existed, and motorised traffic was almost non-existent, even in Kathmandu. Ang Pemba lifted my sleeping bag and rucksack and tossed them into the bamboo basket strapped to his head. I fished them out and loaded them onto my back; I couldn't just saunter along without carrying anything. He stared at me and smiled.

Our route took us through rich green forest spotted with blossoms of every hue. Higher up, small blue flowers covered springy turf. We passed men with long, curved knives tucked into their belts, and huge baskets of leaves for fodder on their backs, strapped round their foreheads. Traders with heavy bundles of firewood or woollen cloth paused for a chat, or sometimes stood for longer and entertained us with a tune on a pipe.

On the first few nights, we unrolled our sleeping bags on the verandas of houses along the path, beside chickens and piles of wood. We slept in our day clothes. One evening I felt queasy after the meal and vomited all over the steps. The lady of the house rummaged around inside and produced a pair of silk liner gloves as a consolation gift. A trekker must have left them behind. I slept well despite flea bites. By morning a pair of fluffy chicks were curled up near my feet.

Ang Pemba and Dorje waited on me hand and foot. So much for my independence. All I had to do was walk from six in the morning until late afternoon. We woke at dawn and Ang Pemba sent Dorje off to collect water and wood. They took turns to prepare tea with sugar and tinned milk, or fresh, if we'd been able to get any from the villagers. That was followed by coarse wheat porridge. We ate without speaking, sitting cross-legged on the ground. Afterwards my companions chatted quietly to one another, occasionally bursting into laughter. In the late morning, they cooked a lunch of rice, or *chapatis*, with lentils and potatoes – and the same again in the evening. Sometimes they supplemented the meal with chicken or eggs, or anything we could purchase along our route. It was delicious, but it didn't change much. Sweet and sour pork would be good when I got back to Kathmandu.

My guides couldn't have been more discreet. Whenever I disappeared behind a rock, they walked on ahead and waited. I didn't need to say anything. But on one occasion, when I was trying to bury toilet paper, a gust of wind blew it straight back to the hamlet below. Villagers rushed out to help, thinking I had lost valuable documents. It was time I learnt to use leaves or earth.

Communication with Ang Pemba and Dorje wasn't difficult. We shared a handful of Hindi words like *food, water, yes, no, thank you* and *please stop,* and speech wasn't needed for practical purposes. I simply followed their lead. But how was I to express all my feelings about this long-awaited world of mountain and rock? Letter writing wasn't an option; there weren't any post offices outside the Kathmandu valley. After days of enforced silence, I began keeping a journal in an exercise book.

April 1964: 'Writing this in a broken stone hut, a bit like a sheep shelter in the Pennines, huddled up in a woollen shawl. Clouds of dark brown smoke from the wood fire that Dorje has just lit are making my eyes smart. Patches of snow scattered around. We are very high up now, on an old track to Tibet. I picture myself as some inspired missionary woman of the early twentieth century, making her way across uncharted territory, battling fear and exhaustion, like Bunyan's hero-pilgrim, Christian, on his journey towards the Celestial City. It's only eighteen months since I wrote an essay about him for my seventeenth-century literature course. Only I am not heading for a Celestial City, but for Gosainkund. A special place of another kind, with a special view, high in the Himalayas. Maybe that will be the transforming moment of my life. I am leading – or being led – on my own expedition, with my own two Sherpas.'

Some days later:

'Mists have descended and it's gloomy, so I'm burying myself in my notebook. We haven't seen any houses, or people, for several days. At night, we put our sleeping bags on the edge of the path, anywhere that's sheltered. The mountains terrify me now – almost as if I slipped off a ledge, I would go on falling forever. But life is not without hope. Down in the plains all hope evaporates. Thousands of miles of never-ending flatness, the earth dry and cracked, with the sun burning down on the same patchwork of fields, and trees, and little clumps of mud huts. People seem so unimportant. Could that explain some aspects of Indian philosophy?'

My journal undated:

'Ann and Jim told me I would be going over a pass of 17,000 feet, but we've been up and down so many times, I don't know if we've been over it or not. We haven't met a soul for five days. Today the country was harsher and bleaker. A few stunted trees clung to the edges of craters which fell away down the mountainside. Then a thick mist blanketed out that world of eroding rock.

'We heard water dripping, and smelt decay, as our path entered a forest of rotting trees, leafless and covered in mosses. Many were an awful pink, like human limbs with the outer skin peeling off. Some sported large, red, bell-shaped flowers, but the petals were withered at the edges. I plodded on.

'Out again, to a barer, more open landscape, the track hardly a ledge. Across scree, over the shoulder of a mountain, then down and up again. Separated chunks of cliff stood ready to sheer off and bring down half the mountain in the next storm. This is a land still in the making.

'We kept listening for water and looking down for faint signs of the track. In the late afternoon we stopped, halfway up a cliff, perched on a ledge, beneath overhanging rock. From outside, it looked grim, but from within, it was a warm shelter. And water was nearby, so we spread out our sleeping bags and lit a fire.'

Next entry:

'Today we passed through a yet more godforsaken land, colossal in scale, without any shelter. Up and up we went to a high pass – picking our way across the snow, wondering whether it might give way and plunge us into some ravine – sneezing and wheezing, like three old men, my guides picking up wood whenever they saw any.

'At last we came across the first lake, half frozen over, even now in summer, and then a little later, looking down across the snows, we glimpsed another below, and then another, down the steps of the mountain. Mist rose from each level, like hot steam from the crater of a volcano. Along the edge of the first lake, to a clump of stone shelters, grey and deserted.

'"Gosainkund, memsahib," said Ang Pemba.

'He picked up one of the coconut shells left behind by the annual Hindu pilgrimage, fingered it, and tossed it aside.

'This was our destination. But what an anti-climax. Where was the larger view? Dense cloud wrapped itself around us. The shrine of *Nanda Devi* loomed up out of the mist. A sheaf of corn sat on top of its image of the *lingam*. I wasn't expecting this, after all the *mani* stones with their Buddhist symbols and inscriptions. But, by now, I was craving more for signs of human life than religious variety. We continued our cold, lonely trek, hardly able to see our way through the mists, seeking somewhere to rest. We found many rough shelters but no water.

'Late in the day, we dropped down from the heights, through dense woodland, like some Scottish estate. The path well kept, yet nobody using it. All seemed unreal. Continually changing height in relation to the clouds. At last, on the steep slope, we found an empty hut with a torrent far below, but near enough for Dorje to bring up water.

'In the morning we struggled to trace the path through tall trees without leaves or branches. Occasionally a white trunk, contorted in shape, appeared near the path, or we passed through a clearing, spattered with head-high stems bearing monstrous yellow flowers. A wet silence hung around and the mist dripped over us. Distant voices and the crack of wood under an axe broke into the silence. Ahead, a large stone building appeared, with a Buddhist flag flying above. Smaller shacks huddled nearby.

'A middle-aged, rosy-cheeked, Tibetan-looking woman beckoned us in to sit cross-legged by a huge log fire. She was wearing many layers including a long, felt skirt, apron, waistcoat and cap.

'"Lama," said Ang Pemba, pointing to the woman's husband, a man of Indian appearance, with the intense unsmiling expression that I so disliked. The other man in the household looked East Asian. We drank salty, buttered tea. Even that was welcome. And we tried to converse in my Hindi/their Nepali.

'The temple area was gaudily painted by English standards, like the awnings of a fairground, with symbolic designs and images of gods. The Lama pointed to his ornate bed and ran his finger along strings of carved Tibetan words – the *panch silas*, he said – the five forms of perfect conduct. Behind it, a huge image of a standing Buddha dwarfed the room. A row of small figurines fronted it, and, on a central platform, oil wicks sat next to musical instruments, drums, pipes, and coloured plastic toys: anything, no doubt, that they had found exotic. This included a beer bottle labelled 'bier van Holland' with an incense stick stuck inside.

'"Maha Guru," said the Lama, gesturing at piles of huge tomes. In among them small beaded pedestals supported upright coins. I took a photo and they asked me to send them a copy but could only write

The lama and his wife

their address in Tibetan. I transcribed the sound as best I could into the Hindi *Devanagari* script.

'My old longing for Tibet swept over me. "We go Tibet?" I asked Ang Pemba, using my hand to point to the three of us, and my feet to make walking movements in a northerly direction. "Enough food?" I gestured at the baskets, and at my mouth, and again to the North.

'He pointed to four fingers, and mimed sleeping. Four sleeps to the border. He and Dorje looked questioningly at one another. For a moment, they seemed half-persuaded.

'"No, memsahib."

'Leaving our hosts, we took a steep path that plunged downhill to a river far below. A man with long, wavy hair walked past, guiding his herd of black cows through the dense forest. He scowled in our direction. Thank goodness Ang Pemba was beside me. Bamboo shelters appeared, with one side open, woven roofs held in position by stones, and heaps of bamboo strewn on the ground. A few small fields were scratched out on ledges. Suspicious faces appeared and disappeared just as suddenly from beneath the thatch, but nobody emerged to speak to us.

'An hour later, we reached a river gorge, hundreds of feet deep, spanned only by a bridge made from two tree trunks, tied together in the middle by bamboo branches. No handrail. I could never cross this. The Sherpas walked slowly over. They looked back sympathetically and then disappeared behind a rock.'

I sat down for a few minutes. My chest pounded. I stood up. Then sat down again, head in my hands. Blanked out. For how long, I don't know. This was impossible. A bridge to hell. Couldn't we return the way we'd come? Why had they vanished? Waves of heat and cold surged through me. I couldn't do this. I couldn't. If I wobbled, I'd be finished. But I had to do it. I had to shut down my mind. Just focus. Just focus on each step.

Do it now. First step. Step by step. One foot after another. No thinking. Nothing except my feet. And now it's done. Standing there on the bank, trembling.

My companions showed no response when I joined them but stood up as if nothing had happened. I stumbled after them like an automaton, like a patient emerging from an anaesthetic.

'We passed more and more houses, and by late afternoon came to a dark-grey stone village on a steep valley slope, with peaks in all directions. A pack of snarling dogs rushed out, followed by a man who escorted us to the headman's house. It was built into the hill, the ground floor for cows and goats. We walked in at the upper level. One wall was woven, letting light enter and smoke escape. The others were of stone. Clothes, boots and leather straps for baskets hung from a rope.

'The headman, though old and lined, was still good-looking, with a lithe body and alert face. He passed his water pipe to his wife, who had a hole where one eye should have been. Her hair was knotted and unkempt, and she scratched herself continually, clinging to a small child on her lap. She stared at us without expression. Her voice was husky, in between bouts of coughing. Two gentle-faced infants huddled beside her.

'In the morning, we were off again, passing homes all the way. The route was now well-marked and easy to follow, but less interesting than on our outward journey. In the evening we arrived at a wayside hostel managed by a brisk, flirtatious woman, twirling a drop spindle. A stringed instrument hung on the wall. Traders came and went, leaving their packs outside against the *mani* stones. They settled down in a circle to stare at me, the men and women relaxed with one another, so unlike Indians. The landlady handed out barley grain for porridge as travellers arrived. They put it into pouches around their waists. One girl put it in her bodice.

'I couldn't find anywhere private for calls of nature. No alternative but to squat alongside everyone else at the edge of the path. After eating, we spread our bedding on the veranda. Just before I fell asleep, a small boy with a sweet, timid face, and soft fair skin, came across to play with my pen and paper. He dragged one lifeless leg behind him.

'The following day our route flattened into a wide valley. A gigantic hydroelectric scheme blocked all vistas. The site swarmed with Sikh workers whose eyes glinted through faces whitened with quarry dust. We plodded on through a military area, with only the profile of the mountain, Trisul, to keep us going. A motored vehicle revved up nearby. The Sherpas jerked in terror and raced away to the side. These were the men who walked fearlessly across perilous peaks and fragile bridges. We spent that night in a filthy, flea-ridden *dharmshala*, another hostel for traders, filled with Tibetan refugees and small boys, begging for food.

'From there on, every inch of land was cultivated in tiny terraced fields, with neat thatched cottages. By noon, sweat was streaming off my face, and every step was a labour. The river was now wide and shallow. We sat at its edge, knees hunched up, and heads hanging down. I fell asleep and woke to find myself dribbling, and a tall man with a basket on his back gaping at me. I looked around, and saw my two guides, sitting on stones in the middle of the river. I walked out to join them, washing for the first time in three weeks. My feet were sore and my socks were yellow. I had been wearing the same clothes without discomfort, night and day, since we started our trek and, only now, in the heat of the lowlands, did they smell.

'That night the *dharmshala* was again dark and uninviting. Ang Pemba deposited the baggage outside, above the path, under huge trees. Watched by all, we prepared our food and drew out our sleeping bags, the ends outermost, with our possessions stacked between us, to prevent theft. In the night it rained, so we had no option but to move inside. Soon it was pouring with the intensity of the monsoon.'

In Kathmandu I parted from my companions, exhausted but content. We arranged to meet again after I had found a cheap place to stay near Durbar Square. A cracked mirror hung on the wall, the first I had seen since setting off on my trek. My face was red and swollen, disfigured with all sorts of lumps and bumps. Had I picked up an infection? The chemist on the corner of the street took one look at me, said, 'Sunburn' and pulled out a tube of something.

All I wanted now, in this busy city, was to drink tea in the Sherpa restaurant. It was small and dirty, but friendly. Ang Pemba was waiting at the entrance with a white farewell scarf for me. I said goodbye with tears in my eyes. We had not spent a moment apart for three weeks.

As I walked out into the street, a woman in a blue silk sari turned towards me.

'Why you people like the Tibetans so much? Very dirty, they are. Eat dirty things like meat, and drink liquor. Women have no shame. Very backward people.'

Just like the British, I thought.

I stayed on for a couple of days, washing clothes and catching up on letter writing. I wasn't sure whether I should send a letter to Toofan. It was some months since we had met and I didn't want to lose touch. Nor did I want to seem too keen. In the end, I sent him a three-page account of my adventures. I don't know what he made of it. It must have sounded bizarre. But the things foreigners did were bizarre. That was part of the appeal.

CHAPTER 20

BACK TO THE ASHRAM AND ONWARDS TO SRINAGAR

LAKSHMI ASHRAM WASN'T ALL THAT FAR AS THE CROW FLIES. But I wasn't a crow. Travelling from one area of the hills to another required lengthy detours through the sweltering plains. A three-day journey for a two-week visit. I had to decide if the Gandhian movement was the place where my future lay. I flew to Patna and slept in the station waiting room, free of charge. I always travelled Third Class now but used the First Class waiting rooms whenever I could. That was one of the perks of being European. White people couldn't really be Third Class, though that was beginning to change. As a Punjabi friend in Banaras later said, 'When we saw the hippies arriving in crumpled, unstarched, cotton clothes, we thought these must be the untouchables of Europe.'

The girls in the ashram welcomed me back with hugs. 'We hoped you would come again,' Sarala Devi said. 'And I have asked Sita and Sundari to take you on a long walk through the forests to a hill-top shrine. I know you'll enjoy that.' We scrambled up the final hundred feet. At last, the much-longed-for view of snowy peaks.

I hadn't seen a panorama like this in Nepal. I'd walked through mist. And I'd been too close to the mountains to see the scale of anything. A bit like my life. Never seeing clearly, never achieving a comprehensive view.

A miniature white-washed temple perched on the top. We rang the bell as we passed through the gateway, and I didn't hesitate before offering flowers to the goddess.

'Now we find wood and water to cook *kedgeree*,' Sita said. 'I washed the rice and lentils before we started.'

'You're still saying please and thank you all the time,' Sundari scolded. 'We're not doing anything special, only giving you food.'

I'd been told dozens of times to save the expression of gratitude for when it was needed – for when a total stranger risks his life for you – but old habits die hard. And it was still difficult for me to remember that eating times are not for conversation.

Back in the ashram I resumed the routine of my previous visit, cooking, digging, cleaning the animal sheds and taking the cattle out to graze.

A parcel of apricots arrived from the family orchard of a young engineer I had met on the bus up from Kathgodam. I thought of Padma, my Hindi teacher, and wondered how often Indian visitors to England encountered such gratuitous generosity. In India I could never predict what was going to happen from one minute to the next. Self-employment in family businesses enabled people to be flexible about working hours. Life in Britain, even for a student in those carefree days of maintenance grants and full employment, was regulated by the clock, and by effective civic administration. The lives of middle-aged people were even more constrained, with their work ethic, and the cult of house and garden that consumed all the spare time that Indians would devote to social life.

I wasn't too sad to leave Lakshmi Ashram. Manual labour in the fields was hard. I was always snatching a look at my watch. It was hot, even in the foothills, and I was weakened from suffering chronic dysentery for almost a year. Perhaps I had the wrong mental attitude.

I hoped I was concealing my feelings. Perhaps I was just a soft townie, incapable of doing anything other than studying books.

The predictable heat of the plains was a relief after the sudden temperature transitions of the hills. The temperature in Delhi was only just over a hundred degrees because of a shower the day before. Why hurry on to meet Sujata in the cooler climes of Kashmir?

I wandered around the old city in the early mornings, admiring austere Mughal monuments set in manicured grounds. In the evenings I relished strolling without the restrictions of prickly, woollen garments. How easy it was, after toiling in the fields for two weeks. Afternoon siestas were another pleasure to be savoured in the YWCA Hostel.

On my second day, I took a high-speed scooter rickshaw from the old city to New Delhi, to meet the Commonwealth Scholars who had visited me in Banaras. My bones and inner organs bounced about as I gripped the frame hood. Tony and Vicky's bungalow was in a wide and spacious road. They were still wearing Western clothes.

'We had such a good time with you in Banaras,' Vicky said. 'Why don't we go somewhere together next year – a desert region, perhaps, or a wild-life sanctuary? Or should it be Burma and Thailand?'

Our plans were still undecided when I left.

I was about to set off for Srinagar when a telegram arrived from Sujata. 'Trip cancelled. War imminent in Kashmir. Permits for Badrinath refused. Going Calcutta.'

How could she do this to me? We'd planned the trip together and now I was stranded. Why should war make the slightest difference? I'd forgotten that she had a Chinese grandfather, and it didn't occur to me that someone of East Asian appearance might be vulnerable. The Chinese were again threatening on the eastern border. Nehru's release of the secular Kashmiri leader, Sheikh Abdullah, in April, after many years of imprisonment, was adding to the unease. Only a few months earlier, major disturbances had followed the theft of a most holy relic, a hair of the Prophet, from its shrine in Srinagar. Calm only returned when the hair reappeared miraculously.

For a day I vacillated, wondering whether to go on alone. The novelty of the warmth was wearing off. The temperature had now risen to around 115 degrees. Early morning strolls couldn't fill the whole day. Anything would be better than a month in the plains.

The night sleeper took me to Pathankot where I boarded a coach for the two-day journey via Jammu. I grabbed a window seat for mountain views. The coach filled with prosperous Indian tourists. Women in silk and nylon saris clucked over children and bags.

'Are you a gypsy?' one woman asked. 'Could you sing some gypsy songs?'

'Are you Kashmiri?' a family from Bombay wondered. Clothing and mannerisms were more important than skin and hair colour. By now I was oiling my light-brown hair to curb the wilder strands, and wearing it long, in a plait. It looked better that way, I thought, not as odd as it had when I'd first arrived.

Sometime after dark, at the end of the first day, we came to a halt in the middle of nowhere. Everyone piled off and started to make their way to a dimly lit building up the hill. They seemed to know where they were going. I ended up being one of the last to extricate my luggage from the back.

'Have you booked somewhere for the night?' I asked a corpulent lady.

Her eyes unsmilingly scanned my crumpled clothes. 'Yes, we've arranged it in advance,' she said.

Nobody had told me it was necessary to book. I turned to speak to the driver, but he didn't know much English and by now everyone else had disappeared into the darkness.

'Is there anywhere to stay?' I asked.

The driver pointed down the road with no change of expression. It was so dark that I couldn't see anyone in either direction. The others had gone up the road but maybe their guesthouse was full. The driver should know, and I didn't want to hang around any longer.

Hoisting my bag onto my shoulder, I set off round the corner, downhill. A wooden shack huddled at the bottom. At the front, benches, and a trestle table, sheltered under a corrugated iron awning. It was the kind of place where men gather to drink tea. I couldn't see anyone except a wizened old man clearing away cups. This was not where I should be. I looked back up the hill. The night had the dense blackness that you find only far from human settlements. I could barely sense the rocky countryside and the large trees on both sides of the road. To venture up it again was as uninviting as to remain where I was.

'You have somewhere for me to stay?' I asked in Hindi. The old man gaped at me for a moment and pointed to one of the two rooms in the hut.

I pushed open the wooden door. A small space with an earthen floor housed a string bed and a straight-backed chair with a glass on it. I put down my bag and walked across to the shuttered window. The hut clung to the edge of a sheer cliff. No escaping that way. I checked the door. No lock. I placed the chair against it. If I heard the glass fall off the chair in the night, I'd have a second's warning. I slipped off my dusty trousers. It was an engrained habit to take off the day's clothes before sleeping, though I hadn't done it in Nepal. I placed my torch on the floor near the bed and climbed into my sleeping bag. Within minutes I was asleep.

After some time – I've no idea how long – I was woken by the sound of the glass falling off the chair. I was out of my bag and sitting on the edge of the bed in a second, with just enough time to grab my baggy Indian trousers and drape them over my legs, hoping it would look as if I was dressed. The door had stopped moving. Now it opened slowly and the old man stumbled in. He stood there for a moment, surprised by the light of my torch. I noted how awake I was. I prayed heaven that my trousers wouldn't slip off my legs.

He hesitated for a moment, shuffled towards me, and touched me on the knee.

'Please go,' I said in Hindi, in as magisterial a tone as I could muster.

He half dropped onto his knees in an awkward position and patted my legs again. I repeated myself several times, focusing my will on him as strongly as I could. He grovelled in the same position for a few moments and then got up and shuffled out again. I don't know what he wanted; perhaps he didn't either. I instantly put on my trousers and replaced the chair with the glass on it back against the door. I padlocked my bag and placed it near my head. Within minutes I was asleep.

Several hours later, I was woken by the sound of the glass falling off the chair again. I was up in a flash. The old man was standing at the door with a paraffin lamp.

'Memsahib,' he said, 'army for you.'

Oh God. I walked towards the door. A huge turbaned Sikh, about six feet in height, was facing me. We stared expressionlessly at one another for what felt like an eternity. Then he asked for my passport. This was absurd at two-thirty in the middle of the night. But I wasn't going to argue. I unlocked my bag and fished it out. He pored over it in the shadowy light before silently handing it back to me.

'You hippies,' he said, 'maybe you spy for Pakistan.'

So that's all it was. My fortress-body crumpled as my terror seeped away. I remembered Prem Chand, the Danish student who had once been arrested as a suspected Chinese spy. What other explanation could there be for bizarre behaviour? I closed the door again, put the glass back on the chair and, for the third time that night, climbed into my sleeping bag, this time to sleep, undisturbed, until dawn. This was one of many incidents not recorded in letters home.

CHAPTER 21

THE HIMALAYAS AGAIN: KASHMIR

At the Srinagar bus terminus, houseboat owners mobbed the passengers. I was the only foreigner in the group, so a few made a beeline for me.

'Nothing above three rupees a day,' I insisted.

It was all twenty-five, fifty. I couldn't believe what I was hearing: nothing like Banaras prices.

They stared at me bemused. A quiet man, wearing a fez, stepped forward.

'Yes, three rupees,' he said, 'but plain and simple.'

His punt barely skimmed the water. It conveyed me to a small houseboat, moored near a tiny island, far from roads or crowds. The 'Kings Panama', number 403, Dal Lake, was awaiting renovation. Not a stick of furniture in the main room. The owner, Mr Abdul Ali Kadli, lived with his family in a boat alongside. Within minutes, he conjured up a string bed, a kerosene stove, and pots and pans for me to do my own cooking, squatting on the floor, as they did.

'Mr Kadli. I want to stay for a month.'

The second room in the boat contained a stand that was soon topped up with a wash bowl. Later my host added an iron bathtub. All I had to do was throw the water out of the window. Flies and smells weren't a problem in a cool climate. Finally, he rigged up a commode, and strung an electric light cable across from his boat. It felt like home when his three young children tripped aboard to inspect my possessions.

'We give you food today,' my host said. 'Tomorrow I take you to market.'

Small bowls of meat and vegetables soon arrived on a steel platter. Hot *rotis* lay crisply at the side. Why on earth had I worried so much about coming on my own without Sujata?

The food stalls clustered near the school of the eldest daughter, Emiena, so I joined them the following morning in the family punt. We passed *shikaras,* slightly larger boats with thatched bamboo awnings supported on four poles. They paddled along, selling flowers, strawberries and cherries, to holidaymakers in houseboats.

At dusk, I perched on the boat's edge, dangling my legs above the water, looking out over a wide stretch of lake at the sun setting beyond willow trees and mountains. In the daytime, I sat on the roof with a book, enjoying the balmy air. How nice it was not to have servants wandering in and out all the time. This was true bliss, and I was the luckiest woman alive.

Srinagar was heaven on earth at that time, at least for a visitor, before all the years of horror began, with the locals squeezed between Islamist militants and the Indian army. Green parks and spacious roads alternated with winding lanes and rivers. Mughal gardens adorned small islands, their terraced fountains and marble shelters decorated with gleaming floral mosaics. Mountains rose, sheer, from the side of lakes. Ranges of snowy peaks lined the horizon.

It was cheap, too, with no need for taxis or rickshaws. And it was very quiet that year, because fear of war deterred tourists. My happiness was complete when I discovered a public library that allowed me to borrow books in English.

Emiena came over on her own one afternoon. She blushed as she pushed a bunch of roses into my hand. My adoptive family often brought me tasty titbits. They took me with them wherever they went.

We would travel by punt down the river, under the seven old bridges, and then alight, and go off into back alleys to visit their relatives or craft workshops.

As I wrote in a letter to my parents:

'Yesterday I spent the whole day in a boat with Emiena and her uncle. We drifted between tall reeds, across all the lakes. The town is more water than land, but the water is more marsh than lake. Kingfishers darted down into the banks. Children bathed, and adults washed clothes, banging them against the stones. Little boys fished near earth stacked on top of weeds, floating gardens, sporting vegetables and melons. Women moved between the rows in boats, tending and picking the ripe fruit.'

The next morning, Mr Kadli dropped in.

'Last night three boys come. They heard English girl here alone. They wanted climb on your boat. I heard sound. Quickly, I made their boat to sink.'

Should I be relieved or horrified?

'Did they drown?'

'Not to worry,' he said.

Sexual harassment occurred all the time in Banaras, but it was worse in Srinagar. A few days earlier, in a quiet street, on the edge of the city, a man sauntering towards me had leaned over and hit me hard in the crotch – before continuing on his way. I stood stunned for a moment. Could this be real?

'You filthy pig,' I shouted, only half-aware of what I was saying. I limped away as fast as I could.

Additional protectors soon arrived, two young couples on holiday from Bombay.

'You would be most welcome to join us. We are visiting a government silk factory. After that we will go in a *shikara* down the river.'

We reclined on embroidered cushions, shaded from the sun by coloured awnings. They sang Tamil songs. And then it was my turn. I had never been much of a singer and didn't know more than the first line of anything other than Christmas carols.

'Just go ahead, you sing something at least, please.'

In desperation, I launched into the one carol that came into my head: "We Three Kings of Orient Are". I was concentrating so hard, and so embarrassed about my voice, that the inappropriateness of the words only gradually registered. Passing *shikaras* paused to listen. A boat with a Western family slid past. They stared. Was I some kind of youthful missionary?

My Bombay hosts took me back to eat in their houseboat. Lined up in a row, on the bank beside the road, it was palatial, furnished in colonial British style, with fussy curtains and carpets. Not like the clean simplicity of my own houseboat in its tranquil backwater. The adjacent boats were empty.

And then we heard the shocking news. Nehru had died. I hadn't even known he was ill, not having read the papers for some time. What a giant of a man he'd been. As one of my new friends said, 'He had the dash of a warrior and the prudence of a statesman. We loved him because… because he was wholly and solely for us.'

After a while, the newspapers became tedious. They never let up on the tragic tone.

'Mr Nehru's ashes go in Shadipur Lake,' Mr Kadli told me. 'You can go see on Monday.'

So on the 8th June, 1964, I boarded one of the army of special coaches ferrying people to the site. The sun glanced diamonds off the water, with its reflections of green trees and mountains. The police were out in full force, blowing whistles continually, and bawling at the owners of *shikaras* trying to sneak nearer to the boat carrying the ashes.

One succeeded in breaking away from the bank. Then they were all off. It turned into a game of chase, with boatmen splashing police. I stared in disbelief. Funerals should be dignified, I thought. Everything should proceed in an orderly manner – choreographed almost. And why were only a few women weeping? But this wasn't a funeral. This was *darshun* – getting close to the last remnants of a great life. The viewers would be imbued with the power of that life for a moment at least. But could they be truly participating in that moment if they weren't quiet and serious?

On the return bus to Srinagar, I slipped into the first window seat I could, not realising that separate areas were allocated to women. Four men piled in next to me and the bus was soon packed. A tall, powerfully built man squeezed closer, so I tucked myself into as small a space as possible. He continued to press harder against my hips. With horror I realised he was masturbating.

'Go,' I said. My Hindi wasn't up to a full sentence. 'Go,' I kept repeating. Men near me laughed and shouted. I had no idea what they were saying. The few women in the bus were silent, with their heads and faces covered. They must consider me contemptible, I thought, for not demanding to get off the bus, even if it is in the middle of nowhere; they must think I'm just another shameless Western woman. The bus came to a halt in the rural outskirts of Srinagar. I extricated myself with relief, looking down to avoid eye contact. As I hurried towards the centre of town, the odious man rode past in a horse-drawn trap. He slowed down and beckoned to me. I kept on walking as fast as possible. A few minutes later, a police jeep drew up. A moustachioed officer, with a perfect English accent, stopped me.

'Some women on the bus informed us that you were being mistreated. Please come with me and make a report about it. Tell me which man he was.'

So the women had not despised me. They'd acted on my behalf. But by now I was so suspicious of South Asian men in the street, including the police, that all I wanted to do was forget the incident and get back to the sanctuary of my houseboat, and the Ali Kadli family.

'I don't want to talk about it,' I said. 'I'm so sick of people like him.'

'But then how can we stop this awful behaviour?' he said.

'It was the man riding in the *tonga*, wearing a *lungi*,' I said, and hurried on. That was another of the incidents not relayed in my letters home.

From Srinagar I made a couple of trips to settlements higher up. Mr Kadli gave me a letter written in Urdu, addressed to the proprietor

Author with Emiena in a shikara

of a hotel in Gulmarg, instructing him to watch over me. I spent my first day pottering near a stream, edged by fir trees. The mountains of Karakorum, and the peak of Nanga Parbat, soared ahead. They were out of my reach, but a frozen lake, higher up in the hills, sounded feasible. But would it be all right to walk there alone? This endless concern about the dangers of being unaccompanied was one of the curses of being a woman. I hired a horse and horseman.

We didn't pass anybody on foot, only locals on horseback, all slim, the women in red cloaks, and with long hair. The earth was so thickly carpeted with flowers, even at 14,000 feet, that we couldn't avoid trampling them. They grew even more densely on the strip where the snow had melted. I walked the last stretch, up to 14,500 feet. I can't leave an area as beautiful as this, I thought. I'll stay in Kashmir for another ten days. Nobody will be back in Banaras in time for the start of term.

From Gulmarg, I moved on to Pahalgam. Prosperous Indians, carrying nothing at all, were shouting at porters staggering under the weight of four heavy cases. I gazed at the vast open spaces ahead and felt a similar distance between myself and the people around me.

Back in Srinagar I applied for a visa to enter Ladakh. Perhaps this time I could manage to get into the Tibetan cultural zone. I was refused at the first attempt. The Indian army had just discovered that the Chinese had built a road there, across an uninhabited area.

'Since it is so important to you,' the visa official said, 'I will arrange for you to meet the Home Minister.' And he did.

I prepared to shout, beg, and even weep: those tactics that had often worked for me in Banaras, though they had begun as spontaneous outbursts. It soon became clear that this time they would not produce results.

'There is no question of entry for a woman,' the Home Minister said. 'Even my own wife would not be allowed in. The Chinese are not the problem. So many young Indian soldiers are there without access to a woman. Just imagine it.'

I had failed again. I trudged back along the riverbank. Coming towards me was Eberhart, with one of his compatriots from Delhi.

'It's a small world,' he said.

Their houseboat was in the regimented row fronting the road. It was crammed with old-fashioned English ornaments and pictures of hunting scenes, with floral beige carpets and bulky upholstered chairs. It couldn't be clean with all that clutter. But it was nice to meet a known face.

I took Eberhart and his friend to see my houseboat.

'You can't be staying in this.' They hooted with laughter.

The friend was about to return to Delhi, so Eberhart suggested a ten-day trip, walking up to the Lidderwat valley. The mountain hut backed onto thickly wooded cliffs surrounding a meadow. We chatted at the door with the proprietor for a few minutes before turning to deposit our hired tents and cooking equipment inside.

'Very sorry that your room not available for today. I unlocked it two hours before, and now a *saddhu* has taken possession of it. Very unfortunate it is but he will be shifting tomorrow.'

'Anyone would think this is just something that happens, like a shower of rain,' Eberhart said.

We wandered around our end of the valley for a couple of hours, looking at fleecy-white peaks, and listening to rushing torrents. That night we slept out on the veranda.

The holy man moved on the next day. A Punjabi lecturer in English literature, from Delhi, occupied the room adjacent to ours.

'I don't mind that you live together,' he said. 'What is marriage in the face of true love?'

'But we're only friends,' I said, 'nothing more.'

'Not to be ashamed,' he said. 'True love conquers all.'

We sat on rocks at the river's edge and washed as best we could. The air was hot by noon, so we made iced coffee by wedging our mugs between two stones. I couldn't stop singing now I was back in the heart of the hills again.

The next day we set off towards the Kolhoi glacier. A shepherd stopped us, holding out an infant with one arm plastered in cow dung. But what could we do? Neither of us had medicine in our bags. This often happened in India. My heart was hardening. I didn't want to drown in a sea of feeling.

We forded rivers, jumping from boulder to boulder. Higher up came snow bridges that were firm underfoot. At 15,000 feet, we kicked steps in the ice to reach a ridge. The glare from the sun exhausted us, and my head ached. But it was worth it, for at the top I saw the view I had been longing for since childhood. Giant walls of ice supported snowy pinnacles that rippled endlessly, on all sides, into the far distance.

'No worry about avalanches here,' the cook-cum-watchman said, over dinner that evening; it would be safe to stroll to the top of the valley in the morning. We took nothing more than packed lunches, and jackets and shawls slung over our shoulders. The path followed the fast-flowing river. The sky was clear and blue and walking was easy, with the snowline a few feet above. We jumped over small tributary streams. Near the head of the valley we began to climb a low spur. Our feet kept sinking into the soft snow, so we stopped at what we guessed was around 14,000 feet. Peaks stretched in all directions.

The sun was burning our cheeks, so we sat down and ate our banana and nut lunches quickly. Further up the valley a large group of *Gujar* nomads trudged slowly out of sight. They were moving up from the plains with their animals for the summer grazing. We watched them for a few moments and then set off down. Ten minutes later a torrent blocked our way. We managed to clamber halfway across, but the water was icy with jagged rocks and deep pools. How could this be? It was the same path we had walked in the morning.

'The midday sun must have melted the snow higher up, and the streams and rivers have risen by many feet. The river won't shrink back to its former level until the early hours of tomorrow,' Eberhart said.

We looked at one another in silence. Crossing was out of the question. And it would be madness, in the mid-afternoon, to go higher, looking for an easier crossing place. We wouldn't survive the night, out on the snow, in our light clothing.

'The nomads,' I said. 'They're our only chance.'

'They're tribesmen. They may be hostile; we'll be helpless.'

'What alternative do we have?'

We didn't know how far up the valley they'd be by now. I guessed they wouldn't climb over the high mountain pass until next morning. So back we turned, retracing our steps uphill. Dusk was falling before we found them camped by the river – about twenty men, and hundreds of sheep, close-packed on the stony ground. Several fires burned in the centre, near a solitary tent. Eberhart approached two men standing by the bank, but they laughed and sneered and pointed at the river. We stood there, shifting from one foot to the other. A group of older men seemed to be discussing us. They sent a younger man over to hand us a blanket. He pointed to a space on the ground. The stench of sheep made me feel sick.

Ten minutes later, an older man gave us each a metal plate with rice, and some kind of green vegetable – stewed nettles, perhaps. He presented me with a large ladle. They must have heard that Europeans don't eat with the hand. And this was all they had in the way of cutlery. I couldn't even get it in my mouth. Small bowls of sheep's milk followed. We were grateful to receive anything. I shivered, pulling my shawl closer. The women must have been in the tent. Nobody smiled at us. They must have thought we were stupid aliens, engaging in some kind of irrational activity only we understood.

Another man produced a small clay pot with hot charcoal in it. He indicated that we should put it under our blanket. Sharing one blanket out of doors, in freezing conditions, with a man who was only a friend, was no joke.

I slept hardly at all and was so stiff in the morning that I struggled to stand. The *Gujars* were up at dawn and soon ready to set off uphill. We tried to thank them but had no language in common.

'We should offer them money,' Eberhart said.

'That might offend their sense of honour.'

Eberhart ignored me and went ahead. They didn't seem too worried about their honour, and stashed the notes in their clothes, still unsmiling.

We set off downhill. Just as we'd thought, the swift flowing torrents had changed back into little streams. It was easy to jump from one stone to another. Before long, we saw our mountain hut in the distance. A small party was coming up towards us. Someone was leading a horse, and next to him was our porter. He burst into loud wails when he saw us. They were coming up with the horse to collect our bodies.

After all that excitement, we spent the rest of our time lounging around, reading, eating, and building little dams to divert rivulets for twig boats. In Srinagar, Eberhart departed to prepare for the new term and I returned to my houseboat for yet another week. I knew it would still be waiting for me. None of the tourists wanted such simple accommodation.

Now I could get back to my academic reading. The following morning, I visited the library to replenish my supply of books. While pausing at the doorway, a tall serious man, in his thirties, came across to speak to me.

'Where are you from?' he asked. 'I see you are carrying books of philosophy. What are you doing here?'

I gave my normal pat answer. He listened gravely.

'You would be most welcome to stay with my family. We are pundits and live in the village of Sirnoo, just outside Srinagar. My name is Omkar Nath Ram. Here is my card. You can come any time, tomorrow, if you like.'

He bowed and took his leave. I made my way back to Dal Lake. Should I go? This seemed too good an opportunity to miss, but what would I find? The next morning, I packed a small bag and set off on foot.

His house lay at the end of a narrow, earthen track. I banged on the door and it was opened by a round-faced woman in a sari.

'Come in, please,' she said, but her face showed she was far from pleased.

She sat me down on a mat and brought tea. After a while her husband came in. He didn't introduce her, and she withdrew to another room. Was he surprised that I had turned up? His face gave no indication. He sat down on an adjacent mat and said nothing. His wife brought him tea.

'I am a teacher,' he said. 'I like to learn – all my life. But I do not understand why you have come to India on your own. Have you no husband?'

I was used to this query, with its hint of accusation. I was some kind of freak, who didn't behave like a normal woman or even like a normal person. Even a normal man did not choose to go on holiday alone, without friends or relatives. But then they weren't individuals, with minds of their own, like me. Or was it possible that something was wrong with me, or with my culture?

'How can I marry before I have found the Truth?' I said.

He raised his eyebrows.

Drops of sweat were beginning to run towards my chin. 'And in my caste, the old people consider that if a woman marries before the age of thirty, it means she cannot control her desires.'

He stared at me. 'I can see you want to study,' he continued, observing my discomfort. 'Please explain why your Western philosophy is so different from ours. I am a follower of the Shaivite School.'

I struggled to say something meaningful and useful. I didn't even know how the Kashmiri School of Shaivism differed from other kinds of Shaivism. But I wanted to talk to this man. I was drawn to his dignity and his love of books. He, too, wanted to learn what he could from this alien from another planet who had crossed his path.

'We Shaiva people want to be in harmony with the power of the universe. We try to find it within ourselves, or to bring it inside. Then we become powerful. Maybe your people do not look within. You are more interested in changing the material world.'

'There are many kinds of Western philosophers,' I said. 'They all have different views.' I was tired of always having to speak on behalf of the whole of Western thought. Nor could I see why power should be considered sacred, if that was what he meant. And by now I knew that all this talk of the spirituality of the East had mainly emerged as a response to British conquest. 'In ancient times, your kings and merchants tried hard to change the material world.'

Omkar Nath paused and furrowed his forehead.

'That is because they lost the true path,' he said. 'That is why your people were able to overcome us.'

I was losing the thread of the argument – both his and mine. I stumbled on for a while, trying to answer his questions.

It was a relief when his wife entered, as dusk was falling, and took me outside to see the lavatory. She walked round to the back of the house.

'Here,' she said. But there was nothing here that I could see: just an earthen area.

'This is the women's place,' she said, in English.

We returned to the house. She led me to the drainage channel and poured water over my hands, before bringing a brass platter of food to my mat. We ate in silence. She poured water again, so I could wash the food off my hand, and rinse my mouth, and rolled out bedding for us both. Her husband had disappeared to sleep somewhere else.

'You and me, we sleep here,' she said.

What could I say to her? What choice did she have but to offer hospitality? I supposed that she, too, must think I was a loose woman. How could I reassure her? I smiled.

On horseback in Gulmarg

'You are very kind,' I said, 'and your husband is a good man.'

'How you know?' she asked, frowning.

Now I've put my foot in it, I thought. Perhaps she suspects I tried to seduce him, and he resisted, like one of those virtuous sages in the old legends.

'Well, I don't actually know,' I said. 'It's just the impression I have.' It was difficult to be sure of what I was saying. My Hindi was unreliable as well as limited.

'How you meet him?' she asked.

'In the library,' I said. It sounded feeble. 'I am studying all the great Indian philosophers.' That sounded unconvincing too. I began to feel like a serious criminal. I wanted to escape somewhere. Perhaps that's what she felt, too.

'Now we sleep,' she said.

With relief, I wrapped myself in the blankets and, within minutes, was gone into the untroubled sleep of youth.

CHAPTER 22

2006 CONVERSATION WITH SHANTA CONTINUES BY EMAIL

August 30th. Mumbai

Dear Mary,

Thanks for sending the next chunk. But I'm still puzzled by this Himalayan obsession. And all this stuff about the perfect view. Hindus go on pilgrimage to Badrinath – and suffer many pains. But they do it in a group, to leave behind the ego, not to puff it up. Maharashtrian Brahmans would think that dragging one's body, over heaps of rock, is for penance, not pleasure. And this search for adventure seems like mental sickness. Sorry, if that sounds unkind. Some of us might admire it among young men of the martial castes.

September 2nd. Manchester

But Britain did have a martial culture, in the imperial age, Shanta. That was why Germany and Britain competed so frantically in the Himalayas, in the first half of the twentieth century. You must have heard English parents saying to their children, 'Let's go exploring

158

*today and have a little adventure'. That's a relic of the same thing –
the urge to map and master everything. And maybe a nation with
a history of overseas trading is bound to value trekking.*

September 3ʳᵈ. Mumbai

Dear Mary,

*I must admit I can't imagine an Indian mother urging her
children to explore and have adventures. But, Mary, I thought
you'd rebelled against all those imperial ideas. And how could you,
of all people, have imagined yourself as some Victorian missionary
woman – crossing frozen wastes? But perhaps you're right about
the trading heritage. I believe the Arabs wrote lots of travel books in
the mediaeval period, in their commercial and maritime heyday.*

September 4ᵗʰ. Manchester

*Yes. And they didn't hesitate to elaborate on their exploits and the
strange wonders they saw. It's not just personal ego, Shanta. The
dream of uniqueness is a script rooted in Protestant Christian
areas of North-West Europe. Or that, at least, was Bertrand
Russell's disapproving observation. As if he was free from it! We
labour under its weight. But maybe you're right. Maybe it is a
negative aspect of my culture. But how can I be free of it?*

*Viewing high mountains makes us feel that we participate in
the power of nature just at the moment when our self-importance
crumbles. That's the paradox. Isn't that a bit similar to the Hindu
concept of darshun of gods and gurus? By seeing, and being in
the presence of a powerful being, your little self becomes imbued
with something higher for a moment?*

September 7ᵗʰ. Mumbai

*I suppose if you people worship anything it is Nature. The
whole thing seems peculiar to me, Mary. But I suppose it's no
stranger than flailing your flesh with knives at Muhurram, or
lying on a bed of nails for years, though I expect it's sent more*

young men to their deaths. But why would women get caught up in this kind of thing? Will read this new batch as soon as I can. Love, Shanta

PART III
THE SECOND YEAR
1964–5

CHAPTER 23

1964 MONSOON SECOND
TIME AROUND

MY APPREHENSION ABOUT ANOTHER SWELTERING MONSOON in Banaras dissipated as I stepped down onto the station platform. A fresh breeze blew in from rain-drenched streets.

I sat on my veranda like a Mughal emperor in his rain pavilion, savouring the sound and scent of warm showers and wet dust. After the next downpour, Ann and I rushed outside and danced. It wasn't so good for nearby villages now under water. The city's central market flooded, and several rickety houses collapsed.

Lectures showed no sign of starting so I had plenty of time to relish the season. That was not what a new batch of American English teachers wanted. 'There's no work ready for us,' one of them complained. 'What are we to do with ourselves?'

I stared at them. Was work the only thing in life?

A year in India had now passed. How much easier everything was the second time round. I was so comfortable in my *selwar-kameez* that I resolved never again to wear European clothes. How ridiculous those short, tight skirts were. You had to keep your knees clamped together all the time. And as for the elastic girdles women hauled up over their stomachs to conceal imagined bulges – they were even worse. I sometimes passed red-faced Western tourists on my outings into the city. They walked awkwardly and their large arms splayed out at the side. The women wore hardly any outer clothes, only underwear, it seemed. One afternoon I stood behind a pillar, watching a large group. They flapped around whenever flies perched on their arms, or wasps hovered nearby.

Flies and wasps were one thing, intestinal denizens quite another. A visit to the pathology lab revealed I was hosting three varieties of worms.

'You will see some of them in your stool. Not to worry.'

Comfort was offered by Sujata. 'Remember, all life is one. There is nothing inherently revolting about worms.'

Ann and Jim found a rat emerging from the toilet late one evening. 'All life is burgeoning,' Ann said.

I gave a watery smile.

'I'm putting out poison for it,' Jim said. 'Sujata needn't know.'

A few days later, Ann pointed to a dead rat in the gutter behind my room.

'That must be it,' she said.

I gave it a quick look out of the corner of one eye. Beads of moisture glittered on its grey skin. By evening, the bloated carcase swarmed with maggots. By morning, it had shrunk; its fluids were draining away. By the time I got back from the library, in the afternoon, only a little slime remained. Better not to think about it.

*

My courses eventually started a couple of weeks later than scheduled. After the first lecture of the new academic year, I arrived in the International Hostel to find that the European students were already sitting around a side table, heads bent forward in earnest discussion.

'It's outrageous,' I heard Jim say.

'We're talking about Father Raimondo Panikkar,' Eberhart whispered, as I approached. 'He's just arrived from Rome. He's a Catholic professor, and a scholar of Sanskrit.'

'So?'

'He's a genius,' Jim said, without bothering to lower his voice. 'He is a philosopher who writes in Spanish, German and English, and is at home in Italian, as well as many ancient languages, including Latin, Greek and Sanskrit. His latest book, *The Unknown Christ of Hinduism*, has just been published. He applied for a professorship here earlier this year. The appointment is scheduled to start as soon as the monsoon begins to ease off. We've just heard that he was rejected out of hand because he's a Catholic priest. And his referees include people like Jean Paul Sartre. What sort of place is this?'

'I don't know if that is so surprising,' I said. 'Would European theologians and philosophers be any more open-minded to a Hindu monk?'

'Panikkar still plans to come,' Eberhart told me afterwards 'He already has a house near the river. He'll write another book. You're bound to meet him.'

*

August is the season of growth, yet a food crisis swept the country. Protected though we were in our pocket of green rainforest, even we could no longer remain unaware of it. The newspapers announced that the effects of a poor harvest had been accentuated by the grain dealers. The government was reluctant to confront the hoarders though wheat was now costing fifty percent more per kilo. Sugar rocketed in price, so we drank unsweetened tea. Rice disappeared from the hostel menu; we ate chapattis and wheat porridge instead. The postman brought parcels from England containing sugar and rice.

Long queues wilted outside ration shops, and the rickshaw drivers went on strike for a day. Conflicting reports circulated on campus. Some said the drivers were forced into it by the right-wing opposition party, the *Jan Sangh*, who wanted to make political capital out of the crisis. Every day, loudspeakers on vans bellowed as they toured the area. Two stone cutters went on hunger strike for nine days near the university gates, lying on lightweight rope beds outside the large modern jewellery shop where they worked. The rotund owner of the shop, a leading light in the local Rotary club, showed no concern. Customers continued to wander in and out, as if nothing was happening.

'We must go and speak to him,' Sujata insisted.

'I feel embarrassed, being a foreigner,' I said.

'We can try to do it with love in our hearts.'

His response was brusque. 'These men don't want to work. You give them something, but they are never satisfied.'

The end of the month brought an annual celebration of fertility, the *Janmashtami* festival for the birth of Krishna, the much-loved cowherd of tradition. The streets filled with stalls selling greenery, earthenware figures, bags of powdered paint, and stones for making model houses. Shoppers carried armfuls of branches and leaves. Men and women busied themselves all day in public buildings, temples and homes, constructing miniature villages, like elaborated Christmas nativity scenes. Toy animals and cowherds, in a rustic setting, surrounded the cradle. Lentils and rice marked fields and riverbanks.

I watched two men constructing a shrine outside a fabric shop. A bystander in a dark suit explained what would happen.

'At midnight, the priests and householders will place the image of the Baby Krishna in the cradle. The people will offer him fruits and sweets of sugar and chestnut flour. After the God's blessing, we call the sweets *prasad*. Then the in-charge will present the sweets to the people.'

In the morning, a neighbour from a nearby bungalow called round with offerings from the night before, including slices of apple and cucumber.

'We offer these,' she said, 'because, according to the legend, Krishna was born magically from a cucumber. We take cucumbers to the river for immersion, after his birthday. Every day we give food to Baby Krishna and we change his clothes.'

After lunch, I wandered into a small temple near the hostel and stood admiring the Krishna shrine. On a sudden impulse, I stretched out my arm and stroked the head of Baby Krishna, before rocking his cradle. An old woman in white, standing nearby, smiled at me.

What would happen in London if I offered food to Baby Jesus, or changed his clothes? Not that nativity cribs were often seen in public in 1960s Britain. They were still mainly the preserve of primary schools and Roman Catholic churches. Protestants often believed they were a hangover of idol worship. Maybe when I returned home, I would arrange my own nativity tableau on a side table. But would my friends think I'd become a born-again Christian?

Krishna worship was widespread throughout India, but especially popular in the North, in the Banaras region of Eastern Uttar Pradesh. Minority groups from other linguistic regions, such as Punjab, Gujerat and South India, focused on distinct traditions in their own neighbourhoods. The largest of these groups were the Bengalis. I knew little of their culture, despite my friendship with Toofan. That was about to change.

Soon after the *Janmashtami* festival he took me to watch one of Tagore's dance dramas at the Annie Besant Theosophical College. I noticed a tall and imposing Bengali swami looking across the room at us. The following morning, he turned up outside the flat I shared with Sujata. 'I would like to invite you both to the Ashram of Mother Anandamayi, in Assi, right now,' he said.

We entered a spotless, marble-floored building, and followed him upstairs into the temple with its Krishna shrine and large image of the Mother's Guru. Stillness and peace enveloped us. Through an open door we saw young Bengali girls in ochre robes.

'They have renounced the world and their families,' explained the swami. 'They have freely chosen to devote their lives to God, to be married to Krishna. Just now they are studying Sanskrit. Meet this lady.' He gestured towards an elderly woman with a shaved head and large, beautiful eyes. She smiled brightly, twice clasped our hands and then patted our cheeks.

'She was the daughter-in-law of the poet Tagore's brother. Now that her family has grown up, she has become a nun and lives here, teaching the girls to sing and play instruments. We Bengalis believe music is a route to the divine.'

I remembered the faces of the men listening to Ravi Shankar's music. I had never seen audiences look like that in Britain.

The swami and the nun were waiting for me to say something. I pulled myself back to the present.

'Don't the girls ever want to go outside?' I asked.

'They do, but the Mother does not allow it,' he replied.

How could ten-year-olds decide to renounce the world? I squinted at the woman in a white sari, now joining us.

'This is the Mother,' the swami said, bending his head.

She led us to meet the girls. We folded our hands in greeting and stood motionless, staring at them as though they were objects in a showcase. I hurried out as soon as possible.

From there, the swami took us by rickshaw to meet a Bengali yogi living down an alleyway, near the central market. He was a disciple of Sri Ananda of Rishikesh. We climbed steep, narrow stairs to his small room. He gestured at the white mattress that covered the entire floor and asked his servant to bring tea and salt biscuits.

'I stayed in England for five years,' he said. 'Now I seek mental freedom. What is needed is for the mind to concentrate itself, to free itself from distracting ideas. A great musician, artist or scientist, can find freedom through concentration. We Bengalis believe it is easier for a woman to achieve because her mind is softer.'

Sir John Woodroffe's book on tantric philosophy lay open on one side. How odd that the yogi was studying from an English author.

'We should try to put ourselves in helpful situations but, after that, to be oblivious to our surroundings. We can make tea weak or strong, well or poorly, but the tea cannot make us,' he explained. 'But let us leave that subject, Miss Mary. I would like to give you an Indian name, Shanta, because you speak so calmly.'

'But I've already been given an Indian name,' I said. 'Sarala.'

It wasn't uncommon for Europeans in Banaras to adopt Indian names. An Italian student of philosophy was known as Uma Vesci.

'Very good. I call you Sarala.'

Another member of the Bengali community arrived outside my door a few days later. A knock on the door revealed an Englishwoman in a sari, Barbara Mukerji.

'I grew up near Bolton in Lancashire and met Dr Mukerji while nursing at the hospital. He was a wonderful doctor, but I insisted on coming here for a holiday before agreeing to marry. We live in a joint family, with his widowed mother and aunt, in a Bengali neighbourhood. His mother manages the household finances and makes the main decisions.' Barbara spoke English with a strong Indian accent and moved her head and hands in an Indian way. But she was too tall for an Indian, and she wore her hair short, in the English style.

'I hope it is not difficult for you, adjusting to the life here,' she said. 'We would be very happy if you would visit us for tea, in Ramapura.'

I wondered what it would be like to be married to a Bengali in Banaras.

The rickshaw deposited me at a gate, opening into a large garden and house with an imposing veranda. A watchman led me into a huge living room, with small rooms leading off from the sides. This was a multi-purpose space, furnished with chairs and small tables, a large double bed at one end, and several teak cabinets around the walls. Barbara welcomed me and asked a servant to bring in fried *pakoras* and sweet tea.

'I live a restricted life, focused on the family,' she said. 'I don't like the staring and comments in the street, so I hardly ever go out, except in the car with the family. In any case, I am busy with a baby, and I help my husband in his surgery.'

Barbara was trying to behave like a good Indian wife and daughter-in-law, knowing how the locals disapproved of European women.

'I haven't abandoned my own views,' she added. 'I am still a Christian, though I don't go to church.'

I couldn't live like this, I thought. But then any life as a wife and mother was unappealing.

It wasn't only other people's lives that were hard to comprehend; so, too, were their words. Toofan dropped round before breakfast one morning, with a pot of guava jam made by his mother.

'Can't stop for long,' he said. 'I'm on my way to play cricket with a university team before my office opens.'

I looked at him, standing in the doorway in his cricket whites, radiating vitality. We chatted for a while. He mentioned his house in Calcutta. I was puzzled.

'Isn't that where your oldest brother lives?' I asked.

'Yes.'

He is boasting, I thought; he's trying to give the impression they have two houses. 'Then it's not your house, it's your brother's house.'

'No, it's my house... our house.'

How was I to know that houses could be owned jointly by brothers? How was he to know that I couldn't grasp that?

And it wasn't only Indians who used English words differently from me. One afternoon, when I got back from the College of Indology, I found a policeman sitting on our veranda. He was taking notes on a theft from Jane, an American living in the adjacent flat. She was becoming irritated. Sujata had invited them in to try and calm things down. She was pouring tea from a dainty green china pot.

'This sure is time-wasting,' Jane said, sighing. 'There was a lot of money in it.'

'Please, miss,' the policeman said, 'it is a must to establish the nature and size of the said item. First you said it was a purse, now you are saying it measured about ten inches square and had a leather shoulder strap. So, it was not just a purse.'

'Of course it was a purse,' she snapped. 'What difference does the size and style make?'

I tried to be helpful. 'It must have been a big purse, if you had room in it for notes as well as coins.'

'Of course she put notes in her purse,' said the policeman. 'Where else would she put them?'

'Well, in her wallet, presumably,' I said. 'Did she lose her wallet as well?'

They both frowned. 'Wallet?' the policeman said. 'What is wallet?'

'Jane,' I said, trying to clarify things, 'was your purse pulled out of your handbag or was the whole bag taken?'

'I told you already that the purse was taken. It wasn't in a cloth bag. The purse strap was pulled off my shoulder.'

The penny dropped. All three of us were using the word 'purse' differently. The others listened with surprise when I explained. The tension eased. The policeman completed his notes. We finished our tea and went our separate ways.

*

At the end of the monsoon, the controversial philosopher, Panikkar, arrived in the city. My Italian friend, Uma, took me to meet him. She enjoyed a private income from family estates near Rome and pursued long-term studies of Indian religion from her base in a small rented flat near Panikkar's house. She wore her hair in a bun and dressed in saris.

'He believes it is perfectly possible to be a Christian priest, and also a Hindu,' she explained in the rickshaw, 'but the Pope is not happy about it. Raimondo's last stay in India ended suddenly when he was called back to Rome. The Pope gave him a warning, but, thank God, stopped short of anything worse.'

We got down and picked our way through the maze of alleyways to his house.

'He knows many, many languages,' Uma said. 'His father was from South India but he grew up in Spain with a Spanish mother – one of those fortunate people with a foot in two cultures.'

She led me up some steps to Panikkar's domestic chapel, a room furnished with a low altar covered with red and yellow silk drapes.

Paintings with Christian themes in Indian styles hung from the walls. An image of Ganesh sat near the doorway, and, on a low side table, incense sticks smoked in front of sculptures of Hindu gods. We joined a group of students, South Indian Christians, and Europeans, sitting cross-legged on mats. Two young men from Kerala played a plaintive melody on flutes. A small man in silken robes started the ritual; Father Panikkar moved slowly with theatrical style. After the service, he invited us out onto a terrace overlooking the river. I watched the boats drifting past as I drank my sweetened milky tea. Four Tamil students were discussing the *Katha Upanishad* scripture.

'It's better now for us to focus on a single *Upanishad*,' Matthew said, 'though it was useful for us to start by discussing St John's Gospel, in the light of the ancient Indian texts as a whole.'

'I agree,' George said, 'and what matter if the context is different today? The key point is that the spirit of it still speaks to us. We need to work out what we can do with that, in our ordinary lives.'

This is academic discussion with a point, I thought.

Father Panikkar nodded his head. 'We'll be meeting regularly after the October holiday, Mary. Would you like to join our weekly Upanishadic discussion group?'

'Very much,' I replied. 'I should be back by then.'

My preparations for an autumn vacation visit to Tamilnadu and Kerala were well under way. But Toofan had additional ideas. 'October is the best time to learn about Bengali culture,' he said later that week. 'The *Durga Puja* festival is the highlight of our year. Would you like to come with me to Bengal, to Burranpore, the town where I spent my early childhood? We'll only be away for a few days. You'll have plenty of time for your trip to South India.'

I remembered my taste of the festival the year before. How I had woken in the early hours to hear the thick darkness echoing to the sound of an ethereal voice, half-singing, half-chanting, 'Oh Goddess of all graciousness and beauty, come now and dwell among us.'

CHAPTER 24

PUJA IN BENGAL

'My mother wants to meet you before we go,' Toofan said.

She's bound to see me as a brazen, foreign woman, I thought – though he again insisted that she was westernised, with liberal attitudes.

'She studied at the Diocesan College in Calcutta University. The British Viceroy always went to their graduation ceremonies. A student tried to assassinate him when my mother was there. The bullet narrowly missed. The Britishers carried on as if nothing had happened. That's what they were like. The girl was executed, after a long court case. Everyone said her brother was behind it. My mother was like you. She never wanted to be a housewife. After her graduation she worked as an inspector of schools. My father made her give up the job. After he died, she lit a fire on the roof and burned all her certificates in a rage.'

That sounded like me.

We agreed on a time when I could join them for a meal. I was to meet him at the central crossroads in town. As usual, he was late. I had to huddle in my rickshaw, hiding from prying male eyes. We stepped down in Bhelupura, at the entrance to his narrow lane and walked towards the little sand-coloured house at the end. Faces peered from behind barred windows, and shawls flashed out of sight, as we threaded our way forward. A small woman, in her early sixties, dressed in a white sari, opened the door.

I bowed and pressed my hands together in greeting. She inclined her head and smiled. Toofan led me into the inner courtyard and poured water over my fingers in readiness for the meal, before leading me back into a small room at the front of the house. We sat down on hessian mats. His mother brought in pots of hot food and served us on brass platters. She sat next to us, topping up our plates whenever a space appeared, with mildly spiced aubergine and okra. Much tastier than our hostel food. What beautiful expressive eyes she had, just like her son. A faint current of air passed between two ventilation holes in the thick walls. A dove's nest half-blocked a third one.

'It was my mother's own choice to wear white after my father died,' Toofan said. 'The family did not put pressure. And it was her decision to become vegetarian. We feared her health would suffer. Bengali Brahmans are not like Brahmans of other regions. We eat fish and meat.'

His mother didn't say much but asked a few questions about what I was studying. Her English was better than her son's. I liked her straightforward manner. She used words in the same way I did. Toofan's style of talking often seemed to come from another, more mysterious world.

'You can't imagine, Mary, how it was when my father was still alive, before we moved to this little house. Musicians and poets would gather at our place. My father would recite verses for hours, in Bengali, English, Urdu, even Persian. Who could think of retiring to sleep when the moon still shone brightly, and nightingales sang sweetly? And the way they would eat. You see these two milky sweets we are eating now, *rasogollas*. In those days they would consume forty at a time.'

The soft murmuring from the bundle of straw in the blocked ventilation hole suddenly erupted into a raucous clatter. We finished our food and they both stood up.

'Can I help wash the dishes?' I asked, determined to behave well. They burst out laughing. I didn't know why. Still, I felt I had passed some kind of test. Toofan saw me back by rickshaw to the University gates. He was in a bad mood and didn't place his arm on the back of the rickshaw behind my shoulders, as he usually did.

'That's the worst meal she has ever served,' he said. 'I don't know why she was so stern and severe.'

'Oh, I thought it was all right,' I replied.

He snorted.

Our trip to Bengal was definitely on now. Ann was accompanying us as far as Calcutta.

Two days later a telegram arrived, saying my maternal grandmother had died. I wouldn't see her again. She was a lively, fun person. But England seemed so remote, like a fading dream. I couldn't take it in. And new beginnings were emerging on all sides.

We didn't get round to reserving berths, or even seats, on the night train. It took so much time and energy to trail across town in a rickshaw to the station, and then to queue for hours in the heat, without a guarantee that anything would be available. Ann and I arrived at the station in the evening to find Toofan already there, with a squad of friends, prepared to fight their way through the crowd on our behalf. The great monster of a train steamed in slowly, belching clouds of smoke.

The friends divided into two groups for the assault on the targeted compartment. They jumped on the running-board, elbowing people back, hauling themselves over heads and shoulders. Legs and arms stuck out of doors as they dived in headfirst. One man rushed between legs and somersaulted himself into the fray. A great mass of bodies congealed. Men were lying, sitting, standing, wedged on the floor, on luggage racks, and in the lavatory.

I forced my way into the compartment where Toofan's supporters were camped. An elderly man lay on a wooden bench, guarding it.

He was wearing the uniform of the State Bank of India. 'He's the night watchman,' somebody said. Was this where he was supposed to be at this time of day? Ann was already in the compartment, red-faced, sitting screwed up in a corner. A few minutes later, the train began to move off slowly, with a fanfare of whistles and hoots. Half the passengers leaped off, leaving unexpected spaces. Some of those wedged on the luggage rack now toppled off and fell in a heap into the newly vacated places.

'What happened?' I asked.

'They were only friends and relatives, helping to hold seats,' Toofan explained.

The three of us had got places together. I couldn't thank the squad. They had all disappeared into the dark. My heart was still pounding with excitement half an hour later. Nothing was ever as exciting as this in England. Maybe a rugby scrum. But then I'd never been in a rugby scrum. My previous train journeys in India had been hectic, but not on this scale.

I rummaged in my bag. 'I've made these for us,' I said with a flourish, doling out sandwiches made with white, sliced bread from the Sikh grocery store. Toofan struggled through one. We drank sweet milky tea from earthenware pots that suddenly appeared from the basket of a boy who had jumped on board as the scrum departed.

'Toofan is so gentle and courteous,' Ann whispered to me. 'Anyone would be charmed by him.'

I looked at him and smiled. He was different from most of the male students I had known in England, not unkempt and gawky. After a brief chat, we dozed off, hunched up against one another.

The Calcutta sky was grey with the fumes of traffic and coal fires. Cars and buses cut across one another, weaving in and out like dodgems. Ann and I refused to cross our first main road. Toofan had to hail a taxi to get us to the other side. Banaras was greener, and more human, crowded with pedestrians and cycles, not vehicles. But it was exhilarating to walk among monumental buildings and liberating to escape from the judgemental eyes of a conservative, provincial city.

The Salvation Army Hostel provided a room for three. We collapsed onto our beds and slept for most of the morning.

After lunch, Toofan announced that he would take us to the zoo. Perhaps that was one of the things you did as a visitor. You went to see the marvels. I dressed in a sari; it bunched in some odd places. He gave it a quick look and frowned. After an hour of wandering around, staring at dejected-looking animals in enclosures, we reached a small patch of open space. The three of us sat down under a tree and, within minutes, fell asleep again. When I opened my eyes, I saw that the stream of visitors moving on from the tiger enclosure, to our right, was stopping to stare at us for a few minutes before moving onto the reptile section, on our left.

The next day, Ann departed to join friends. Toofan and I caught a train for the six-hour, one-hundred-and-fifty-mile journey, to Burranpore. Once out of the urban sprawl, fragrant air flooded in through the windows. Green clumps of dense forest alternated with marshes and lakes. In the evening we arrived in the town where Toofan's father had long ago been an honorary District Magistrate. His brother was away in Delhi but had invited us to stay in their flat. One room had already been turned into a base for the local *Durga Puja* committee. I was so tired after the journey that I slept without waking until the early hours.

We were still eating breakfast when the first neighbour wandered in. Old ladies, who had known Toofan as an infant, rushed in with screeches of joy. He was the much-loved youngest son of the family. Girls in the street approached and asked his permission to invite me into their homes. His mother had warned him to avoid one elderly couple, known for their strict traditionalism.

'They saw you in the road,' Toofan informed me the next morning. 'I can't believe it. They've invited us for a meal.'

As we entered their veranda, I bowed, and greeted them with a *namaste*. Toofan bent down and touched their feet.

How could a modern man like him, with his fashionable Terylene shirt and fitted trousers, do such a thing? But it shows the depth of his rootedness, I thought.

The couple didn't eat with us but sat on the edge of the day bed and chatted. Toofan's shoulders and face relaxed. They beamed at him.

The neighbourhood celebrations had begun several days earlier. I sat on the veranda, watching the painting and adornment of the huge bamboo and plaster image of Durga, her foot pressing down hard on the defeated demon, Mahishasura. Everyone else chatted in Bengali. Women draped the image with flowers. It was the sixth day now and the ceremonies were hotting up. Coloured awnings were installed above the platform. Toofan changed into a white silk tunic and *pyjamas.*

A priest read passages from the scriptures and chanted verses as he performed rituals inviting the Goddess to enter the image. The power of beauty and graciousness was now entering our world for a brief period. Small boys jived, pounding on huge drums with one hand, and brandishing pots of steaming incense in the other. Balloons and fireworks shot up to the heavens, and neighbours placed offerings of sweets at the feet of the Goddess. We sat outside, listening and watching, going backwards and forwards, from one house to another, sampling everyone's special food.

At the close of the eighth day, the ritual intensity increased. The focus was now on Durga's cosmic defeat of the world-threatening buffalo demon. This had to be re-enacted every year.

'The last day of the festival is very important,' Toofan said. 'Banaras is the place to be for that. We must leave early tomorrow and hope the train arrives in time.'

Whenever I woke in the night, I heard chanting and the thundering of drums.

Could the rituals in Banaras possibly be more exciting than those I had just seen?

I managed to get a seat on the train, but he had to stand, or squat, for most of the sixteen hours. Everyone was on the move. We arrived as planned on the tenth day. It was time for the Goddess to depart. Toofan jumped onto the first available rickshaw in the Varanasi station forecourt. No time wasted in haggling.

'Puja committees will already be taking the images of Durga out of the shrines in the Bengali neighbourhoods down to the Ganges for immersion,' he said. 'We must go straight there otherwise we will miss it.'

The processions were still arriving at Dasasamedh Ghat. Groups of young men carried the images down the steps and out onto boats festooned with drapes and lights. By four o'clock in the afternoon, most had been brought down.

At half-past nine, ascetics in white, or ochre, robes, began dancing in front of the images, some swaying gracefully, others in what looked like an intoxicated frenzy. Clouds of incense billowed around. The close-packed crowd surged in all directions. Police with long sticks, on horseback, were at hand to prevent stampedes. I stood close to Toofan, at the back, wedged against temples and crumbling palaces, near small stalls with kerosene lamps selling sweets, or peanuts and roasted corn cobs.

Graciousness and beauty could not remain for ever in this imperfect world. The Goddess had given us a momentary vision of herself and of her power. She could not be allowed to depart without a spectacular send-off. She would need to return year after year. Evil would never be finally defeated. The throb of drums filled my ears and extinguished all thought.

CHAPTER 25

SOUTH INDIAN ADVENTURES WITH CHRISTIANS AND MUSLIMS

My four-week trip to the South was scheduled for two days later but neither of my prospective travelling companions had materialised. My Thai friend, Chun, had cancelled because the students on her pharmacy course were all going south to a chemical factory in the new term. An acquaintance in the Women's Hostel had dropped out because of the likely costs. I could afford to live at a level well beyond most Indian students because of my Commonwealth Scholarship. This disparity of incomes was an ongoing problem.

Ann accompanied me to the station to see me off on my three-day train journey. I was determined not to travel First Class, despite my parents' entreaties. They couldn't understand that it was safer for a woman on her own to be packed in with the crowds. Leonora, a new Italian student in the International Hostel, had arranged for a Tamil acquaintance to meet me off the train in Madras. Raju was still waiting on the platform even though I arrived four hours late. It was easy for him to pick me out in the crowd.

'Miss Mary,' he said, 'I very happy you come to visit my city. I have book bed for you in dormitory in University Women's Hostel.'

He fussed over me for four days. But India was like that: incredible kindness, interspersed with much harassment. Wherever I went, someone would take care of me. Often it was young men. They enjoyed more freedom and were generally more curious about Europe.

'Are you sure you can spare the time to show me around?'

'Not to worry. I am an insurance agent. Not getting many commissions nowadays.'

Another young man, met earlier that year in Delhi, had said he was recovering from a cough and not fit for work. I didn't yet know about 'Casual Leave', that employees had an annual quota of days so they could respond flexibly to unexpected family demands. I must sometimes have been the beneficiary of that. And I was a novelty, an opportunity to practise speaking English.

Wide roads, free of beggars, led to my hostel. Flat-roofed houses with balconies framed sumptuous courtyard gardens. A red carpet mounted the stairs of a clock tower. And luxuriant palm trees and gracefully designed modern buildings, painted white or yellow, faced spotless golden beaches that stretched for miles. What wealth. So different from Banaras. An imposing mansion must be the seat of the Vice-Chancellor. But no. It was the headquarters of the Slum Clearance Project. Odd, then, that across the road, on the beach, fishermen lived in bamboo huts. They caught fish in woven baskets, from boats made of tree trunks, lashed together with ropes.

Three girls befriended me as I passed through the hostel doors. Vasu wrapped my hand in hers after the evening meal.

'Mary, if you like, after two days, we are free to take you by bus to Mahaballipuram. It is near to sea, forty miles from here. Greatest artistic achievement of the *Pallava* period of the fifth to ninth centuries.'

We stepped down in a small village. Temples, carved from boulders and cliffs, sprouted like vegetation. Sculptured figures spilled from rock, rich and disordered, unlike anything I had seen in the Hindu north. And utterly different from Islamic architecture, with its distinct separated shapes, and geometrical forms. Islamic architecture created pattern and symmetry. It imposed order on disorder. Mahaballipuram made the order of that world look limited and artificial. The world of Hindus was stranger, more exuberant, and difficult to argue with, except in the writings of the philosophers. One thing flowed into another. That was its attraction.

My young travel-mates from the Women's Hostel looked after me well, but they too came from another world. They talked endlessly about saris, and the boys they knew. I can't stand anymore of this, I thought, so the next day I boarded a bus to Kancheepuram, one of India's holiest cities, and the ancient centre of the *Pallava* dynasty. Its huge, towering temples, every inch covered with sinuous sculptures of gods and animals, flaunted the wealth of the region's maritime trade with South-East Asia in the first millennium.

A train took me on to Pondicherry, the old French colony. The Government Rest House offered plenty of beds. I woke early and made my way down to the grand dining room. Paint was peeling from the ceiling. I sat on a carved mahogany chair and ordered a breakfast of *idlis* and *sambar*, steamed fermented rice balls and lentil sauce. Only one table was occupied. A serious, bearded man, aged about thirty, was drinking coffee and reading *The Hindu*. After a few minutes, he lifted his head from his newspaper and swivelled his chair so he could speak to me.

'From where are you coming, and what are you doing in this place?' he asked.

I gave my usual explanations. I knew by now that they would be greeted with a mixture of pleasure and incredulity.

'You have come so far to study philosophy?' he commented with surprise. 'I, too, am interested in philosophy, though I am an engineer. I have worked on several dams. My new job is at a government research institute where I study coastal erosion. My name is Hussein.'

I introduced myself.

'If you have not made any arrangements, I can show you the sights of Pondicherry, if you like.'

I was grateful.

We spent the day wandering around, enjoying the sea air.

'I am studying coastal erosion even now,' he said, as we strolled along the beach. 'Perhaps you can tell me, what is this Existentialism I hear about?'

I enthused. 'You become yourself when you lose yourself in the things you are creating.'

'I think I see,' he responded. 'But why must you create these things? Can you not find them? I try to lose myself in God. I do not have to create God.'

I hesitated. 'It is not always easy to know whether you have found something or created it. But maybe it doesn't matter,' I added, backtracking.

'Well, I can find God in my tradition. Of course, he is not just sitting on my plate. I have to work, to find him. Maybe your Existentialists say you have to create something because they cannot find any God.' He stopped and looked at me, and then, in a kindlier tone, said, 'But I understand that there are many good things in your tradition, and many things we need to learn from you.' He offered me a guava from his bag.

We looked at the sea defences and he wrote something in his notebook. He began to quiz me hard about England, including family and religious life.

'We hear that you force your old parents to live alone, or to stay in homes for the elderly, and that you turn your children out of the house as soon as they finish their studies,' he charged. 'It's not surprising they neglect their elderly parents. But it pains me to think of my mother living alone.'

I didn't know how to answer. It was true that my grandparents lived alone. And I could not remember seeing older people in my friends' houses.

'I think they prefer to live alone,' I said. I really had no idea. 'Not many go into homes. And most parents don't throw their children out.'

'But isn't it true that you live away from your parents and they have no control over you? See yourself, only twenty-two, and you are here on your own, so far from home.'

'Yes, but I wanted to come on my own. I wanted to study philosophy in India. I am seeking the Truth.'

'I see,' he said, looking mystified.

'My parents know I am very capable,' I added, straightening my back.

He looked at me doubtfully. 'No doubt you are a sincere and serious person. I believe Hindu philosophy is interesting and has depths, though I am a Muslim. Islam is more clear and straightforward. It tells us how to live a moral and disciplined life.'

We walked past the famous ashram of Sri Aurobindo and he pointed out houses dating from the French period. Lunch was a savoury *utthapam* pancake at a small café just off the front.

'And where might your next destination be?'

'I am thinking of Madurai,' I replied, 'to see the Meenakshi temple. From there I shall go to Kerala.'

'I have some free time,' he said. 'If you like, I can show you more places. I have work to do in Madurai so I can accompany you there on the train from Madras tomorrow.'

I had ceased feeling surprised by the way things like this happened. He seems all right, I thought.

'Now,' he said, 'I suggest we take the bus back to Madras today. Then we can catch the morning train from there to Madurai. If you like, you can stay at my house in Madras tonight.'

That would be a good opportunity to see something of Muslim life. I didn't suppose there would be any problems.

His family home was a traditional mansion, with wood panelling on the interior walls, quite different from the modern buildings I had seen near the university. I had no idea what part of the city we were in.

Hussein showed me into a large and gracious room, furnished only with a few antique chairs. He disappeared somewhere. Various male relatives came in and bowed. A young cousin brought fried savoury snacks and coffee. I sat there, eating them on my own. I wondered if anyone was watching me. The cousin returned with an array of dishes for my evening meal. He spread a white cloth on the floor and placed the dishes on it. Hussein reappeared and ate with me, hardly speaking.

It was odd that I hadn't been served food by a woman; I hadn't even seen one since I entered the building. Perhaps they would come in later. After the meal, Hussein asked me more questions about the political situation in Britain.

I changed tack. 'Aren't there any women in your family? Or are they in another part of the house?'

'They don't live here,' he replied briskly. 'They stay in our hometown.' Then he got up to go. 'You can sleep at the other end of this room.' He pointed to a pile of thick hand-woven rugs. 'I shall see you tomorrow.' Then he disappeared.

No women. But strange things were always happening in India. That's just how it was. I didn't feel unsafe. So I made my way to the end of the room, lay down on the rugs and covered myself with a sheet.

The following morning, we took the Janata Express from Madras to Madurai. Hussein looked more at ease. He sat closer to me this time.

'Well, Mary, what are we going to debate today?' he asked with a glint in his eye.

While I was wondering what topic to suggest, he started again, with more questions on aspects of British life. It was hard for me to answer. What did I know apart from my family and friends, and what I had read in the newspapers? A degree in English Literature, mainly pre-twentieth-century texts, and European Philosophy, had not equipped me to expound on the current social system and changing cultural norms. Much of my knowledge of social trends came from angry leaflets produced by the student Socialist Club, detailing such facts as the numbers of houses still with outside toilets in the early 1960s.

I improvised as best I could. Having always attacked the injustices of the British social system, I now found myself taking on the role of defender. Hussein listened intently, watching my face. Occasionally he laughed out loud when he saw me floundering, and sometimes he laughed when I caught him out in an inconsistency.

In between discussions, he read academic papers in his bag, underlining sections in pencil. I gazed through the windows at the post-monsoon rice fields with their soft-green shoots.

Hussein returned to the issue of religion.

'I do not understand how you can deny the existence of God,' he said. 'You don't look like an atheist. Maybe your God is Truth. But my God has many names and I am sure Truth must be one of them.'

My religious beliefs were far from clear, so I did no more than defend myself, and avoided making a frontal assault on his ideas. He is getting off lightly, I thought. When the time came for his prayers, he went out to wash his head and feet, before spreading a cotton sheet on the compartment floor, and prostrating himself. He prayed with his usual intense concentration.

'I usually pray five times,' he said afterwards. 'Sometimes I feel more need for it.'

Did he feel more need for it in the company of a foreign female atheist?

I had already arranged to stay for a few days in the Fatima Catholic Christian Degree College for Girls in Madurai. Hussein said that he needed to look at coastal erosion in Kerala, and suggested we travelled together when I was ready to leave.

'If you like,' he said, 'I can accompany you to Trivandrum and show you the beautiful places.'

How helpful he is, I thought. What a lucky encounter. And I enjoyed the challenge of his questioning. It was all new territory: exciting, too. So we arranged to meet up again three days later.

I passed from his care to the hands of a couple of girls who caught hold of me as soon as I crossed the threshold of the Christian Girls' Hostel.

'Come,' one said, 'we have very nice Home Science Exhibition.' They pointed at large wall posters of chubby and, to my eyes, over-fed, pink babies, in the Child Care Section.

'Nice, no?'

I grunted ambiguously, thinking how much more attractive the little imps playing in the streets looked, with their lithe bodies, if ragged clothes.

'After one day, we are free to take you to temple at Cape Comorin,' one of them announced, 'the most southern point of India, where the Pacific Ocean meets the Bay of Bengal, and the Arabian Sea. It is a must for you.'

The Meenakshi temple was on my list for the next morning. It was a city within a city. Sculptures flowed across the walls and ceilings of its vast labyrinth of courtyards and passages. I wandered around, observing rituals and worshippers, until fatigue led me to a stone ledge, close to a group of performing musicians. A door opposite opened into a hall with a huge bronze statue of Shiva Nataraja. He balanced on one leg, a still point at the centre of his cosmic dance of dissolution and reconstruction. His eyes, half-closed, were unseeing, indifferent. The minor movements of mortals were mere froth in this scale of things.

My new friends were more at home in the English language than the students I knew in Banaras. They often laughed and hugged one another, so unlike students in England. It was nice not having to pretend to be worldly-wise. New Delhi might have been different. They didn't have to cope with the parties of my undergraduate days where couples spread-eagled on the floor and twined against the doors. Not that I had lasted long at such performances. My family lived far from such activities, far from friends and school. And I had never dared to brave my mother's wrath by listening to the new pop songs coming over on the radio.

We took a train to Trivandrum, and then to Cape Comorin, where we made our way to the Kumari Amman temple. They all trooped in. The gatekeeper barred me.

'Hindus only,' someone on the door said. But the doorkeepers had not checked the religious identity of the girls from the Catholic College. My companions looked shocked.

'It's because you are white,' one said.

This had only happened to me once in Banaras and, in the end, they had let me in.

We returned to the college and the girls related the incident to an American nun.

'I once brushed against a middle-aged woman in the street,' she told us. 'She glared at me and rushed to the nearest public water tap where she washed the portion of her sari that had touched my arm.'

But, on the plus side, there weren't so many leering men hanging around everywhere in the South. And people looked healthier.

'Why you not study in a clean place?' one of the girls from the hostel asked me. 'Banaras the most dirty city in India.'

I leaped to the defence of my current home. 'I don't think it's much dirtier than other North Indian towns, though the pilgrims produce a lot of rubbish. Most of that gets eaten by goats. Broken pot is the only thing that doesn't rot away.'

'And the cows?' she asked.

'Well, people keep them in outhouses, so they can rely on pure milk. Then they let them out to roam all day, eating waste food that's been thrown out. And the Milkman castes are very powerful in North India. Local politicians would soon get voted out if they tried to move the commercial cowsheds out of the city.'

Hussein and I met up as planned and set off for Kerala. I wanted to spend at least a week there. First stop was Trivandrum again, to look at the famous Shri Padmanabhaswamy temple. It was totally out of bounds for me. A soldier with a rifle was guarding the entrance to keep out non-Hindus. Hussein didn't even try. I wasn't permitted in any temples in Kerala.

We walked through the rural outskirts of the town. Hussein told me more about his life.

'I get up every day at four o'clock. After bathing, I pray and then read until eight.'

'Does your mother cover her face?' I asked.

'She wears the full, black *burka* whenever she leaves the house,' he replied.

I gulped. What must he think of me? I checked that my *oorni* scarf was properly draped over my chest. It tended to ride up if I wasn't careful. Did this mean he was from a very traditional family? Most Muslim women in India didn't cover their faces. Many covered their heads, but that was true of lots of Hindu women in the North. I had steered clear of raising feminist issues in India, so I wasn't going to start now. They muddied the waters and made it difficult to move on to anything else. It wasn't as if Britain was perfect for women.

'Did you ever hear about the massacre in January of almost a thousand Muslims, at Rourkela in Orissa?' Hussein asked.

I remembered the faint rumours that had seeped through to us in Banaras.

Hindu staff at the Rourkela Indo-German steel factory, he said, had connived at the manufacture of steel hand weapons. When German technicians realised what was happening, they wrote to Nehru, but it was too late.

'He never recovered from the shock. The atrocities were concealed. Muslim editors who attempted to publicise them were arrested. The police took no action.'

How was something on such a scale possible outside war? And how could this be true in a peaceful country like India?

I gazed at the tall coconut trees swaying above densely packed greenery. Small clearings accommodated thatched, or whitewashed, homes. Woven fences enclosed the compounds, not mud walls as in the North. We wandered past streams and lakes, pretty boats with curved prows and tiny, thatched shelters for sun and rain protection. That afternoon, Hussein took me by bus to the new Nayyar dam and irrigation project. I still preferred the countryside, though that was shaped by human hand too. We passed a patch of woodland.

'Every tree on that land,' he said, 'has a purpose, and produces fruits, nuts or spices. The land is so fertile – it's hard to believe that food shortages are causing riots, even now, in Kerala.'

I was happy to follow him, often hardly registering the names of places, though I had some ideas about where I wanted to go. We did the standard things, watched forest elephants drinking from a lake, and took a boat from Kollam, through the backwater lagoons at the foot of the Western Ghat Mountains. Unspoilt, empty beaches, fringed with swaying palms, skirted the sea.

'But Alleppey is like Kashmir, with its canals and bridges,' I exclaimed.

The locals puzzled over my identity. My skin was still pale, or reddish, but my hair was plaited and oiled as usual, and I was wearing my *selwar-kameez*. On one of our longer rural bus journeys, back towards Trivandrum, I sensed that the passengers were discussing us in Malayalam, not realising that Hussein would understand. He translated some of it in whispers.

'Perhaps she is a dancer from Bombay. Just imagine.'

How could anyone imagine I might be a dancer, me in my crumpled cotton clothes, not starched and ironed? And, anyway, Bombay dancers always wore synthetics or silk.

'But then she might be hailing from Punjab, or Kashmir, perhaps,' countered a thin man with a large cloth bundle.

We began to play to our audience, to draw them further into a thicket of confusion. I alternated between Hindi and English. Sometimes Hussein addressed me in Tamil or Malayalam and I pretended to understand. To add to the joke, I pulled my *oorni* over my head, even half over my face. Whenever it slipped off, he made me pull it up again. By now the whole bus was agog. Two elderly Muslim men were sitting behind us. They beamed with delight. Hussein whispered more translations of what they were saying.

'It isn't common these days to meet a young couple so steadfast in the old traditions. He must have met her away at college somewhere. But still he is seeing that she behaves properly. Could she be Anglo-Indian?'

Hussein kept silent for a few minutes and then turned round suddenly, as if outraged, and addressed them in Malayalam.

'How can you say such a thing? She is from the holy city of Damascus itself.'

Our audience went silent with shock. The elderly men goggled with admiration. We saved our giggling until we got well away from the bus. It made a break in the serious discussions.

That evening we found our way to the training college for the Kathakali School of Temple Dance Drama. The late-night performance was about to begin. Two bare-chested men, clad from the waist down in white *dhotis*, held gorgeous drapes of silk to mark off the edge of the stage. An ornate brass candelabra, with many wicks, cast flickering lights on the backcloth. Incense burned at the side.

A thunderous din from drums and cymbals heralded the entrance of tottering figures, wearing bell-shaped skirts and massive silver headdresses. The dancers swayed, like bloated, dying beetles, about to collapse from their ungainliness. The endless movement of their hands was at odds with the fixity of their eyes, and with the heavy immobility of the masked faces and grotesque costumes. At three in the morning, we left. The performance had still not finished.

We shared a room with four beds that night. It was the only one available. Hussein closed the door and looked at me for a moment. He stepped forward and wrapped his arms around me so tightly, I could hardly breathe. After a second, he pulled away with a groan. He turned the light off and threw himself on to one of the rope beds.

I was woken in the morning by the sound of a mynah bird tapping on the shutters. Hussein was lying with his hands folded underneath his head, looking up at the ceiling. Two lizards were racing in circles on the wall.

'Let's go to the coast today,' he said.

He was unlike anyone I had met before in India. I loved the way he would catch hold of an idea I'd tossed at him, weigh it up, and then throw it back. After breakfast, we sat on a sea wall, watching gulls wheeling and swooping. Hussein talked about the problems faced by the communist government in Kerala.

'They try hard,' he said, 'but nothing is straightforward and corruption creeps in everywhere.' He moved onto religion. 'There is no caste system in Islam,' he said. 'The idea of human brotherhood and equality is of its essence. I don't understand you Westerners. You talk about equality but you confuse it with self-assertion. Where is your discipline and obedience to higher laws? There must be laws higher than any government or politician. Some people here say you make a god of the Self. Your individualism is a madness to us. What can a grain of sand do on its own? Combine it with others and it becomes strong. I have seen how sandbags hold back tons of water. Our family system is like that.'

How should I reply? I also wanted to believe in higher laws though his certainties were too like the Christianity of my past. Perhaps he was right. Perhaps I did believe that developing the self, keeping it independent and autonomous, was the most important thing. Now I was in India I could fleetingly sense the absurdity of that, but I could no more abandon it than I could change the colour of my eyes. And I was still hoping for a vision to show me what to do with myself.

'You've gone very quiet, Mary. Surely you have not lost your words?'

'I am thinking,' I said.

He smiled, and we continued, walking silently along the outskirts of an old palace. Monkeys were screeching in the trees behind the wall. He wouldn't argue so much and ask so many questions if he really was completely certain about everything, I thought. An argument is a way of putting ideas to the test. And it's a way of being alive. As for me, my stay in India was providing so many alternative ways of thinking that it was becoming difficult to be sure about anything, or to see anything sacrosanct in European ideas. I needed a sea wall.

On our last day in Kerala we walked through fields and drank coffee at wayside stalls. Hussein saw me to the station. We didn't exchange addresses.

'Now we continue our journeys alone,' he said, with a sideways smile. He turned sharply on his heel and disappeared.

I sat on my wooden berth in the train, looking through the window bars, watching the fields flash past. I felt forlorn. Where was I going? What did I want? Was independence really a life buoy; could it be a god?

I lay down and was soon asleep. When I awoke, at six in the morning, I found a thin blue blanket covering me. Where had it come from? I looked across at the woman sitting cross-legged on the berth opposite and held up a corner of it with an enquiring look. She pointed to half a dozen older men further down the coach. I walked along to them. They were chatting as they played cards.

'Is this yours?' I asked.

'We thought you would be cold in the night,' one said. 'The temperature drops as the train goes north.'

'But didn't you need it?' I asked.

'No matter,' he replied.

CHAPTER 26

STUDYING IN
THE COOL SEASON

THE COOL AIR OF WINTER WELCOMED ME HOME AS I STEPPED down onto the station platform. A rickshaw whizzed me back to the Multi-Purpose Flats. More parcels of rice and sugar were stacked near my door. My parents still refused to accept that food shortages only affect poor people. Jim called in with a long white greetings scarf from Ang Pemba. Their five-month climbing trip in the Himalayas had achieved the desired summit. His tutors hadn't noticed his long absence.

I joined a *tabla* class. If only I could learn to play like the drummers at *Durga Puja*. The other students could bend their fingers backwards in a deep arch. Was it genetic, or due to the oil massage they received as infants? Mine, like iron rods, refused to budge. I gave up after one session and returned to my study of Indian thought.

*

The Seventh Congress of the World Federation of Buddhists was about to be held on Indian soil for the first time. I had to go. It would be a chance to observe living Buddhism at last. Would it be as clear-sighted and unsentimental as the Buddhist philosophers I had been reading? 'I'll borrow a car,' Toofan said.

Dr Radhakrishnan, the philosopher-president of India, opened the proceedings. This was the man whose book, *The Hindu View of Life*, had helped to bring me to India. Would he live up to my expectations? I leaned forward to scrutinise this tall, imposing figure in a white turban and robe. What a beautiful voice he had. But how disappointing his speech was, full of the usual platitudes on curbing the passions.

'He is known to be a womaniser,' someone whispered.

A Thai princess came next, and then the Dalai Lama. Odd that he didn't look much older than me. He addressed us in Tibetan, and his interpreter relayed a series of modest and homely exhortations. Pompous speeches by dignitaries cashing in on the prestige of the occasion ended the first phase of the proceedings.

The special guests now withdrew into a large tent for deeper discussion. The rest of us remained at a distance behind a cordon. The Thai student monks from the International Hostel brandished permits, allowing entry to the tent. Our hopes rested with them. Once inside, they gathered up their tickets and two slipped out to redistribute them. We sneaked in under their protection.

Five minutes later a huge roar erupted, as the crowd burst through the cordon and across the grass towards the tent. People of all persuasions wanted *darshun* of the Dalai Lama, to benefit from the aura of his presence. That was more important than any theoretical lectures, or *dharmic* doctrines. Police with batons turned back the crowd at the last minute. We kept out of view at the back of the tent.

An unknown tall American girl was standing nearby. 'All you need,' she said, 'is poise. Then you can get anywhere. At a big function in Delhi, somebody offered me a chair next to the Burmese ambassador. Everybody assumed I must be important.'

Being from the West must have helped too, I thought. But I lacked her confidence and sweat was trickling down my forehead. The discussions resembled a staged performance. And I was sick of self-satisfied religion. What's more, we hadn't eaten or drunk for hours. All I wanted now was to go home to the Multi-Purpose Flats.

In a rash moment, I had offered the spare places in the car to all and sundry. That amounted to seven of us. We squeezed our way out of the tent, past the policemen, and piled in. The car refused to budge. The extra five passengers got out, and scrabbled around, trying to find the rickshaw drivers they'd dismissed. With vast crowds milling everywhere, they had little hope of finding a rickshaw that wasn't pre-booked. Toofan remembered he had invited three friends to lunch. My watch showed four-thirty. 'Not to worry,' he said. 'They'll have gone home by now.' Three hours later, the car cranked into life again.

What a disappointment that outing was. Nothing more than comforting mantras to anaesthetise the mind, no more plausible than the claim that chemicals could offer an instant route to insight. Not that I wouldn't give chemicals a chance if a suitable occasion arose. An opportunity arrived in early December. Franco, an Italian-American student, invited me to his farewell party on the river front. His Nepali friend, Pramodh, had organised a small gathering of foreigners. We spent the late afternoon on a boat, enjoying the gentle breeze, and watching the sun set. At six o'clock we returned to the steps of the main *ghat* and followed our young host to an old man, clad in white, sitting on a small platform. He handed us leaf cones containing small greenish-brown balls that looked like dung and smelt and tasted very bitter.

'*Bhang*,' Pramodh said. 'Eat it and then drink from the clay cups.'

'It's hashish, a shortcut to a higher consciousness,' Franco whispered.

I munched my way laboriously through the balls and drank the rich, sweet beverage. I wouldn't say no to a vision.

Nothing happened.

'No hurry,' said Pramodh. We climbed back into the boat to pass the time. On the other side of the river we strolled around, kicking up sand on the almost deserted shore. A solitary young ascetic stood inside a bamboo shelter. He supported his arms on a wide plank suspended by ropes from above. Long, matted hair framed a face covered in ashes. A typed sheet of paper announced that he had vowed to stand for twelve years. Another eight to do.

His eyes darted about restlessly. Maybe his legs were damaged. But no. A few minutes later, he slipped out of his support and moved to kindle his cooking fire. An earthen pot contained donated coins.

'He gives them to fishermen, and they buy him food,' a passer-by explained. 'When the monsoon comes, he moves his shelter higher up, above the river.'

I watched him for a few minutes. He wasn't prepared to go with the flow. He was trying to put his own mark on it, to be in control of something.

By now we were hungry, as well as unusually cheerful. Back on the city side of the river, we climbed up the steps, joking and laughing. My legs wobbled and the city smelled more intense than usual. Half a dozen coiffed and manicured Western tourists walked past, frowning in our direction.

A Chinese meal followed, high on mirth. Diners at the other tables were staring at us. I couldn't see why. In the hostel we lay around, listening to records. Nothing happened so three of us ate more of the little balls. American Jane announced that her body felt light and empty. 'I am worried I may take off,' she said.

Disappointed, the rest of us returned to our own rooms, only later to experience bliss, or horror, as the case might be. Reports percolated through over the next few days. Jane floated up to the ceiling and stared down with astonishment at her body lying on the bed. Another American girl melted into the colour blue. Jim began laughing uncontrollably a day after the celebratory meal. Ann was afraid he would damage an internal organ. Then he started to sob. His groans could be heard all along the corridor of our block of flats.

Afterwards he explained, 'I had a terrifying vision in which Good battled Evil for control of the planet. The outcome rested on my actions.'

Author with Nepali friends

No such luck for me. Why couldn't I float to the ceiling or be shown the meaning of life? Not that I wanted the future of the planet to depend on my actions. Not totally. As usual, I fell asleep immediately. In the morning I still felt normal. In the evening, after dinner in my professor's house, I wept a bit. At ten o'clock I started vomiting. Every time I rushed to the bathroom, I heard sounds of manic laughter from above. Like something from the underworld. I, alas, experienced enervation rather than elevation. My diarrhoea and vomiting were uncontrollable. This weakness of my bowels was my Achilles heel in India. How would I ever rise to a higher level?

The next morning Sujata rushed me to hospital by rickshaw. A circle of solemn doctors quizzed me on my problem. I averted my eyes and hung my head, as I told them about the party. A burst of laughter greeted my confession.

'We usually take *bhang* with friends on a Saturday,' one said.

Hashish was not illegal in India. They advised me to pack a bag and return to the hospital where I could remain under observation.

'Don't do that,' Ann said. 'Stay here so we can look after you. We'd have to carry food into the hospital, and you'd be more at risk of infection.'

'It might be the polluted Ganges water that caused the problem,' Sujata suggested, 'or the copper they sometimes add to intensify the effect of the *bhang*.'

I was still in bed two days later. The other co-diners all visited to provide consolation and unsuitable food offerings such as fried garlic omelette, Thai prawn soup and iced chocolate drink. At six o'clock the next morning, Toofan called round to check that I was still in the land of the living. Somehow the news had reached him.

I stumbled around for almost a week after my recovery. That wasn't a new sensation. Perhaps my short-sightedness was another factor. I'd stopped wearing glasses. The locals were always telling me that eyesight is just a matter of mental discipline. And glasses weren't so necessary in Banaras, with few street signs to read. We rarely saw a bus, and when we did, it was uninviting, with hundreds of people clinging on. We always walked, cycled or travelled by rickshaw.

Ann showed me a photo taken at another party with Nepali friends. The photographer had been kind enough to enlarge my eyes. I wasn't surprised that I looked excessively tall at five feet four inches but why did I look so pale and sickly? I'd regained weight that winter. Or was it only the contrast that made me colourless?

*

A few weeks later, the Banaras crowds thickened in readiness for another eclipse of the moon. Pilgrims camped outside by the river, though the temperature had dropped so low that I couldn't read, even indoors with warm clothes on. The papers announced that large numbers of street sleepers had died in Delhi. Sujata insisted that we go into the city to check the situation. I didn't like the role of Lady Bountiful but thought I had better go.

Our rickshaw forged a way through the crowds until we reached a police barricade. The emaciated driver tried to reverse but in the confusion and confined space went a few inches over the line. A policeman swore at him and struck him across the shoulders with a stick. The driver bent his head and said nothing. Sujata exploded.

'This man is not an animal,' she shouted.

A few minutes later, we saw another policeman striking the bowl a beggar was holding. He held on to it with steely determination. The policeman struck it over and over again, until it fell to the ground. Rice grains flew in all directions.

Thousands of beggars were lining up along the lanes leading to the river. Many sat happily in family groups; others looked desperate. One was lying on the ground, immobile, not hunching himself up against the cold, like the others. His cotton wrap only half-covered his body.

A well-dressed man was looking down at him with concern. 'He is dying.'

I leaned forward. 'How can you know?'

Sujata turned towards the nearest shop. 'We must buy him a blanket.'

'No point,' said the well-dressed man. 'Already I presented him with one, a few hours before. Someone has taken it.'

We asked the beggars on either side if they would watch to see that nobody took another blanket, but they refused.

'Better to give to the living,' someone said.

'He was sitting up yesterday but the weather worsened last night,' a fabric shopkeeper across the lane said. 'It is only just above freezing temperature now. Maybe he had eaten nothing.'

Sujata ran over to a nearby tea shop and persuaded the owner to sell her a cup of warm milk. She poured a few drops down the beggar's throat. He gulped it in, still lying like a statue. A crowd gathered. By now it was about seven-thirty, and dark.

'Why waste milk on a man who is dying?' someone said. 'It is time to give sacred Ganges water.'

But nobody offered to go and get any.

Sujata felt the man's pulse.

'He is dead,' she announced.

He looked the same as before. It didn't seem to matter to anyone. Nobody knew who he was. The dying man too had seemed indifferent. Was death so insignificant? I shuddered.

We stood for a few minutes. Then everyone moved away. None of the nearby shopkeepers got up from their seats. Was there any point in us staying?

'We must buy blankets for others before it happens again,' Sujata said.

We bought a cheap wrap and gave it to one of the most wretched-looking. He snatched it and wrapped it round himself without looking up.

Funeral processions often passed us in Banaras, with male mourners carrying their dead relatives aloft as they made their way to the cremation *ghats*, chanting 'Rama, *nama, satya hai.*' That evening I was more aware of them than usual. Sujata and I sat in silence in the rickshaw home.

*

Christmas was a modest affair in Banaras. Not a frenetic search for perfection, or an orgy of consumerism. Just an opportunity to leave the university for a week.

'We could visit Lucknow,' Toofan said. 'That's the old courtly capital of the kingdom of Oudh. You'll see something of Mughal architecture.'

And more of him, I thought. Just the two of us.

We arrived early on Christmas morning. Wide, gracious avenues resembled Georgian London more than Banaras. Our rickshaw bowled along unclogged streets, passing fashionable shops and elegant parks. We wandered into a public garden and sat down in a spot with a good view of the ruins of the British Residency. Banaras had no parks to speak of, and certainly none that any woman, or family, would venture into.

A small group of Muslim children were playing nearby. Every so often they stopped and held a conference about me. Shrieks of laughter interrupted quiet whispers. One of the bolder boys crept as close as he dared before retreating in giggles. Gradually they gained confidence. One of the girls invited me to join in their game. As soon as I got up and moved towards them, they ran away, screaming. After a few minutes, they edged nearer again. This continued for some time, without any progress.

'Their parents have warned them to be careful,' Toofan said, 'told them that a big white man might kidnap them if they're naughty.'

But I wasn't a big white man.

In the evening we dropped in to the Roman Catholic cathedral. Candlelight illuminated the building. Six priests at the front adjusted gold headdresses. They walked backwards and forwards several times, before taking them off and placing them on the altar. What on earth was going on?

Toofan gaped. 'I thought you people had abolished rituals,' he whispered.

We moved on to three other Victorian churches, all locked up outside the times for congregational worship, even on Christmas Day. Why didn't they stay open like most temples?

Toofan had booked a room with two beds in a cheap hotel. He began to fill in the registration book. I saw that he was putting me down as his wife.

'You can't do that,' I said. 'It's not true.'

'But it will avoid trouble for you.' He lowered his eyes. 'Otherwise they will treat you badly.'

'That would be cowardly. It would be contemptible to lie, just because of public disapproval.'

His face froze. This girl had so many abstract ideas. But what could he do?

The hotelier said nothing. My only problem was fleas and bed bugs. I slept hardly at all.

On Boxing Day, we browsed the market. The shops displayed their goods behind plate-glass windows rather than on open stalls. Decorated gift boxes containing miniature dolls in the traditional costumes of different Indian regions caught my eye. How enchanting. But it would be pointless to buy them for myself. Would they be suitable as a gift for anyone? Perhaps my mother? I hesitated.

'It's bad to have a calculating attitude like that,' Toofan said. 'You should follow your heart and buy something if you like it. Not act like a regimented soldier. You people even walk like machines. Are you mechanical robots or humans?'

I jerked my head in his direction. Why was he angry with me? And should I be apologetic, or defiant? I knew we weren't on the same wavelength. I looked up at his face. My shoulders sagged. The worst thing would be to get sucked into the quagmire of desire and dependence. To end up imprisoned with children in a house with curtains across the windows. Toofan came from a world in which an honourable man would respect the chastity of an unmarried woman. I was safe with him – just. I wanted to go away and sit down somewhere.

*

By the time we returned to Banaras, Christmas parcels had arrived from England. They contained tins of French paté and ham. My parents had subscribed to *The Guardian Weekly* on my behalf. It was strange to read articles about 'colour prejudice', and hard to be interested in the English news. Britain was so far away, so irrelevant.

My presents had not been a success. My parents had not known what to do with the tinned milky balls in syrup, so they had fried them. Of course, they fell apart. My brother began vomiting after playing on his side flute, so my mother washed it in Dettol. Afterwards it smelled so bad he refused to go near it. She took the vomiting as a sign that the paperback novels by Indian authors should be fumigated; she put them in the oven on a low heat. Two caught fire.

Now that the weather was becoming milder, Ann and I spent free afternoons on the steps that led down to the Ganges. She painted river scenes in pastels while I watched people and animals. On one occasion I noticed a young woman with a shaved head, sitting cross-legged on the next *ghat*.

'That's the American yogi,' Ann said, 'the one who got herself fitted with a metal chastity belt, in full view of a crowd of priests and passers-by.'

'You're joking.'

'No, I'm not. She locked it ceremoniously and hurled the key far out into the Ganges. She lives and sleeps out in the open, down by the river front. Men treat her well.'

Was that really the only way for a woman to find respect and to retain her independence?

We sat for an hour before hiring a boat and crossing to the other side of the river in search of a more peaceful location. Three boys laughed and leered when we landed so we set off again until we found a quieter spot downstream. A woman and her daughter were planting vegetables in the damp earth. Men shovelled sand into boats. Others fished from small dinghies with huge nets, propelling themselves along slowly with bamboo poles. Shirts dried on masts.

Back on the city side, beggars jostled for prime location. Presumably, another festival that evening. At a sharp corner in the lane we almost fell over our regular shoe-shine boy, with his large black eyes, and the impish face that had tempted Ann to paint his portrait in oils. What was he doing here? He found plenty of work. Students in the hostel often gave him clothes and food. There he sat, along with all the destitute, a bandage, smeared red, around his arm. Instead of his usual cheerful smile, he wore a miserable expression while holding a howling baby.

'Pinching it, I should think,' Ann said. We gaped at him until he noticed us. At once his face lit up in a huge smile, not at all abashed.

That evening, over dinner in the Hostel for International Students, we mentioned the incident. A heated discussion was soon in full flood. Opinions were divided. The Japanese students, and Eberhart, argued that begging should be prohibited. The Indians from overseas listened in silence, astonished by the idea that anyone would want such a curb on freedom.

'And what about the beggar I saw die just before Christmas? He was destitute.'

Could any liberty be more basic than the freedom to beg? My freedom was limitless in comparison. So vast that I couldn't decide what to do with it. Except to make sure that I didn't lose it.

I was hurtling towards the crossroads of departure on an unstoppable train but everything else was rolling round in a never-ending cycle.

CHAPTER 27

1965 FINAL MONTHS

IT WAS GOOD TO FEEL LIKE AN OLD HAND, NOT ALWAYS THE little newcomer, tagging along behind. I now had no hesitation in responding to a letter from my parents requesting cross-cultural advice on entertaining two Gurkha soldiers. I replied with four pages of detailed instructions on food taboos and body language. Not that I had more than minimal knowledge of Nepali customs. Every injunction I gave was qualified with the proviso that there must be many exceptions. Of course, a few don't eat meat, I added, and the odd one might even eat beef, and not be unhappy to make body contact by shaking hands.

My parents wrote back thanking me. They would ignore all my advice. They didn't want to be completely inhibited.

The usual start-of-term arrivals in mid-January gave me a chance to flaunt my cultural skills. Two history undergraduates from the London School of Oriental and African Studies appeared in the hostel dining room. At last, I wasn't the only English person in the hostel. They were wearing strange flowery frocks.

'We're only here for four months,' Cathy said. 'I'm studying Religion. Gillian is doing history. We don't know where to buy toilet paper or sun cream.'

Her roses and cream complexion might need protection. But I didn't know if sun cream was available. Gillian might be okay. Her hair and eyes were dark.

'I've stopped using toilet paper.'

Their eyes widened.

'Thank goodness you're here,' Gillian said. 'You're so Indianised. Maybe you can tell us where to buy Indian clothes? And can we drink the tap water?'

I tried to look modest.

Two new Americans invited a dozen of us to a meal. They talked about the risk of nuclear war. 'Worrying about it keeps me awake at night,' one said.

It was the first time in nineteen months that I had thought about the danger. It seemed ages since the Cuba crisis and the imminent threat. I remembered phoning my mother to say goodbye. All over England people were doing the same. But shouldn't we be detached from these things? We could continue to campaign, even to go on Aldermaston marches. After all, they were about more than disarmament. They were a communal witnessing to a faith in the possibility of a new world. But why get agitated?

The newcomers were keen to visit the festival at Allahabad at the end of January.

'I can take you,' I said to Gillian and Cathy. The Americans came along too. Officially, it was only the annual *Magh Mela* – as in the previous year – but some of the priests and astrologers in Banaras announced that, according to their readings, it was time for the *Kumbh Mela*, the much bigger and more auspicious, but less frequent, event. Extra pilgrims were streaming into Allahabad because of the confusion. At the previous *Kumbh Mela* in 1954, four thousand people had died in a stampede caused by an encounter between an elephant and renouncers wielding tridents. The police and army were not taking any chances this time and large numbers stood in position at regular intervals among the crowds.

Five Western men sauntered past us, wearing long, flowing robes and large nose rings. Brightly clothed Indian families wound their way through naked ascetics, lying on nails, with thick steel needles piercing their tongues. Dwarfs, smeared with white ash, sat at the side of the track, hoping to benefit from the supernatural power produced by a particular conjuncture of the stars. But by midday I was hot and bored, and ready to leave.

'We can't go yet,' Gillian said. 'This is far too exciting.'

*

A series of letters from my parents filled me in on excitements back in England.

'I'm going to buy a derelict croft house, in a remote part of the Scottish Highlands, Mary,' my mother wrote. 'I went up there to look around. And guess how I travelled – in the sidecar of Richard's motorbike. He's going to study forestry in a college in Pitlochry; he'll be the only English student there. The mountains will be nearby.'

That would be a lot more thrilling than studying in England. I knew my mother would think so too.

My father referred to current political issues, and to a housing racket in which tenants were being forced out so that rents could be raised. Property developers were becoming so excessively rich that they were retiring from work at the age of thirty-five. The newspapers were debating whether parents should hit their children.

Hit children? I hadn't seen anybody hit a child for almost two years.

He enclosed the information I had requested on courses leading to diplomas in Education. I wasn't keen to teach children, but I had to do something when I got back to England. Did I really want to spend my life reading tomes in Sanskrit? That would be my future if I continued along my present path. And I wanted to do something useful, something with people. But why were the brochures so parochial, with no awareness of a world beyond Europe? The 'History of Education' courses didn't mention anywhere other than Britain. They were light years away from my life in India. I didn't want to return to all that. I stuffed them in a box, resolving to look at them later. Why waste the time left to me?

*

Better to think about the annual five-day Music Conference about to start again. One evening wasn't going to be enough this year. I sat through three nights in the huge tent, not leaving until after dawn. We chatted, or snoozed, while the musicians warmed up. The *tabla* player at first followed the lead of the *sitar*. After a few hours, he could anticipate where the *sitar* was heading and sometimes leapt in first with his own composition. The crowd roared its appreciation. By early morning, all fidgeting had ceased, and a deep calm suffused the audience. The purity of the sitar swept clean the night air. Tears came into my eyes. I looked around. How could I leave a place with music like this – where it affected people in this way?

'Time is running out,' Toofan said when I next saw him. 'How about a trip to the Taj Mahal? Three days to coincide with a full moon. You can't leave India without seeing that.'

He did all the bookings as usual.

The sublime beauty of the white tomb pulled me up short. A marble monument that seemed to float. Built by an emperor, maddened by the loss of his love. A defiant attempt to halt the remorseless flow of time. But something about it was too perfect. Could symmetry really compensate for the monstrous shapelessness of life?

Two American families, with cameras and tripods, crossed my line of vision, and distracted me from my reveries. The older women, with bleached and permed hair, looked like teenagers. Hard to tell which were the mothers and which the daughters. They walked in the same self-conscious manner, prancing around, posing for photos. I turned to look at a group of older Indian women. So poised and grounded.

We sat in the moonlight, gazing at the tomb. Toofan turned to smile at me, giving an English rendering of an Urdu love poem. A voice from behind cut into the flow of his lines.

'Toofan.' It was one of his Banaras friends, Shokti, with a young woman.

'On the spur of the moment we decided to follow you. Rani has never seen the Taj,' he said, indicating his companion with a flick of the head. 'We came on the overnight train. But we didn't know where you were staying. We phoned all the hotels in Agra. We guessed we'd find you here.'

Toofan and Shokti embraced.

'Who is the girl?' I whispered.

'His sister,' Toofan said.

She didn't look like his sister.

We returned to the guesthouse by rickshaw, and all piled into our room. The men shared one bed, top to tail, and Rani and I occupied the other. The following morning, we boarded a pony and trap to the palace at Fatehpur Sikri, the abandoned Mughal capital, some way outside Agra. I admired it from a shady corner. Its pavilions and courtyards spread across a wide area, but it was subtle and human in scale. In the evening, we savoured the Taj again for the final time.

On the train back to Banaras, Toofan and Shokti could not get seats and, worse still, had to stand outside on the running board, gripping the bars of the door, for several hours. The train shot forward. By the grace of the gods, we all arrived safely.

Toofan dropped me off at the Multi-Purpose Flats.

'My mother wants you to come again for a meal, this weekend,' he said. 'But remember she is always punctual. It was drummed into her by her father who was a Latin lecturer at a Christian college. And by her English teachers in Calcutta.'

I flagged down a rickshaw and directed it along the maze of alleyways, towards his home. After twenty months in Banaras I'd given up being obsessive about timekeeping. Still, better to be careful. I didn't want to annoy her.

'I'm sorry I'm an hour late,' I said, as she opened the door. She smiled but said nothing.

At least I wasn't as bad as her son. He wasn't back yet.

I deposited my shoes in the hall and sat down on a mat. Toofan turned up after another hour. It was easy now for me to eat properly, cross-legged, leaning forward and using only my right hand. I still had to be careful not to get food above the second knuckle.

'My mother is worried that you haven't seen any of our great films yet,' Toofan said. 'She invites you to a matinee showing, on Wednesday, of *Apu Sansar*, by the famed Bengali director, Satyajit Ray.'

On Wednesday I arrived at their house only half an hour late.

'I have been waiting for you,' she said quietly.

How strange, I thought.

The film told the story of a young man, ready to launch into independent adult life. He is pushed into marrying his best friend's sister when catastrophe strikes in the middle of her wedding ceremonies. Gradually his resentment changes into love. Her death in childbirth unhinges him so much that he flees, abandoning the child. After years of numbed depression, he returns to find the boy. The film moves forward slowly, giving us time to savour each image, like a sequence of paintings in an art gallery. We weren't bombarded by hectic movement. I had never before seen a film of such psychological truth and delicacy. Tears streamed down my cheeks.

*

Everyone was still trying to teach me something new about India – I'd only scratched the surface – but how could I assimilate it all? Simple things like making butter by shaking buffalo milk in a jam-jar weren't too hard. Sujata soon got me to master that. She failed to teach me how to prepare medicines from leaves and roots gathered on campus.

But nor could she grasp why I always wanted to know where, and when, a particular philosophical theory had come into being. 'All that matters,' she insisted, 'is whether or not it's true.'

I was finding it hard to believe that any truths could have universal application. Yet somewhere at the back of my mind I did now believe in the *advaita* doctrine of the unity of everything. After all, wasn't that what modern physics was all about? And, as an undergraduate, I had always admired Spinoza's holistic model of reality. But how could I ever grasp the vastness of that unity in my little mind?

The looming deadline for applications to join one-year courses in Britain was weighing me down. Did I have to return? But what was the alternative? The other foreign students didn't have to struggle with such decisions. Jim had an academic post waiting for him. Sujata had several more years in which to complete her doctoral thesis, and my Thai friends were nowhere near the end of their courses. Pramodh, and several of the Nepalis, had already gone home to government jobs. My friends in the Multi-Purpose Flats urged me to apply for grants to continue studying Indian Philosophy in London.

'Get properly qualified,' Jim advised.

The prospect of spending the rest of my life in an airless library still didn't appeal. The hoped-for vision showing my destiny had not materialised. I remembered how, in my final year as an undergraduate, I had toyed with the idea of opting for a life of self-sufficient simplicity in a Hebridean cave, if I didn't secure the class of degree I was hoping for. The Commonwealth Scholarship had pre-empted such fantasies. Now I was back in the same vacuum. Britain was a bleak prospect after the richness of the present. I didn't want to waste time thinking about it, so I dispatched an application to the London Institute of Education.

An incoming letter from the Commonwealth Scholarship Commission in London enclosed a ticket for a cabin on an Anchor Line boat, leaving Bombay for Liverpool, on the third of June, via Karachi, Aden, Port Said and Gibraltar.

First, I needed a certificate confirming that I had paid all my taxes. I dragged myself to the Income Tax Office, on the far side of the city, ready to wait three hours for a five-minute task. I sat there under the fan, quietly reading, not getting irritated at all. This is wonderful, I thought. Here is the fruit of a long and painful process of learning. Only after two hours did I decide to force the pace.

What a relief the onset of warm March weather was. I now disliked the coolness of a North Indian winter, and sometimes shivered in the high eighties. But as the temperature rose higher, I succumbed again to my old lethargy; reading was too much effort. None of the other Europeans suffered so badly. They sweated more than I did. And probably tossed back more water. I always sipped.

By the month of May my only refuge from the mid-day sun was my small, dark room, with its wooden shutters closed. My body slumped like a sack of rice. I could only drag it a few feet to sip tepid water from my large earthenware storage pot. Exhausted with the effort, I would lie down again on the cool concrete floor, my spine softening into crumbling material. The heat melted my surfaces and I could no longer sense where I began and ended. It was best to lie still, almost naked, dissolving into the room, faintly aware of the whirling of the ceiling fan, its rhythm alternating with fluctuations in the electric current.

Ann was also suffering from diminished health. She thought she might be pregnant when her intestines swelled up with amoebic dysentery. To make things worse, mosquitos invaded our flats. Whenever I opened a cupboard, a cloud would fly out. At night-time, the little wretches hovered by the openings on my net, ready to leap into bed with me. In the morning I would crush some in my hands. The red stain glared like a warning. Toofan offered to bring a spray.

'You people have no idea how to live in this climate,' he said.

As if the inexorable rise in temperature wasn't enough, I had to prepare for my final MA exams. The first day arrived. What a tiresome interlude. On the 'Indian Religions' paper, five questions had to be answered in three hours. The temperature was now 110 degrees in the late morning, and I nodded off briefly in the middle of the exam. The more interesting the question, the more impossible it was. I spent two hours struggling with the first one – 'Explain the meaning of life according to the Hindu tradition'. Then thirty-five minutes for 'Summarise the Religious Consciousness'. How could even a saint and mystic do that? Never mind me. That left half an hour for the last three. The final one was completed in two minutes.

I hadn't seen much of my English classmate outside lectures during the two years we had studied together. He rented a house, with his wife, somewhere near the Anglican Church on the far side of the city – and lived on another planet as far as I was concerned. He wasn't trying to find enlightenment; he had found it already, probably born with it in his mouth, like a silver spoon. The courses had given him what he needed to further his missionary work.

I hadn't found enlightenment either. My studies had liberated me from the residues of Christian belief and unsettled many of my assumptions. Often, I felt they had opened doors to a vast and promising landscape; occasionally, I felt simply confused.

The students in the first year of the English medium MA course organised a farewell tea party for the two of us. Our lecturers joined the gathering. Servants in uniform spread a starched white cloth across a large table and brought in plates of fried *gulab jamuns* in syrup. One of the students presented us with English translations of stories and poems by Tagore. The Professor of Sanskrit recalled his time in England.

'The family I was lodging with asked me, "Is it not true that Indians have oppressed women?" I replied with another question. "Is it not true that the English have oppressed mankind?"'

Everyone roared with laughter. I smiled too.

It was time to buy presents. I called in at a large silk shop down one of the alleys. Removing my sandals, I climbed up onto the white mattress covering the raised floor and relaxed among bolsters and cushions. The shopkeeper threw open rolls of fabric. A lilac silk sari with silver thread embroidery caught my eye.

'I'll have that one.' It didn't make sense to buy a sari for myself at such a late stage. I didn't care; I wanted it. I sipped cardamom tea and reflected on designs and shades while Muslim weavers arrived with their boxes. The shopkeeper haggled quietly over prices, but power was in his hands. Saris woven entirely in gold and silver thread, each with a unique design, spilled out of half-open cartons.

The preoccupations of packing blocked out thoughts about the changes ahead. I bought several trunks to accommodate my new acquisitions. My luggage now amounted to nine major items, including a basket, three small cases, two large and three small trunks, one of which belonged to Gillian. She had already returned by air. Three trunks bulged with books on India and Indian philosophy. My Gandhian principles of simple living had got lost somewhere.

In my last week, invitations poured in. Toofan and his mother took me for a boat trip, followed by a visit to a restaurant.

'I want to give you something to remember your time in India,' Toofan's mother said at the end of the meal, after we'd freshened our mouths with betel nut. She handed me a packet in tissue paper.

I unwrapped it. An ivory necklace rested on a turquoise silk scarf with silver embroidery. My favourite colour. I wasn't expecting this from her.

'But why… thank you…' I stammered.

She smiled. And stood up abruptly to leave the restaurant. Our rickshaws were waiting. I followed them mutely like a crumpled scrap of paper at the mercy of random winds.

But by late May I was ready to leave. Hot gusts, carrying clouds of dust, burnt into my cheeks, even when I veiled my face with a scarf.

I had never once felt homesick in Banaras. I'd been too busy living in the present. Only occasionally had I hankered for the open horizons of the Yorkshire Moors. The night before my departure, I dreamt of England for the first time. I was in a cake shop; I woke up drooling.

CHAPTER 28

BACK TO A FOREIGN ENGLAND

Toofan stacked my luggage in the corner of our First Class coupe. For two days we sweltered on that train at forty degrees centigrade. Stupefied, we slipped in and out of sleep. Glazed eyes stared through barred windows at the fleeting world. We didn't talk much. This train was not moving forward to new adventures. It was a departing, a winding down, and the beginning of a return to ordinary life.

We spent a further night sleeping on benches in the Bombay station waiting room. The humidity was welcome, for once.

'You've got time to visit Ajanta and Ellora,' Toofan said. 'Whatever the heat. Those Buddhist and Hindu cave frescoes and sculptures are almost two thousand years old. We can deposit the trunks in Left Luggage.'

Hours of more travel. Slumped in a rattling bus. Up on the inland plateau, away from the sea, the heat obliterated all thought. I trailed after him. I didn't want to return to England, but my scholarship was ending. And I had to proceed with my life, to accomplish some of the great tasks that surely, surely, must be awaiting me. I gazed blankly at glimpses of cave paintings illuminated by intermittent flashes of torchlight. Only one image was able to break through into my consciousness. The face of the compassionate Bodhisattva looked down at me, feeling my weariness and confusion.

In Bombay, we checked into a luxury wood cabin on the beach of an affluent suburb, Juhu, home of Bollywood film stars. English money stretched even this far. Coconut trees lined spotless sands. Wealthy Indian women in European skirts moved around freely without being hassled. Would they have found Banaras any easier than I had? They bathed in swimsuits, not saris, so I wore mine for the first time in two years. We swam in the early morning and dried off over Western breakfasts of eggs and toast under a canvas umbrella. This was a waiting room between two worlds.

A cab carried us back into the city. Motorised traffic hurtled along speedways, and electric trains zoomed past. People with drawn faces queued quietly for buses. Many spoke English. But how much easier it was in Banaras – you could flag down a cycle rickshaw whenever you wanted. And how peaceful it was, after an evening out, to ride home slowly, packed cosily in a covered rickshaw for two, with only the sounds of bicycle bells and bullock carts, and the light of cooking fires. How fortunate that I'd chosen to study there, not in Delhi or Bombay.

I sleepwalked towards departure. We had never talked about the future. We came from different universes, and we were young. I was weeping when I boarded the ship. As the boat drew away from the shore, I watched the crowds pressing against the railings in their bright, flowing clothes, waving and shouting farewells to their relatives. Toofan became a pinprick on the horizon.

Blonde-haired people, wearing Western clothes, filled the ship. Where had all those blue eyes come from? I hadn't seen them in India. Even more boarded a couple of days later, in Karachi. Their children ran everywhere, shouting, trying to hoist themselves up onto the railings. I couldn't see anybody else wearing *selwar-kameez*. The denim dress I had worn on my outward journey had long since been abandoned. It was far too heavy and showed too much of my legs.

A tall, self-assured young woman with dark hair and eyes, dressed in a fashionable linen trouser suit, came over and introduced herself. She was from Calcutta. Anglo-Indian, I guessed.

'I'm domiciled Irish,' she said. 'We've been in India for generations.' She steered me towards a quieter corner of the deck and pulled two chairs together. June told me the story of her life, the bitterness of family problems that had sent her off alone to Britain in her mid-twenties.

'I'm a beautician. I ought to be able to find work, though I don't know anybody there. I was a gangling, unattractive teenager, and far too tall for a girl, but I worked hard to make myself confident. That was why I became a beautician.'

What an impressive story. 'That's amazing,' I said.

June was less alien than the boisterous families, the couples relaxing on sunbeds, or swimming in revealing swimsuits. And she didn't get annoyed as they did if I forgot to say thank you. I'd spent two years learning not to mouth that mantra. It was hard suddenly to go into reverse.

'They're so formal,' she said, 'not natural.'

That evening she eyed me sideways with a determined look. First, she targeted my nails, all covered in ink, and insisted on giving me a manicure. Next came my clothes.

'You can't dress like that in London. I bet they don't wear their hair in plaits. And a little lipstick wouldn't do any harm.'

'I line my eyes with *kargil*.'

'And maybe you should forget your boyfriend. I saw you crying when we left the shore. I know what those North Indian boys are like. And Bengalis are no better, especially the youngest sons.'

I said nothing. But June helped me return to my old life. And I tried to prepare her for what lay ahead.

The temperature plummeted as we entered the Mediterranean. We shivered and wrapped ourselves in shawls. The British families donned coats. A week later the boat chugged out of the Mediterranean, past Gibraltar, and into the Atlantic. We sighted the English coast at seven in the morning. It was silent and remote, veiled in thick mist, a fragile outpost floating in far northern seas. The shore glimmered with phosphorescent light.

*

We berthed in Liverpool. My parents stood stiffly by the exit, and, behind them, my brother with a blanket over his arm. We stared at one another for a moment, and then hugged, but it was formal.

'What's all this?' my father asked, eying my nine items of luggage. He beckoned a porter.

'She's been to India and brought books,' he apologised, as the man crumpled under the weight.

'Don't let her go again. That's all I can say,' the porter replied, laughing.

I smiled. English humour. But why was the platform so quiet, and the train corridor too, and the compartment? Nobody spoke, nobody shouted. As if speaking wasn't allowed. And the countryside had the perfection of a miniature. Immaculate houses lined the roads like children's toys. Through the windows, I gazed at the soothing soft-green grass. Neat, bounded fields rose in gentle undulations. No vast plains to strike awe into the eyes of the beholder. The horizon near at hand. Human beings were master here, and every stretch bore their imprint, yet they were nowhere to be seen. Nor could I observe any animals, apart from an occasional cow.

'Where are the crops?' I asked. 'I can't see anything growing, only grass.'

They stared at me.

A couple with a small daughter sat opposite. The girl read a story to a blue velvet bear cradled on her lap. Her book showed a family of pigs seated at a dinner table, wearing frilly pink dresses.

How weird.

Our taxi from the Beaconsfield station drove through streets almost as silent and orderly as the countryside. Who would I ask if

I lost my way? Cars moved up and down the roads with clockwork regularity. The detached houses sat on display. I stood transfixed in the living room of my parents' home. It must have been recently redecorated for it wore a look of indescribable luxury and opulence. No flaking plaster, or bulges in the walls. I pinned my arms to my sides, fearing I might damage something.

'What have you done to it?' I asked.

'But it's the same as when you left.'

*

I slept late the following morning. The house now looked familiar; gone was the palace of the day before. But other things remained strange. I pulled out the storage boxes from under my bed in search of warmer clothes. Not a trace of dust or mould. Could things in England really be invincible to assaults from nature? In Banaras the forces of decay mass on all sides. Could that be why Indian philosophy enjoined non-attachment to material things?

Outside, the only people to be seen in the street were walking their dogs. Dogs could drop their dirt wherever they liked; people could not. Posters for animal protection shouted from notice boards. And the pets slept in the kitchen, of all unlikely places. How unhygienic.

English people asked if I had enjoyed myself in India. And then never mentioned it again. Why weren't they curious? Was it too remote from their experience? Nor was there much sign of social life. A knock on the door would be someone collecting for charity, for Society in the abstract: never just to say hallo. Neighbours met in the shops would unburden themselves of their news but listened only as a precondition for the right to self-expression.

My parents dragged me along to summer fairs. Serious-looking adults competed in competitions of every kind: egg and spoon races, three-legged races, and football matches of women against men, dressed as women. Grown people took part in obstacle races: jumped in sacks, struggled through rubber tyres, over metal drums, under bamboos and tarpaulins. They dunked their heads in water to bite floating table-tennis balls. Men pushed prams, containing teenage boys, in a race to the far side of the field. People of all ages and classes laughed together. But what a relief not to be harassed, not to be made conscious of one's sex or foreign-ness all the time.

'You should go up to London for a day and meet Great-aunt Daisy,' my mother said. On the train the passengers sat upright with their feet on the floor. How could they relax like that? I tried to tuck my feet up on the seat, but it was difficult in a short skirt. I looked around at the women. All with knees glued together.

I offered a sandwich to the woman sitting opposite.

'No thank you,' she said, avoiding my eyes. Nobody talked. People smiled as if with the brake on. I missed the warmth of India, and of hostel life.

My great-aunt met me at the Marylebone station, and we boarded a London double-decker bus in the street outside. She sat with her basket on the long seat near the door.

'So, what are Indians like, dear?' she asked.

I floundered for a moment.

'They're very musical, Auntie.'

'I think all foreigners are, dear,' she said.

*

For six months I rented a tiny bedsit in Knightsbridge, in the same block of flats as June. Occasionally we cooked curries together. My room provided only a single electric ring. I plodded on with my one-year teacher training course at the Institute of Education. Lectures on comparative education brightened the week. June hadn't yet found employment as a beautician and was working long hours to pay her way, including a late shift as an usherette at a local cinema. One evening I joined her to watch *Dr Zhivago*, and we walked back together. Children, of no more than twelve or thirteen, shuffled past, boys and girls wrapped around one another, kissing desperately, the girls' faces plastered with make-up, their hair bleached and permed like hideous effigies.

We didn't talk much about India. Banaras faded into a far-off dreamland, something to file away at the back of my mind. Ann and Jim started a family and gave up writing. I kept Toofan's photo in a drawer and we exchanged letters for a few months. A few men crossed my path, but none displayed his charm. In any case, I had no time to think about the past. I had to get on with my new life, and my health was still below par.

*

The following September I moved to West London to teach Asian children in a girls' secondary modern school in Southall. It would make good use of my knowledge of Indian culture. The Head allocated three-quarters of my time to reception classes for Punjabi girls. I teased my pupils in Hindi, and we played language games. Their English came along in leaps and bounds. That's where I met Shanta. She was teaching Maths.

A handful of white fourteen-year-olds extended their racial hostility in my direction. Their ringleader shouted, 'I hate all wogs' when she passed in the corridor. The Commonwealth Immigrants Act of 1962, four years earlier, had made it clear that workers from South Asia and the Caribbean were not wanted, unless they were lucky enough to get one of the rationed employment vouchers. Landlords displayed signs saying 'Coloureds Not Welcome'. But how odd that the girl's arm was wrapped around the shoulders of a black girl.

I spent the evenings in my bedsit preparing my lessons. Sometimes I put my papers aside and looked around at the empty room, or sat, staring out of the window, onto a street where nothing moved or breathed. Why had my friend, Gillian, the English student I'd met in Banaras, and who now lived on the other side of London, not answered my letters? A month later her reply arrived. She'd been too depressed to make contact. And I'd assumed the cause was some deficiency in me. How egocentric. I wrote again.

'I also sometimes I feel I don't want to live,' I said.

A rapid response landed in my post box.

'I'm glad you've been depressed,' she said. 'Maybe now you'll realise that even you can't be a self-sufficient individual. Nobody can. You need people like everyone else.'

The letter fell out of my hands. Gillian, the charming diplomat, always spoke the hard truth.

Thoughts of Banaras now resurfaced. If only I could find a forum in which to make sense of my Indian experiences. University seminars were restricted to enrolled students. And Hindu-inspired groups for seekers of 'Union with the Divine Soul of the Universe' made me want to run a mile.

'We'll have to start our own cross-cultural discussion club,' Shanta said. A Jewish couple of Central European origin joined us, and South Asians of various backgrounds, all people who knew more than one world. At last I'd found a group I could relax with. And they all enjoyed the tongue-and-groove style of argument. Gillian joined us occasionally. I met her once a week to swim and chat.

Other friends from Banaras flitted through my life. Eberhart turned up one day, with Nicky, his American fiancée. She'd been in Banaras in our second year. He was teaching German in the USA. Chris Byrski, the Sanskritist from the International Hostel, now lectured in Warsaw University. That summer I visited Poland with my old friend Judy, and we stayed for a few days with his family. We moved on to Krakow to visit a couple she knew from a Socialist International Work Camp.

'You're a wonderful cook,' she said to the wife.

'Not so special,' said the husband.

'That wasn't very nice of him,' Judy complained afterwards.

'Oh no, it's not that,' I said. 'He identifies with her, so he's just being modest. It's not the English individualistic approach.'

India had made it easier for me to spot cultural differences – so all that experience hadn't vanished into thin air, even if I was no nearer enlightenment. It had opened my eyes to the fascination of cultural diversity, and of the quest to make sense of it. The social roots of ideas now interested me more than the philosophic doctrines themselves. Perhaps I should take up anthropology. And it would be good to get back to the reflective world of university after a couple of years teaching in schools.

In 1968 it wasn't difficult to secure funding for a two-year conversion MA. London was too big and impersonal for me. Manchester would be more manageable. And it had a large department. India and its caste system featured in one of the courses on offer.

Anthropology opened new vistas. I learnt that ideas can be implicit in ritual as well as explicit in texts. The first year raced by. The summer of 1969 might be the last long vacation I would ever have. The future might contract again. What was more obvious than to go back to India, overland by public transport, even if I didn't know anyone else who wanted to go? The hundred pounds unexpectedly inherited from my other grandmother would, hopefully, be enough to get me there and back. I would be able to investigate prospects for future research.

I hadn't been hankering for India. It had become no more than an idea, even a puzzle, and a stimulus for intellectual thought. Once I made the decision to return, I dreamt of Banaras twice in succession. I was sitting on the *ghats,* looking out across the river.

'The only thing that worries me,' I confided to a fellow student in Manchester, 'is a friend I had there. I don't know if it would be a good idea to see him again.'

'But you don't have to see him,' she said, 'if it's a city of half a million people?'

'Oh, I couldn't not see him,' I said.

CHAPTER 29

2007 CONVERSATION WITH SHANTA CONTINUES BY EMAIL

January 5th. Manchester
Dear Shanta,

Thanks for your message of encouragement. I'm attaching the last section of my account. I wasn't sure where to finish, because of course it hasn't ended yet. Those two years at the University of Banaras were only the first episode in my encounter with the city. Hopefully, we can discuss these chapters when we meet here in March. I know you'll be in a mad rush until then. Mary

PART IV
1969 BACK TO INDIA OVERLAND

CHAPTER 30

1969 JOURNEY TO ISTANBUL BY TRAIN

'WELL, I CAN'T GIVE YOU A RETURN TICKET AS FAR AS INDIA, love,' replied the ticket clerk, throwing back his head and laughing. 'There isn't a railway line beyond Eastern Turkey. Erzerum's the name of the last station. I can give you one to there. Your student card's valid up to Istanbul. You'll get a good reduction on that.'

I filled in my cheque and reread it several times. This was the point of no return. I tucked the ticket in my money belt and walked over to my parents.

'Let me carry your bag,' my father said. 'It weighs a ton. I don't know why you didn't bring a rucksack.'

'I don't want to look like a hippie. People treat them with contempt. It's heavy because I'm carrying food for the first four days, as well as extra tins of meat. The journey's going to take about three weeks if all goes well. I can't carry much money because of the new currency export restrictions. It's going to be difficult to get through three months and still have enough left for the return journey. But I should be all right if I'm careful.'

The train to Dover was already in. Only First Class passengers, with proper sleepers on the *wagons-lits*, could go all the way to Istanbul by the Orient Express. The rest of us had to change at the coast, and again in Munich.

'You're not going to be on your own, thank goodness,' my mother said, looking around at the rosy-cheeked girls with round faces, clutching maps of Europe and *All You Need to Say in Greek*. All I wanted was to be off. The future was opening up again – at last.

Crowds of young people milled around: men in jeans, with long hair and untamed beards, some with ponytails and rings in their ears, others in baggy trousers and long smocks. The women mostly wore jeans or minis. A few sported flowery cotton skirts, red and black bodices, and jangling bracelets. No sign of suits, or safari shirts, twin sets and pearls, high heels or polyester dresses. Just the odd tweed jacket. All carried bulging rucksacks, sometimes with a dangling guitar attached, or a copy of the *Bhagavadgita* poking out of a side pocket.

Who would have thought we were citizens of the country that had ruled the largest empire the world had known, the country that had been the first to industrialise and develop a railway system?

The procession of seekers and adventurers en route for India was well underway by now. And for every person who stood awaiting the train, there were others who were glad someone they knew was going. They couldn't go, perhaps didn't want to, tied to their partners or set in their jobs, but they were happy that someone was doing it, on their behalf, almost.

"India" had the allure of an Eastern melody. It had drawn me on as irresistibly as the magic of a pied piper. And now it was drawing thousands more overland: travelling from Germany and France, from Belgium and the Netherlands, and especially from London. Transport was train and local bus, sometimes car or jeep. In Iran and Afghanistan there wouldn't be any tourist offices waiting for us, but we didn't care because we all dreamt of treading in the footsteps of a Heinrich Harrer, or a Freya Stark.

Most of us didn't have much money: only earnings from cleaning electricity pylons in the previous vacation or wiping floors in hotel bedrooms. A few enjoyed endless access to Daddy's bank account in Los Angeles. They could have flown for the same cost; instead, they chose to head east on the India trail, the greatest adventure playground of the era.

We descended on the unsuspecting inhabitants of Eastern Europe and the Middle East like a Mongol horde – a giant wave that rolled out of the West, crashed on Istanbul and unfurled itself in a thousand little rivulets across Turkey and Iran. Unsettled, we made a religion out of movement. The world watched with astonishment as the trickle of dishevelled travellers turned into a torrent. Was this pilgrimage the dying gasp of the old world, or the birth pangs of a new one?

But I knew little of all this as I stood on the platform at Victoria Station in London on the 1st July 1969.

Turkish workers crammed into the train at Munich, thin men with lined faces and shabby clothes. They squatted in corridors blocked with bags. It was hard to fight your way through to the toilet. We were all tired by now, squeezed among people speaking unknown languages. I managed to get a turn sleeping on the luggage rack. Every few hours, a figure in uniform woke me, shining a torch into my face, pushing people aside with the butt of a gun, and demanding to see passports. It was hard to know what country we were passing through. The voices of the border guards all sounded the same, harsh and guttural.

The train disgorged its human cargo in driblets as we moved eastwards. I tried to focus on the view from the window, to hold the image of each moment as it passed, but my mind wandered from one thing to another: hopes for the future, thoughts of the past.

'We're going overland to India as well,' said an English girl in my compartment. 'We've got full instructions from people in Cambridge who've already done the journey.' She brandished a wad of typed papers.

All I had was a series of maps on which I'd marked major towns in red. The whole trip had been planned in haste. I had posted off letters to India only two weeks before my departure.

'This sheet tells you places in India where you can get food for free. You just have to queue with the beggars. Nobody asks questions. It's really cool.'

I frowned.

'You don't have to feel bad about it,' she said. 'That's their custom. And whatever you do, don't go by train from Istanbul. You'll be mauled alive by Turkish males.'

'It's even worse for young men,' her not-so-young companion volunteered.

They moved next door after a long, unscheduled train stop. What a relief to find the compartment emptying after the crush of several days. Now only two middle-aged Turkish men huddled in corners. The European stretch of the journey would soon be over. This was merely the prelude. In southern Yugoslavia, a couple of large women with baskets, and several bottles of alcohol, entered the compartment. They beamed. A torrent of foreign words hit me. I beamed back like an idiot. They roared with laughter and offered me a swig of the bottle. I took a sip and coughed and spluttered. This made them laugh all the more. They made themselves at home without any ceremony, spreading their bundles around. Their warmth spilled out across the carriage. Soon everyone was drinking, even the men in the dark, crumpled coats.

But before long, the women were gone, and their places filled with the greyness of evening. I turned to my food bag and trimmed the brown edges off the lettuce. It was time to start purchasing hunks of bread and cheese through the windows at stations.

Dawn showed us winding along ledges on the side of cliffs, dwarfed by rock faces towering above and falling away below. The puny train continued, undaunted, chiselling its way through the bellies of white limestone mountains. It was single-minded, unconstrained by residues of the past. We, too, could surmount unknown obstacles.

Clouds parted before us, horizons crumbled, and futures came and went. Shadowy glimpses of other lives flashed past: fleeting snapshots of people rooted in place.

I hadn't packed a camera. I couldn't see why it should be a ritual obligation to convert the moment into a durable object. I would allow the tidy cypresses, doing sentry duty in the vineyards and olive groves, and over the terraced fields and the tumbling streams, to flow by unimpeded.

On the fourth day, a young Turkish woman moved into the compartment for an hour. 'Excuse me,' she said with an American accent, 'but I would advise you to wear trousers, not that short skirt. Better even to wear tight jeans and show the shape of your backside than the bare flesh of your legs.'

'But it's so hot!' The only dresses I had were minis; nobody was wearing anything else in the late 1960s, not even the least fashionable of us.

'Whatever the heat,' she said.

On my way to the toilet, I chatted to three English students sitting in the corridor on top of their rucksacks.

'You're going to India on your own? Why don't you join us? We're taking the night train to Erzerum.'

I hesitated.

'I don't think I can face the thought of moving on again this evening, after four nights on this train.'

It was late afternoon by the time we reached Istanbul. I had to find somewhere to stay before dark. The station was a mass of people, crowding in on all sides: thousands of men, hardly any women to be seen. Was this what it meant to be in the East? I'd forgotten my first visit to the State Bank of India in Banaras, when all the queues of men turned round to stare. Now, again, a thousand eyes were pressing in on me.

An information office at the end of the platform promised assistance. The portly woman at the desk did not waste time on a smile. She rifled through her files for the names of cheap hotels. The first she suggested was too expensive. It would be humiliating to have to depend on the mercies of a British Embassy to get me home.

'Well, this is all I can offer,' she said, pushing a piece of paper with two addresses on it towards me. 'I can't promise they will have any vacancies. You'd better go at once, as it's not a good area after dark. You'll have to take a bus and then keep asking.'

What if I couldn't find the place? I tried to screw my cheeks hard into position but could feel them getting out of control. My eyes began to leak.

'You're too old to cry,' the woman said. The blood rushed into my face and I ran out. What a feeble character I was, disgracing my country. Perhaps Turks never showed weakness. Probably they had a proud, martial tradition. They'd had an empire too.

I showed the piece of paper with the hotel addresses on it to several men walking past and managed to board the right bus. After a ten-minute ride the driver stopped and pointed to a slow-moving taxi, with a sign indicating its destination. I flagged it down. Several men were already aboard, all going somewhere near the San Sofia Mosque. It was dark when I arrived in a small back street at the hotel *Sosyal*.

The gentle-eyed proprietor greeted me in the reception hall.

'That price she give you is for one bed,' he said. 'Not one whole room. Nice room. Only four beds.'

'Not my own room? Who will be in the other beds?'

'No women come here. Turkish men come later.'

Tears streamed down my cheeks.

'No worry,' he said. 'I'll do something.'

And he did. He gave me a room on my own, with three iron beds and one chair.

'Nobody else come,' he said. 'And here is name of good café for you, just round corner.'

A few men were eating at the front near the window. A waiter directed me to the curtained space at the rear. I was famished after my Spartan diet of bread, browned lettuce and tinned meat, and wolfed down a huge bowl of lamb and vegetable stew with okra, aubergines and green peppers. Back in the hotel, I collapsed onto my bed and didn't wake until ten o'clock next morning.

I couldn't spend more than a couple of days in Istanbul, so, after coffee and bread at the café, I hurried towards the two major mosques soaring high above the congested streets, the Suleymaniye, and the Sofia, a Greek Byzantine church until the Ottomans overran the city in 1453. That cataclysmic event increased the flow of Greek scholars, carrying to Italy their volumes of ancient Greek science and philosophy, as well as Arabic commentaries and scientific treatises informed by the mathematics of India.

At the Sofia Mosque, I removed my shoes and placed them in the rack outside. The huge doorway opened into a vastness of space, broken only by glistening chandeliers. The man at the entrance thrust a scarf into my hands. I covered my head with it, before sitting down on the sumptuous old carpet in the women's section. The huge dome absorbed and extinguished the clatter and heat of the streets. A low murmuring of voices wafted over from the entrance. Old men sat cross-legged, swaying backwards and forwards as they recited the comforting words of familiar prayers. Others pored over well-worn volumes. I was far from the prying eyes of the crowds, refreshed and tranquil.

The only women on the streets of Istanbul were middle-aged and plump, wearing black skirts or frocks that ended halfway down their calves. They scuttled along as if they didn't want to be noticed. Probably Jewish or Greek, someone informed me later. How drab and plain they looked, compared with women in Banaras. India was my yardstick for everything outside Western Europe.

The arches of the covered market tempted me into a sparkling treasure house of unknown objects and people. Red-haired Circassian families mingled with the crowds. I peeked like a child with its face pressed against the glass panes of a sweetshop. But I couldn't savour the sights for long; I had to reach the main post office before it closed.

Was it unrealistic to hope for letters from Banaras? I hadn't corresponded with anyone for several years. And I'd left it so late. I didn't even know who would still be there. Would Sujata have returned to Bali? The clerk fished out a single blue air letter from under the counter. I recognised Toofan's handwriting at once.

By seven, I was sitting in my eating place. That was my rule. To be inside by dusk in the sex-segregated societies of Islam and South Asia. The proprietor welcomed me back into the hotel. 'No need sit alone,' he said. 'Please, you like come on my roof terrace? It very nice.'

His friend poured me coffee and *sherbert*. The air was sweet with the scent of yellow roses, their outlines silhouetted on the white-washed wall. A full moon hung suspended from the ceiling of the night. I gazed at the sweeping curves of the two mosques towering above. The men offered me almonds from a silver bowl and talked together in low voices. Sometimes they would switch into broken English and speak about poetry. Then we would sit in silence, allowing the night to lap around us.

'Why all you people want to go India? India not a good place. Why India so special?'

What answer could I give? Would they understand if I talked about the Ascent of Everest, and about Tibet, and the *Upanishads*, and everything else? And did I any longer know?

They looked at me with incomprehension. I didn't live by the rules they lived by, but still I was a woman to be protected.

CHAPTER 31

ONWARDS TO AFGHANISTAN

Six Australian men arrived at the hotel the following morning – travelling from India to London. Five blonde and beefy travellers who all laughed loudly, and one, of slighter build, quieter, Italian in appearance. I approached him.

'What's the train to Erzerum like?' I asked.

'It's bad for women,' he said. 'Why don't you cash in your rail ticket and go on the coach? It'll be three nights instead of four, and you'll sleep in guesthouses, cost included. That's what we did this time. The only hairy bit's when the coach races on hairpin mountain bends. You can see the wrecked vehicles in the gorges below.'

I set off for the station, not sure if death at the bottom of a gorge would be preferable to sexual assault on a train. The station didn't look so menacing in the bright light. Not far from the entrance, an elderly north European man was standing at the side of a railway track, next to a huge steam engine. He was surrounded by a large pile of luggage. Tall and gaunt, with a black umbrella hooked over one arm and a cotton sunhat perched on his head, he was gesticulating with some agitation at a green canvas bag. A few minutes later, I saw him again near the ticket office, carrying a briefcase, accompanied by two porters.

'They have put me on the wrong train,' he said, with a strong French accent, noticing that I was looking at him. 'I desire to go on the Taurus express to Baghdad. It's not here, so I go now to have some coffee.'

'I think I'll have some too,' I said, on impulse.

It took him a few minutes to rearrange all his belongings. 'I have to carry many things,' he explained. 'I am retiring to India.'

'Oh!' I said. 'Have you spent much time there?'

'I regret that I have never been before. I shall travel until I find the special place, but probably I shall stay finally in Pondicherry, at the ashram. First, I desire to visit a few of the religious places.'

'You've never been before?'

Who would think of retiring to India without first having a look at the country? A great shock might be awaiting him. Perhaps his odd collection of luggage represented all his worldly goods? Had he sold his house in France?

He emptied his right-hand pocket and placed the contents side by side on our table. A small grey notebook was followed by a blue pen which lay next to two paper clips and an olive-coloured eraser.

'But supposing you don't like it. Wouldn't it be better to go for a holiday first?'

'I travelled much when I was young,' Monsieur Clausse said. 'My father was a diplomat. We're of an aristocratic family, you see. People say that the family rank made no difference after the Revolution, but that is not correct. My daughter's husband is very successful but you can always know that he is of a peasant family. Travelling in Europe was easy in those days. It was not necessary to have a passport. They came in after the first war.'

He seemed to be going off at a tangent.

'How wonderful that must have been,' I said, thinking of the border guards poking me in the ribs, as I lay contorted on the luggage rack. 'I wonder what's happened to our coffee.'

Monsieur Clausse swept on.

'I was not able to travel much after my marriage as my dear wife was ill, frequently. In Europe she suffered bad arthritis. Eventually, we had to settle in Morocco. Also, we had some problems in the last war since my mother was German. So it was better to go away.'

The coffee arrived. I eyed the heavy deposits at the bottom of the glass.

'What was Morocco like?'

'Unfortunately, it was bad for my son. I had to spend much time with my wife and our baby daughter. He was at a difficult age and then he mixed up with a criminal Moroccan gang. In the end, I understood that I had to finish with him – for the good of us all. Then my dear wife died. Now I have a house in Spain. My daughter stays there in her vacations.' Monsieur Clausse leaned back, exhausted.

I was finding it hard to take it all in. It was a relief to turn my attention to the challenge of sipping coffee without making contact with the grounds. We sat in silence. Out of the corner of my eye, I could see two men in well-tailored suits at the next table. One was Indian, and the other sounded African. I heard the Indian saying loudly in an outraged tone, 'I couldn't believe such a thing was possible.'

'Exactly,' said the African. 'It's ridiculous not to know English, in this day and age. Even men in suits don't speak it properly. How is one supposed to manage?'

'Now I know the time is ready,' Monsieur Clausse continued, 'for me to see India and complete my life.' He took a framed photo of a young woman out of his briefcase and placed it on the wooden table. 'My daughter.'

I turned to look at the image of an elegant young woman who returned our gazes a trifle coldly. The old man sighed a little. I explained that I was returning to India and going to a holy place, like him.

'So you, too, are a seeker,' he exclaimed. 'I knew it as soon as I saw you.'

'Well, not exactly,' I said, avoiding his eyes. 'I studied philosophy there. I'm just going back for a visit.' I hesitated and thought for a minute before saying, 'To see old friends.'

'But you studied philosophy,' he burst out. 'You are seeking something.'

At that moment, a porter approached and indicated that the Baghdad train was coming onto the platform. Monsieur Clausse grabbed his pen and wrote down my English address.

'I will write and tell you everything,' he said, stuffing the framed photo into his pocket.

I watched him disappear at speed, with his two porters, through the door of the station restaurant.

Three months later, I received a letter from him. An elderly Iraqi was praying on a rug the full length of his train compartment. He waited in the corridor with his thirteen pieces of luggage, before he was invited in. It turned out that his travelling companion could speak perfect French. They had excellent conversation about the higher things of life all the way to Baghdad. Monsieur Clausse maintained a regular correspondence with me for several years, until finally I received a letter with a Spanish postmark from his daughter. He had died in India, and never gone back to Europe.

I walked over to the ticket office. As feared, I could get a refund only in London. Should I post the outward portion home and keep the return part in case I ran out of money on the way back? The newspapers were full of stories of over-landers who ended up penniless on the doorsteps of some far-flung British Embassy, desperate to be repatriated to the once-despised safety of a suburban English home. I wasn't going to end up in such ignominy. And I could probably afford the bus.

So there I was, at five o'clock the next morning, hurrying towards the coach station in Istanbul, with the hotel proprietor struggling with the bag he had insisted on carrying. He shook hands with me.

'I not understand why you make this journey. But I do my duty. I hope you are safe.'

*

The luxury coach was packed with Iranians travelling from Munich back to Teheran. I took the first spare gangway place. An English-speaking engineer, returning home from a year in Germany, was in the window seat. He'll be good company, I thought, until he fondled my hand. I jumped up and moved further back to sit near a young couple with a baby who bounced happily on their laps, not crying once. Their contentment fanned out to everybody around them. We halted at regular intervals for meals of rice and kebabs, and mounds of what seemed to be raw spinach. Breakfasts were fresh flat bread and white butter and yoghurt.

A large, middle-aged German woman chatted in Persian to other passengers. She was returning home to her Iranian husband. 'Why are you eating this tinned food?' she asked at one of our meal breaks.

'We're not allowed to take much money out of Britain at the moment. I have to make it last for three months.'

'You'll be unhealthy. Tinned food isn't the same,' she said, ordering me a plate of meat and rice.

What was I to do? Courtesy struggled with self-respect. I remembered the girl who'd shown me a typed handout on how to bag food for free in India.

'I must pay you for it,' I insisted, annoyed that my careful plans for economical travel were disintegrating.

'Nonsense.' She did the same thing at the next meal stop.

This time I refused to eat the food.

'Pride is bad,' she said. 'You must learn to receive with grace.'

True to forecast, the bus driver raced against other coaches, vying for pole position along spectacular mountain roads. The passengers waved across to one another, cheering the drivers on to greater feats of daring. The carcases of dead dogs littered the route. Huge precipices of grey rock reared above us; white-flecked torrents danced in the chasms below. We spent two days crossing Turkey, staying at Sivas and Erzerum, each time arriving at eleven o'clock in the night and departing at five in the morning. Crumbling earth houses clustered forlornly in the villages of eastern Turkey.

I chatted with a Persian student, Mohammed, who was returning home after three years at Sussex University. We compared notes about courses, and exchanged addresses, with vague plans of travelling back together. He referred to the terrors of the Shah's regime.

'I've never been politically active, but if you've been outside the country, anything can arouse their suspicions, even a poem.'

He panicked as we approached the Iranian border. He checked all his bags and pockets in case there was a scrap of what might be deemed incriminating evidence – an old theatre ticket for a play with the wrong title, a Students' Union membership card, a friend's letter with a passing political aside. Might he have overlooked something that hadn't seemed significant when he'd packed in Britain? He tore some letters into strips and tossed them out of the window. At the border, the bus was held for five hours and all the Persians were searched minutely. Nothing amiss was found. Mohammed relaxed again.

Our overnight stop in Iran was Tabriz, city of honey-coloured limestone. The sound of music and shouting woke me from my slumbers. I peered through a chink in the shutters into the large courtyard below. Crowds of men applauded male dancers who leaped and whirled with ever-increasing energy.

'Have you somewhere to stay in Teheran?' Mohammed asked on the final day. 'I'll see that you and the three American girls at the back reach a hotel safely.'

I was grateful, though I had no wish to be bracketed with the girls at the back. They giggled noisily with the bright-eyed men who approached them with talk of the night clubs of the capital.

We arrived in Tehran at eleven that night. What an ugly modern sprawl. I stumbled out into the glaring lights of the bus station. Mohammed sprang out into the warm embrace of forty relatives: parents, brothers, sisters, aunts and uncles, cousins many times removed. For ten minutes he was absorbed in hugs and handshakes. What a lucky man. At last he broke away. There must have been some conversation about the four crumpled, and not very appropriately dressed, Anglo-Saxon females. Mohammed's cousin offered his car, or perhaps it was commandeered. They insisted that we climb in. The relatives would wait. Having seen us safely installed in the *Girouldi*, a suitable cheap hotel, endowed with a green courtyard and fountain, Mohammed turned to me and shook my hand.

'I've completed my responsibilities,' he said. 'Now I'll wait and see if I get a letter from you. Then I'll know if you're just like all the other selfish Europeans who only take and never give.'

I winced; I wasn't like that. But I lost Mohammed's address in India, so I ended up just like all the other selfish Europeans.

The American girls were out all evening and night, dancing at clubs, and in all day, sleeping it off, so I hardly saw them. Teheran was no more endearing than it had appeared the night before. Concrete blocks overshadowed gracious buildings surviving from an earlier age.

A walk to the main post office brought another letter from Toofan, reiterating his welcome, and a note from my parents exuding anxiety. They enclosed a copy of a long article, published in *The Times* the day after my departure, on the dangers of travelling overland to India. Under no circumstances, it said, should women travel alone. This was followed by the latest horror story about a young couple who had camped between towns in Afghanistan. They had been kidnapped by bandits. The man had been found with his throat cut.

On the way back to the hotel I dodged the clusters of young men who occupied the pavements. They strutted along in tight trousers and well-tailored shirts, leering and occasionally lunging out at me. How I longed to be a man, and invisible.

What a relief to sip black tea in the hotel courtyard. I leaned back and watched the water spurting from the fountain. Four years had passed since I left the sub-continent. Britain was in flux at that time, but India was consolidating the changes set in train by Independence. After the trauma of partition had come the struggle to develop a secular state, a constitutional overhaul of caste and marriage legislation, and centralised economic planning. Kashmir had been an ongoing concern, and the newer problem of China had been in the foreground. Now, in 1969, it seemed that India might be entering a period of instability. Nehru's death in 1964, when I was in Kashmir, had weakened the central government.

At five o'clock the following morning, I boarded a local bus to Mashhad. A European couple were already sitting halfway down. It was good to be on the move again, always with that same sense of excitement as the vehicle pulled off, heading for new and unknown worlds. Our route lay along a smooth, modern road with glimpses of snow-capped peaks. The earth became drier, with only a few trees distracting from the bare outlines of hills and rocks. The bus bumped and bounced as we manoeuvred our way around fallen rocks. A picture of the Shah in military attire, the universal protective talisman, glared down at us from above the windscreen.

We paused at small wayside shacks every few hours, to sit on rugs at low tables to drink black tea, served in dainty little glasses standing in glass saucers. At one of these stops a Dormobile, with a blonde couple at the front, zoomed past in a cloud of dust. The man sitting near me turned and stared at it in silence until it became a blur in the distance. Who were these people and why were they all going to India?

The land became steadily barer and dustier. Even the low scrubby vegetation disappeared. A man boarded, selling cucumbers from a basket. Anthropological theories of gift exchange flitted through my head. I bought half a dozen and cut them into slices for the family sitting near me. They smiled and gave me pistachios in return. I could see their faces poking out from behind a heap of bags and babies.

We reached Mashhad, the last important town before the Afghan border, after twenty-two hours. I sorted myself and my luggage out on a bench by the wall of the bus station. Three women wearing long, dark *chadors*, with their faces half-covered, turned and stared at me. One was much taller than the others. She pointed at my head and pulled at her robe. What right did she have to tell me how to dress? But maybe I did look indecent. I turned away sharply and hurried out.

Men filled the streets, with only occasional huddles of blackly cloaked women, scurrying with their heads down. No concrete to be seen anywhere. I hurried towards the mosque and tomb celebrating the founder of Persian Shiism. Tiles, in shades of blue and green, blazed from the walls.

A handful of women entered the tomb compound, so I made a cautious approach. A man at the entrance threw me a black *chador* and pointed at the shoe rack. I wrapped myself in the voluminous robe and walked slowly ahead until I found an empty place to sit. Not wanting to stare, I squinted out of the corner of one eye. It wasn't difficult to seem pensive, even devout. I always enjoyed these little forays into Islamic religious places, more like retreats from the hurly burly. And I had never before seen any buildings as vivid and lovely as the mosques of Iran.

Half an hour later, I was out in the sun again. Passing a small side alley, with lots of busy little shops on each side, I turned to wander down it. A man in his thirties, wearing a long woollen coat, walked briskly towards me. He paused for a moment, and said, with a perfect English accent, 'Under no circumstances go down any of those side streets.' Then he was gone. I hesitated, startled, and turned back. But who was he and what was down those streets?

With the aid of my little list of useful Persian words, compiled with the help of Mohammed, I found a cheap place to stay near the bus station. I secured a space on the floor, and use of a shower, for a few pence. A handful of Americans were swapping stories of discomfort and danger. With their wild beards, dry un-oiled reddish-brown hair, and tall, uncoordinated bodies. What a contrast they were to the sleek and well-groomed Turks and Iranians. And they talked endlessly about rates of exchange and the best bargains en route. Still, they were from a semi-known world even if they seemed like a throwback to colonial times.

'There was this guy. He had forty bites from bed bugs when he got up next morning.'

'It's no use expecting anything to be done on time here. I had to wait a week for my visa. They're all the same, still backward. Nothing changes. You've got to show them you mean business.'

'I met this character who gave me some dope. I was stoned for three days. You can't trust them.'

Should I tell them about my problems getting a visa for Iran in London? How the elegantly coiffured Englishwoman with the public-school accent had pushed my laboriously filled-in application form back across the polished desk?

'You haven't given your religion,' she'd said.

'I haven't got one.'

'You have to have one,' she snapped, 'otherwise you will not be allowed into Iran.'

'But that's ridiculous. Why should I have one?'

'That's the rule.'

'What's the reason for the rule?' I was feeling mounting hatred for her well-manicured refusal to express any kind of reaction.

'That's not my concern,' tight-lipped as ever. And then, exasperated, 'Can't you just put Church of England?'

Those were words I never would write. But then the penny dropped. Probably they wanted to check if I was Jewish. Or maybe atheists were seen as a Communist threat. 'Write down Hindu,' I said.

Expressionless as ever, she filled the crucial space with immaculate italic script and took the form off to receive the magic stamp.

'I'm turning in,' one of the Americans said. At the other end of the room a handful of Iranians were already asleep. One was snoring loudly. I rolled over and was lost to the world within minutes.

In the morning I caught a local bus heading for Herat, across the border in Afghanistan. The Americans had already taken the seats at the front, so I moved towards the back. Once out of the town, the road was not much more than a dusty track. Before long, the bus got stuck in the ruts of a dried-up ford, and we all had to climb out.

It was late before we reached the frontier. I followed everyone out of the bus, clutching my dirty canvas bag. The lights of wood fires and paraffin lamps peppered the darkness. A few single-storey buildings were scattered around on the sandy earth. I had no idea what was happening and was too tired to care much. An Iranian passenger muttered something about customs officers. We sat on a step waiting to be told what to do. I could faintly see the Americans but in the dim light, couldn't distinguish one from another.

After what felt like several hours – my watch had stopped – someone shepherded us inside. Four Afghan men in long, flowing clothes and loosely tied turbans reclined on rugs, smoking water pipes. The air filled with an unfamiliar aromatic scent. One of the men laughed a lot and leaned back against another man who pulled him down and ran his hand inside his clothing. Then they were all rolling around, pushing and laughing, in a heap of heaving cloth. Another surfaced and drew something out of a small pouch. He offered it to an American who sniffed it gingerly. Money was changing hands. The customs officers were rolling around again on their rugs.

Shadowy figures wandered in and out. Three Afghans began dancing. Sinuous movements alternated with fast gyrations. The others roared with laughter. Hours passed. The Americans were smoking. Some passengers dozed on the mat. I fell asleep too. Someone tapped me on the shoulder. Through half-opened eyes, I saw people filing out. I followed a line of figures back to the bus, climbed in and we were off again, rattling our way forward.

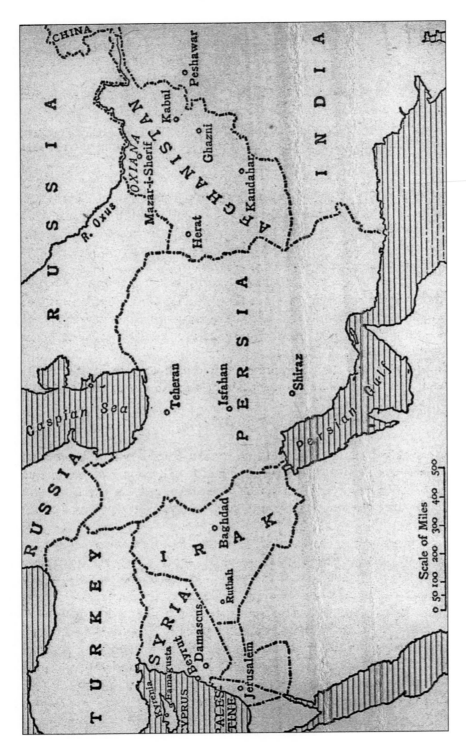

Overland to India

CHAPTER 32

ANOTHER BEGINNING
IN THE SUB-CONTINENT

HERAT SMELT THE SAME AS THE CUSTOMS OFFICE ON THE border – even the aubergines and potatoes on the street stalls. Could I be imagining hashish everywhere? Once again, my hotel in this pleasant little town cost only a few pence a night for a rug on the floor. I slept heavily after the twenty-three-hour wait the day before. After breakfast, I dashed out to look at yet more melancholy ruins of long-departed empires, citadels, mosques and tombs, before finding the bus for Kabul.

I wriggled my way onto a seat next to an Afghani family with six children. The women were wearing black *chadors* but smiled and guided me to the toilet whenever we stopped for glasses of tea. They offered me peaches, and I gave them chunks of bread and cucumber. Their youngest child prised my Indian bamboo fan out of my hand and played with it until her head sagged onto her mother's arm.

At the final tea break I buttonholed an elderly French-speaking Iranian and asked him to suggest accommodation in Kabul. He recommended a guest house near the bus stand. The proprietor was dressed in tight trousers and a nylon shirt. That should have been a warning signal, but I had to stay somewhere. I deposited my bag on the floor and began to sign in.

'Fine,' he said in English. 'Now we go nightclub.'

'No thank you,' I said, grabbing my bag and retreating to the safety of the street. The *Waliyar* hotel next door was equally cheap and gave no grounds for concern. I filled in the required forms and whizzed out to do my normal tour on foot. I didn't have time to see much because of my self-imposed curfew. Weren't Pathans bloodthirsty men who flashed scimitars as they galloped off into the mountains? I was going to be even more careful than usual.

It was hard to read the cultural clues in men's clothing. Their flowing grey robes displayed none of the Indian insignia of respectability; they were un-ironed, unbleached and unstarched. Yet they made no attempt to intrude on my personal space and I suffered none of the harassment routine in North India. They neither stared, nor made eye contact but remained aloof and self-contained. Was this because they lacked curiosity about the strange aliens passing through their land or were too proud to show interest, or because staring is a threatening act?

The following morning, I boarded a bus for Peshawar. It wouldn't be long now before the Khyber Pass. We followed the river as it narrowed into the main escape route off the plateau, and cranked our way precariously down between desolate, eroded mountains. For thousands of years, this had been the entry point to India. Through this long and narrow defile, traders and troopers had stormed out of the dry wastes of Central Asia, down into the promise of the fertile plains below. But what an anti-climax. High peaks menaced the road, but no more dramatically than in parts of Turkey, or the Scottish Highlands. The pass was marked only by a dreary British-built brick tower. Small groups of men with rifles over their shoulders walked along the side of the road.

I chatted for a few minutes with a couple of Dutch over-landers. 'We've taken a year off from teaching,' the man said. 'We wanted to see India before we settle down and have a family.'

The bus dropped out of the mountains into the Pakistani foothills. We clambered down outside the station in Peshawar. Men dressed like Afghans, and with the same lean, wiry bodies of mountain people, swarmed through the streets. This wasn't yet South Asia. But what a relief to have reached the sub-continental railway system, with its waiting rooms, retiring rooms and restaurants. What did it matter if the British had built it only for economic and military reasons?

I managed to dredge some Hindi from the depths of my memory. 'A single ticket for Lahore, please.'

'You speak very good Urdu, memsahib,' responded the clerk.

That was kind of him.

The train descended further into the plains. Beads of perspiration trickled off my forehead, and my clothes stuck to my body. The sounds and smells of South Asia assailed me. Tin shacks and kiosks replaced the stone houses of Afghanistan. Emaciated women carried heavy head loads. Faces were darker, with larger eyes.

I planned to reach the border as fast as possible. Indians had filled my head with stories about the awfulness of Pakistani men. Yet, as in Afghanistan, men troubled me less than in North India. They were formal and distant. Perhaps I was an object to be avoided. At one station, a group of schoolboys in uniform boarded and crowded round me, firing off questions and giggling, but they were polite enough. And I wasn't pestered by vendors, or people desperate to practise their language skills.

Palm trees and tropical vegetation replaced the barrenness of Central Asia. The towns were greener, with leaves poking above buildings and bushes sprouting on waste ground. Meals on the trains included vegetables, not just meat and flat bread. And it was good to be in a country where so many people knew at least a little English. I was tired of being a silent observer, able only to use a handful of words backed up by mime. I had flown past like a dragonfly that skims across pools, alights briefly, and hastens on.

With my face pressed against the bars of the train window, watching the flat, lush fields flash past and feeling the hot air rushing in, I wondered what had brought me back. Did I really want to explore possibilities for research in the following year? Had it been so wonderful the first time? Had I forgotten the exhaustion and the sickness, the harassment and the mental confusion? Had I only remembered the exhilaration of encountering a world where every moment impinged, where people wanted to engage with others?

Indo-Irish June, after a few months in London, had once said, 'English people are odd. They don't see anything or look at anyone. They walk hunch-backed with their eyes down, absorbed in themselves.' I didn't want to be like that. But was it masochism to seek again a bombardment where my taken-for-granted values would be shown no respect? Did life have to be a journey the whole time? Was there no other way to keep windows open?

I dozed off, weary with the effort to put my thoughts in order. From Lahore, a bus took me to the edge of the no-man's-land separating India and Pakistan. A rickshaw carried me further toward the border, along a dirt track, through fields of maize. The scent of moist earth, and the rhythmic creaking as the pedals turned, lifted my spirits.

Indian army officers with moustaches checked my documents. 'You must be mad to return overland.' They laughed.

An unexpected rush of joy flooded over me as I stepped onto Indian soil again, encountering that unpredictably alive mix of human warmth and hassle. An Indian rickshaw took me along a rough path through fields of sugar cane, growing to shoulder height. Occasional rickshaws passed in the opposite direction. At Ferozepur station, I reluctantly exchanged the rickshaw, and its intimacy with the land, for an enclosed metal carriage.

Five hours in Amritsar to wait for the rail connection to Delhi. Enough time to visit the Sikh Golden Temple. I walked through the domed entrance, into the courtyard with its huge marble water tank. Crowds of male and female volunteers prepared *rotis* for the daily communal meal. Hands slapped dough balls with lightning speed and tossed them along the lines for rolling, and then for cooking on gridirons. Men with muscular arms prepared *prasad*, stirring *ghee* into huge vats of semolina *halwa*. I tasted a generous dollop. No god could be impervious to an offering like this.

Once on the Delhi train, I moved further into the rich greenery of the monsoon zone. We arrived in the capital the next morning and I set off on foot to the main post office. Coming towards me was my old philosophy professor of four years back, N.K. Devaraj. How astonishing that he recognised me. And nice, too.

'Mary Surly,' he said, 'back again at last.' He had always struggled with my surname. But he had never been given to effusiveness, and he moved on at once.

At the post office I collected a pile of mail: from my parents, from my flatmate in England, and from Toofan again. Most helpful of all, in the short term, was a note from the Delhi relatives of a Bengali friend in Banaras, insisting that I stay with them.

I flagged down a scooter rickshaw and went straight to their flat in a tree-lined avenue of New Delhi. A short, round-faced couple, Mr and Mrs Roy, opened the door and drew me in warmly. Their teenage son and daughter beamed at me from the sidelines, and Grandmother Roy rushed into the kitchen to organise tea-making. They sat me down in a polished wooden chair with a comfortable wicker back. Mosaic floors and high ceilings freshened the air. My shabby, crumpled appearance did not discomfort the family. I showered and changed, and was fed like a long-lost, prodigal daughter. Then I was directed to a divan for a siesta. What a wonderful homecoming to people I had never met before.

Within a few hours of arrival my bowels began to shake, just as they had six years earlier. I retched in the bathroom like a wrung-out rag.

'Not to worry,' said Mrs Roy. She and her daughter, Rita, busied themselves preparing bland food: plain yoghourt and soft rice, boiled with lentils, and potatoes and cauliflower. The Roys looked after me for a week until they deemed me fit to leave. Even a hundred rebirths would not be enough to repay all the kindnesses I received in India.

On my last day in Delhi, I toured around, meeting academics, enquiring about areas of anthropological research. The Punjabi women students stared at my loose *selwars*. Tight *churidars* were now the fashion.

From the capital I travelled on the night train to Allahabad, to stay with my friend, Gillian Buckee. She was now a doctoral student, funded by a Commonwealth Scholarship, working on nineteenth-century legal documents at the Allahabad High Court. Her knee-length flowered dress looked like something from a 1940s colonial wardrobe.

'This is more appropriate in my circle here than *selwar-kameez*,' she explained.

Gillian lodged in a gracious house in the Civil Lines, with a highly educated Christian family, rooted in several different Indian communities. They had taken it upon themselves to interpret Indian culture for her benefit. I accompanied her to a potluck meal in the house of one of the anglophile lawyers in her circle. We sat on heavy mahogany chairs and looked out at a large garden with flowering shrubs and trees. Whisky was served on ornate tables, and salad, as well as mutton *biriani,* and dishes of curried vegetables.

I remained in Allahabad for four days, until Gillian's servant had managed to book me a seat on a train to Banaras.

'Where are you going to stay when you arrive?' she asked.

'In Istanbul and Tehran, I received letters of invitation from Toofan,' I replied.

'I met him briefly, six months ago,' she said, 'at the house of a friend I was visiting in Banaras. It wasn't long after his mother died. He must be from an upper-class background to have such poise and courtesy. He wasn't at all ill at ease, though my friends are from a prominent local family.'

I gaped at her. That wasn't how I had seen him. His relatives were no longer wealthy. And, anyway, I didn't admire high families.

'It will be late when you arrive there,' she said. 'You must send him a telegram so he can meet you at the station. Give me your best *selwar-kameez* outfit and I'll iron it so you can wear it on the train.'

'My best one? On the train?'

Gillian went to her trunk and pulled out a set of matching glass bangles.

It was nearly midnight when I stepped down onto the platform at Banaras. The station was being repainted so there was even more commotion than I remembered. I hoped it wouldn't be difficult to find Toofan in the heaving crowd. It would be easier for him to spot me.

Someone took my arm. Toofan was standing beside me. We stood still, just smiling and smiling. He guided me out to his rickshaw.

Two weeks later, we married in a Hindu ceremony. It was 'Indian Independence Day'. 'An appropriate occasion,' he remarked, 'for an Indian to make a conquest of an English citizen.' But he did promise to consult me if he purchased an elephant.

The wedding

CHAPTER 33

2007 EPILOGUE FOR SHANTA

February 25ᵗʰ. Manchester

Dear Shanta,

Now at last I've finished what you suggested. I've written about the first stage of my life in India. What a long time ago.

When I close my eyes, I can remember returning one summer to our little house in Bhelupura. We'd been away for a few weeks in the hot season. The rickshaw clattered up the alley, bags and cases balanced precariously at the back. And there it was. Such a neat little peach-coloured building, tucked at the end of the lane. We unbolted the door and I walked up the dark hall and into the bright courtyard. Everything was as we'd left it. The doves were still nesting in the ventilation hole. Even the layer of dust wasn't too thick. And the potted plants and creepers were more luxuriant and glossy. The rains had seen to that. Throwing open the shutters of the windows that faced into the courtyard, I poked my head into the little rooms. I looked round at the curtains and the pictures, and the books all in order along the shelves, arrayed by size, as my husband liked.

We stood contentedly for a moment, side by side, enjoying the midday tranquillity. Facing us was a row of poetry books. He pulled out a volume, and I did the same. As my fingers closed over the spine of the book, it disintegrated in my hands, crumbling into dust. In place of the pages was a heaving, jelly-like mass of bloated white termites. As I screamed, they fell and scattered in their hordes, swarming over the floor and along my arm. I was dimly aware that the whole row of books was the same, a hollowed-out, colourful façade. My legs barely carried me out into the light of the courtyard and across the veranda to the washroom. Frenziedly pouring bucket after bucket of water over my head and shoulders, I tried to purify myself, to blot out the horror.

A shudder goes through me as I remember it, even now after so many years. The loveliness of the moment. And the horror of impermanence. The gods laugh at our earnest endeavours and take their tribute. But we fill our shelves with new books and life resumes. We warm ourselves in the sunshine, on temporary landing stages, in protected harbours, and then set sail again, hungry for the hill-top view.

Through the window of my house in Manchester I see the last streaks of daylight, fading behind the holly bush. The old cottage across the road is almost down now. The developer's bulldozer is flattening a row of rose bushes. A doll's leg lies in the gutter. But way beyond the sycamore trees, the night clouds dance and flicker.

Mary

APPENDICES

CHAPTER NOTES

Chapter 1
1953–55 Imbibing English Visions of the East

P.B. Shelley: 'Julian and Maddalo: A Conversation', in *Selected Poems*, Oxford: OUP, 1960, p.70.

Chapter 3
1956–63 The Way Lies Ahead

W.H. Auden: *The Enchafed Flood: The Iconography of the Romantic Imagination*, London: Faber, 1950, p.65.

Boxer disturbances: Local poverty and government incompetence, worsened by pressure from imperial nations, had produced hostility towards foreigners.

The Commonwealth Party: For a detailed account see Angus Calder, *The Commonwealth Party 1942–5*, DPhil., Sussex University, 1968.

Commonwealth Scholarship Scheme: The Association of Commonwealth Universities sent us to India as a symbol of equality in the post-colonial world. Scholarships to study in Britain and Canada were awarded to students of the ex-colonies in far greater numbers. They were to become agents of Westernisation. Students were also to move between Asian and African countries, and between the old members of the 'white' Commonwealth.

History of Commonwealth Scholarships: E. Ashby, *Community of Universities: An Informal Portrait of the Association of Universities of the British Commonwealth 1913–1963*, Cambridge: CUP, 1963, pp. 41, 51; H. Springer, *The Commonwealth Universities: The Story of the Association of Commonwealth Universities, 1963–1988*, ACU, 1988, p.105; *Commonwealth Scholarship and Fellowship Plan Final report*, ACU, 1989; *UNESCO World Education Report, 1991*; C.H. Hassall, *Review of Commonwealth Scholarship and Fellowship Plan*, 1993; Lalage Bown (ed.), *Towards a Commonwealth of Scholars*, London: Commonwealth Secretariat, 1994, p.121; *Student Mobility on the Map: Tertiary Educational Interchange in the Commonwealth on the Threshold: Report of the Joint Working Group of Council for Education in the Commonwealth and the UK*, London: COSA, Council for International Education, 2000; *Directory of Commonwealth Scholars and Fellows 1960–2002*, ACU, 2003; K. Maxey, *International Student Mobility in the Commonwealth – An Update*, London: Council for Education in the Commonwealth, 2003.

Western students in India: By the end of the 1960s, students were financing themselves by other means. In 1970 over one hundred and fifty British students were registered at Indian universities. No other European or North Atlantic country has sent so many students to South Asia. The number of Britons studying there since 1970 has generally been double or treble the number from the USA, though in the 1960s Americans outnumbered Britons. Recent political interest in Central Asia has hugely increased the flow of American students. In 1999 eight hundred and eleven American students were sent to India.

Comment by university administrator on study in India: cited by Hillary Callan and Kate Steele, 'Against the Grain: Student Mobility from Britain to Commonwealth Developing Countries', in Lalage Bown (ed.), *Towards a Commonwealth of Scholars,* London: Commonwealth Secretariat, 1994, p.121.

Views of academics: when a British Commonwealth Scholar, Valerie Simmons (now Gillies), announced to her tutors at Edinburgh University in 1969 that she was going to India for two years to 'to compare Indo-Anglian and Anglo-Indian literature', she met the comment, 'You should be going to Oxford for your PhD, not Mysore. You'll wreck your academic career.' Her tutors' views were not an unusual relic of the past.

Chapter 5
First Encounter with the City of Banaras

Banaras: I have used the place names that were in common usage between 1963 and 1965. This variant is still widely used by ordinary people, along with Varanasi.

Chapter 8
1963 Hostel for International Students

Foreign scholars in India before the twentieth century: G.G. Joseph, *The Crest of the Peacock: the Non-European Roots of Mathematics,* London: Penguin, 1991, pp.241 & 311–316; J.J. Clarke, *Oriental Enlightenment: The Encounter between Asian and Western Thought,* London: Routledge, 1997, pp.38 & 56–70; Michael Wood, *In the Footsteps of Alexander the Great,* London: BBC, 1997, pp.33 &191–2; Burton Stein, *History of India,* Oxford: Blackwell, 1998, p.127; Romila Thapar, *Penguin History of Early India,* New Delhi: Penguin, 2002, p.254; E. Sachau (ed.), *Alberuni's India,* New Delhi: Rupa & Co., 1996; J. Assayag & V. Benei (eds.), *Remapping Knowledge: The Making of South Asian Studies in India, Europe and America,* India: Three Essays Collective, 2005; J. Dreze & A. Sen, *Uncertain Glory,* Penguin, 2014, p.115.

The Political Economy of International Student Migration: See P. Williams (ed.), *The Overseas Student Question*, London: Heinemann (for Overseas Students Trust), 1980; *Open Doors, American Institute of International Education Bulletin report on International Educational Exchange*, Nov. 2003; T. M. Davis, *Atlas of Student Mobility*, New York: Institute of International Education, 2003.

Chapter 9
College of Indology

Indian philosophy: For an introduction see Ram-Prasad Chakravarti, *Knowledge and Liberation in Classical Indian Thought*, Basingstoke: Palgrave, 2001.

N.K. Devaraj: *The Mind and Spirit of India*, Motilal Banarsidass, 1967 repr. 2008; *Indian Philosophy Today*, London: Macmillan, 1975.

Spirituality as a modern European concept: See Margaret Chatterjee, *The Concept of Spirituality*, New Delhi: Allied Publishers, 1989; Jeremy Carrette & Richard King, *Selling Spirituality*, London: Routledge, 2005.

'Defensiveness': it is likely that many of the German idealists quoted had developed their ideas from the challenge of reading about the newly 'discovered' Indian texts or had borrowed them wholesale. Encounters between Indians and Britons in the 1960s were still stimulating Indians to rediscover aspects of their past, just as they were leading Europeans to rediscover traditions of meditation in Christianity. See J.J. Clarke, *Oriental Enlightenment*, London: Routledge, 1997; Richard King, *Orientalism and Religion*, London: Routledge, 1999, p.119; K. Lee, 'Kant and Chinese Philosophy' in B. Avari & G. Gheverghese, (eds.), *The Interwoven World: Ideas and Encounters in History*, USA: Common Ground Publishing Co., 2016.

'British Studies': the academic discipline 'English' has, until recently, been constructed around the notion of a literary canon expressing shared values.

It includes modern as well as mediaeval works, but unlike 'Indology' in Banaras, not philosophical, political, medical or grammatical texts. Not until the early 1990s did the British Council invent 'British Studies', first in Shanghai and later in Eastern Europe – but only for foreigners. They did this with the help of John Drew, a British Commonwealth Scholar in India in 1962. He had acquired an outsider perspective on his culture of origin. *His* British Studies was not based on the idea of a classical canon, though it, too, focused on literary texts. Some of his East European colleagues were unhappy with the title as they feared the course might not be good enough for British people. 'Does Oxford offer British Studies?' they asked him. In India, on the other hand, courses on Indology are primarily on offer for *local* students. The confidence generated by imperialism has meant that, until recently, few Britons have felt a need to define the national civilisation. Britons are the observers and recorders of others, whether in travel writing or anthropology. Their culture does not have to be placed in context. See: Brian Doyle, *English and Englishness*, London: Routledge, 1989; David Easton & Corinne Schelling, *Divided Knowledge: Across Disciplines, Across Cultures*, California: Sage, 1991; Perry Anderson, *English Questions*, London: Verso, 1992. The concept of Indology emerged in areas of German culture and was associated with the nationalist notion that each 'nation' or 'people' had its own essential spirit. Hence the notion of Czech Studies etc.

The idea of a unitary Indian culture: a decade later, when I was lecturing on Sociology in the adjacent Arts College, I was surprised when asked to teach the courses on Indian society. My Indian colleagues were not interested in developing holistic ideas of Indian culture. These were thought to be of interest only to foreigners and to members of the Hindu far right. They preferred to teach 'Modernisation and Development'.

Chapter 12
Banaras: Resident Europeans and Anglophiles

The Beat Poets: Allen Ginsberg, *Indian Journals*, California: Haselwood Books, 1970; Ann Charters (ed.), 1991, Introduction to Jack Kerouac's *On the Road,* Penguin, *1991;* D. Baker, *A Blue Hand: The Beats in India,* USA: Penguin, 2008.

Chapter 13
Autumn Vacation: Ram Lila and a Gandhian Community

M.K. Gandhi: *Gandhi: An Autobiography,* London: Jonathan Cape, 1966 (1949); Ramachandra Guha, *Gandhi before India,* New Delhi: Penguin, 2013.

Chapter 15
1963 Return to the City of Ceremony, Temples and Mosques

Archaeology of Banaras: A.K. Narain & T.N. Roy, *Excavations at Rajghat,* Banaras: Hindu University Press, 1976.

Chapters 19, 20 & 21
The Himalayas

Exploration and Empire: M. L. Pratt, *Imperial Eyes: Studies in Travel Writing and Transculturation,* London: Routledge, 1992; E. Said, *Culture and Imperialism,* London: Chatto & Windus, 1993; E. Shohat & R. Stam, *Unthinking Eurocentrism,* London: Routledge, 1994; James Carrier, *Occidentalism: Images of the West,* Oxford: Clarendon, 1995; Graham Huggan, *The Post-Colonial Exotic: Marketing the Margins,* London: Routledge, 2001; Jonathon Neale, *Tigers of the Snow,* London: Abacus, 2002. For a critique of class-blind 'post-colonial' approaches see: A. Ahmad, *In Theory: Nations, Classes, Literature,* London: Verso, 1992/2008; see also Fred Dallmayr, *Beyond Orientalism: Essays in Cross-Cultural Encounter,* London: State University of New York, 1996.

Arab and Persian travel books: e.g. Ibn Khaldun, *The Muqaddimah,* 3 vols. trans. F. Rosenthal, London: Routledge, 1958; T. Mackintosh (ed.), *The Travels of Ibn Battutah,* London: Picador, 2003; N. Matar, *Turks, Moors and Englishmen in the Age of Discovery*, New York: Columbia University Press, 1999; N. Matar, *In the Lands of the Christians: Arabic Travel Writing in the Seventeenth Century*, London: Routledge, 2003; Tabish Kair et al, *1500 Years of African and Asian Travel Writing*, Oxford: Signal, 2006; Mas'udi, *From The Meadows of Gold*, trans. Paul Lunde & Caroline Stone, London: Penguin, 2007, p.2943; M. Alam & S. Subrahmanyam, *Indo-Persian Travels in the Age of Discoveries, 1400–1800*, Cambridge: CUP, 2007; R.L. Euben, *Journeys to the Other Shore*, USA: Princeton University Press, 2008.

Mountains and Individualism: P. Bourdieu, *Distinction*, London: Routledge, 1984, p.219; K. Eder, *The Social Construction of Nature*, London: Sage, 1996, pp.141–2.

Romanticism. Bertrand Russell, *History of Western Philosophy*, London: Allen & Unwin, 1946, pp.651–660; P. Bishop, *The Myth of Shangri-La*, London: Athlone, 1989; Ronald Inden, *Imagining India*, London: Hurst & Co., 1990; Nigel Leask, *British Romantic Writers and the East: Anxieties of Empire*, Cambridge: CUP, 1992; W. Braun & R.T. McCutcheon, *Guide to the Study of Religion*, London: Cassell, 2000, pp.368–379; Robert Macfarlane, *Mountains of the Mind: A History of a Fascination*, London: Granta, 2003, pp.136,157–60.

Chapter 25
South Indian Adventures with Christians and Muslims

Massacres and food shortages in 1964: See R. Guha, *India after Gandhi*, New York: Ecco, 2007.

Chapter 26
Studying in the Cool Season

Chastity: the contraceptive pill was not available to single women in the UK until the end of the 1960s.

Chapter 28
Back to a Foreign England

The 1960s: S. Rowbotham's memoir (*Promise of a Dream: Remembering the Sixties,* London: Penguin, 2000) focuses on politics, fashion and music but does not mention the fascination with India and long-distance backpacking. Other books on the period include: Alan Sinfield, *Literature, Politics & Culture in Post-War Britain*, Oxford: Basil Blackwell, 1989; A. Marwick, *The Sixties*, Oxford: OUP, 1998; D. Sandbrook, *White Heat: A History of Britain in the Swinging Sixties,* London: Little & Brown, 2006; A. Marr, *A History of Modern Britain*, London: Macmillan, 2007.

Chapter 30
1969: Journey to Istanbul by Train

1960s interest in India: see: Harvey Cox, *Turning East: The Promise and Peril of the New Orientalism,* London: Allen Lane, 1977; David Tomory, *A Season in Heaven: True Tales from the Road to Kathmandu,* Singapore: Lonely Planet, 1998; Sharif Gemie & Brian Ireland, *The Hippy Trail: a History 1957-78,* Manchester: Manchester University Press, 2017.

Chapter 31
Onwards to Afghanistan

Afghanistan: Robert Byron, *The Road to Oxiana,* London: Macmillan, 1937; Rory Stewart, *The Places in Between,* London: Picador, 2004.

GLOSSARY

ashram	hermitage, community
atman	self, spirit
Ayurveda	traditional Indian medicine
bhang	hashish
Brahman	the impersonal Absolute
kameez	tunic
dharmshala	rest house for wayfarers
dhoti	man's outer lower garment
darshun	seeing or being in the presence of a higher being
firangi	foreigner, European
Ganesh	elephant-headed god
ghat	set of steps leading down to a river
idli	fermented rice ball
karjil	eyeliner
khadi	handspun, handwoven cloth
kurta	tunic
lingam	phallic fertility symbol of Shiva
lungi	man's loose lower garment
mela	a fair

namaste	greeting
neo-Vedantin	follower of post-nineteenth-century reinterpretation of Advaita Vedanta philosophy
oorni	scarf, veil
paratha	fried flat bread
peon	orderly or messenger
prasad	food offered to a god and then redistributed to the worshippers
puja	image worship
pundit	person learned in sacred texts
pyjamas	loose cotton trousers worn by men at any time of the day
rasogolla	milk sweet
roti	flat bread
sabzi	fried vegetables
saddhu	ascetic
sarong	woman's loose lower garment
Sarvodaya	Gandhian movement
sannyasin	ascetic
stupa	Buddhist reliquary mound
swami	a Hindu religious teacher
tabla	drum
tonga	horse-drawn vehicle
topi	cap
tuni	woman's wide scarf worn over head and/or chest
utthapam	savoury rice-flour pancake
Upanishads	ancient philosophic texts
Vedas	earliest Indian scriptures
Yogacara	a school of Buddhist philosophy
yogi	skilled practitioner of yoga exercises and disciplines

TIMELINE

1947   Independence from Britain. Partition of India into Pakistan (including East Bengal) and India (including West Bengal).

1947–64   Congress Government led by Nehru.

1948   M. K. Gandhi assassinated by a member of the Hindu far right.

1964   Death of Nehru

1964–6   Congress Government led by Shastri.

1966–77   Congress Government led by daughter of Nehru, Indira Gandhi (no relation of Gandhi).

1971   East Bengal broke away from Pakistan with Indian help to form independent Bangladesh.

ACKNOWLEDGEMENTS

I WISH TO EXPRESS MY GRATITUDE TO THE FOLLOWING FOR encouragement, criticism and suggestions: David Stuart, Neil Chatterjee, Margaret Dickinson, Cornerstones, Ursula Sharma, Sunirmal Chatterjee, Jacqueline Suthren Hirst, Maggie Norton and the Ulverston Writers' Group, Christine Wood, Roger Lindsay, Rosie Betterton, Alison Cahn, Wendy McDonald, Kevan Bundell.

I dedicate the book to the memory of Asha Damle, an inspiring role model.

I thank, and apologise to, former British students in India whom I interviewed some years ago. At that time, I was planning to write an academic study. Somehow this book happened instead.